CLASSIC
HORSE-RACING
QUOTES

CLASSIC HORSE-RACING QUOTES

**Horse-racing history in the words
of those who made it**

Grahame Sharpe

ROBSON BOOKS

To everyone who has been outspoken enough to warrant inclusion in this book

This edition first published in Great Britain in 2005 by Robson Books, The Chrysalis Building, Bramley Road, London W10 6SP

An imprint of **Chrysalis** Books Group plc

British Library Cataloguing in Publication Data
A catalogue record for this title is available from the British Library.

ISBN 1 86105 859 4

Printed and bound by Creative Print & Design (Wales), Ebbw Vale

Contents

Introduction

Earlier anthologies of quixotic quotations from Robson Books have concerned cricket and golf about which, after years of relaxing at Lord's and St Andrews, I may have some scant knowledge.

But of horse-racing and particularly the black art of punting, experience has shown that I am clearly not an expert! Thus after attending race meetings over the past 50 years as a sports columnist for the *Daily Mail* – I love the spectacle, the company, the bonhomie and especially the huge bravery of jump jockeys – I feel fully qualified to answer to the description of the most perceptive observation in these pages. It comes from bookmaker Fred Swindell who says 'There's a mug born every minute and thank God some of them live.'

That's me, the bookies' friend. I would have paid off my mortgage two years earlier if I hadn't been.

I have had only one comprehensive win in all those years and shamefully have to admit that it was following a tip about a race that was fixed. Obviously, for legal reasons, as they say, I cannot be too explicit, but it was while an Australian cricket team were touring England and a friend among them phoned with urgent advice to back a certain horse about whose chances of winning I immediately consulted the *Daily Mail's* top racing expert.

He studied his form books and looked bewildered. 'No chance. Not a hope. Three legs,' he replied. 'Why do you ask?'

I explained the circumstances. 'Back it,' he said. In fact, half the *Daily Mail* did. It duly won and for months thereafter I was pestered by colleagues whispering, 'Ian, any tips today?'

Tips? Don't talk to me about tips. At Newmarket one afternoon a leading newspaper forecaster, with the sly winking and nose rubbing that implied serious inside information, marked my entire card. Result: not a first, second or third all day. We took one of my wife's friends who had never been to a race meeting in her life. She risked all of £2 each way on horses whose names she fancied. She was rewarded with four firsts and a third.

This drove a very expensive thought into my head. Could name association when backing horses trip up the bookies? Well, as something of a royalist I've been backing kings, queens, princes and monarchs – however ludicrous their starting prices – ever since. It has almost driven me to poverty-stricken republicanism.

It did work once, however, though with no regal connection on this occasion. It was Gold Cup day at Cheltenham in 1986 and I was in sufficiently euphoric form after a morning of Guinness and champagne followed by a steadfast lunch to break the habit of a lifetime and back the favourite with a stake that would otherwise have paid for a few days of sunshine in Monaco.

Dawn Run obliged me at 15–8 thanks to a lovely American lady of fond memory named Dawn.

Graham Sharpe has wonderfully captured the thrills and eccentricities of horse-racing in this book, not to mention the eternal hopes of those of us who willingly help keep him in the betting business.

Ian Wooldridge, London

Under Starter's Orders

My oddest racecourse experience has to be seeing Elvis Presley taken out to the stalls before a race at Baden Baden, then acting as official starter for the race – before heading back to perform in the paddock with his rock 'n' roll band. I suspect he was a lookalike, but you never know. That was almost as bizarre as the occasion when the official starter failed to get the Grand National off to a proper start and the world watched in wonder as our greatest race was turned into a farce with no official result. Later dubbed 'Captain Cock-Up', the starter, Keith Brown, received his due reward when he was lambasted and humiliated by every non-racing's (and just a few in racing's) favourite trainer, Jenny Pitman, whose Esha Ness actually crossed the line first in the National-that-never-was.

Jenny was not a happy Pitman (well, she wasn't really actually a Pitman at all, having split from jockey husband Richard, but that's another story) on that day in 1993, and she wasn't too worried about who knew it – 'knicker elastic' was her famous description of the malfunctioning starting tapes. The *Sun* was not best pleased, either, 'Starter cocked it up...Aintree cocked it up...Jockey Club cocked it up.' Even Prime Minister John Major felt moved to comment, 'I feel very sorry for the people involved. It was a very unfortunate incident.'

Captain Cock-Up wasn't too sure that he should be blamed for cocking it up. 'It was bound to happen one day and it just happened that I had to be in charge at the time.' Oh, is that all, well then, that's fine, just the luck of the draw, old boy, think nothing of it. Racing writer Mike Langley soon kicked that opinion into touch – 'Captain Keith Brown still blames everybody else. Racecourse management, impatient jockeys, screaming spectators, a needlessly long parade. And the protestors' smoke bombs. Starter Brown may be right in every detail. But won't you be relieved not to see him on the rostrum for the 1994 National?'

Under Starter's Orders? Order Starter Under, more like.

Who or what links Tim Molony, Bobby Renton, Tommy Stack and Tony Gillam?

'The Oxford English Dictionary defines "classic", from the French *classique*, and Latin *classicus*, as meaning "of the first rank or authority", which gets its racing sense exactly; but the word is not used to describe races until 1885, first of all in the phrase "classic races". The shorter form, classic, is first attested in 1905.' Definitive explanation of the role of the term Classic in racing from English language authority, **Gerald Hammond,** in his *Book of Words: Horse Racing.*

'Totally nuts. But to this day I still don't wear any green.' **John Brown**, now retired William Hill Chairman, who was warned not to show up for work wearing that colour when he started in 1959.

'For the greater Conveniency of distinguishing the Horses in Running, as also for the Prevention of Disputes arising from not knowing the Colours worn by each Rider, the underwritten Gentlemen have come to the Resolution and Agreement of having the Colours annexed to the following Names, worn by their respective Riders.' **Jockey Club order** from 1762, first recognising the use of specific Colours by particular owners.

'Horses the property of Gentlemen who must have, prior to the first day of the Meeting, actually expended in fair adverse litigation the sum of £200. Horses of persons who have expended £1000 allowed 3lb.' Unique **conditions of entry** to a £50 Plate run at Tralee in Ireland in 1805.

'There is no better buzz than racing – it gives me a bigger kick than football when I have a winner.' **Kevin Keegan**.

'I've always loved racing.' World Cup winner **Alan Ball** (*Sunday Times*, September 2004).

They all trained Red Rum before Ginger McCain.

'I was more nervous than when I played before 55,000 at Old Trafford.' Ex-footballer **Mick Quinn** on sending out his first runner as a trainer at Southwell in December 1997.

'Instead of crawling into bed from nightclubs at 6a.m. I had to learn to crawl out of bed at the same time.' **Mick Quinn**.

'Racing in France is largely a silent ritual, played out for the benefit of a rich elite who have no particular interest in attracting the public to the track.' *Sunday Times* writer **Andrew Longmore**, June 2004.

'The odds on the English raider were miserable to say the least. However, so were the odds on the outsiders.' Professional punter **Dave Nevison** concludes after visiting Klampenborg racecourse in Denmark during the summer of 2004, that 'there are few better places than England to get value about your betting'.

'People need to be made aware of the German tax office, as it's spoiled what should have been a great victory.' Trainer **Hugh Collingridge** ('they have behaved in a disgraceful, immoral fashion' – *Racing Post*) who was still trying to get 12, 340.86 from the German fiscal authorities almost a year after they levied a 'withholding tax' from his purse for winning a Group 2 sprint at Baden-Baden with Stormont.

'Apart from the big days, American racing is a wonderful cure for insomnia, and the prospect of four furlong races reminds me of those crash, bang performers in the bedroom – over in a flash, turn off the light and goodnight!' Respected (well, perhaps not in the States, but seemingly in the boudoir) racing journalist **Geoff Lester** in 2004, when asked about introducing US-style four-furlong races to the Brit scene.

Who was born in County Down on 6 August 1955, and rode his first winner on Eyry at Goodwood on 16 May 1973?

'About a dozen of my clients were stranded at the track, so I stuffed them in the back of my mobile kitchen and dropped them off at the nearest metro station.' **Albino Jordao**, who runs the popular tented mobile restaurant at Longchamp, recalls a minor panic at the 2003 Arc.

'Parisians just don't go racing. They prefer playing with their boules.' *Sun* racing correspondent **Claude Duval** (*Sun*, 2 October 2004).

'It was a bit like Chippenham Town, should they be so lucky, hosting Manchester United in the FA Cup.' **Jonathan Powell** on the decision to hold the 2004 Breeders Cup at Lone Star, Texas (*Daily Mail*, 31 October 2004).

'They were not friendly to me because I am Arabic... In Newmarket nobody wanted to help me.' Godolphin trainer **Saeed Bin Suroor** on his reception in England in October 1996.

'It may well be that there are more black people involved in the committees of the Ku Klux Klan than in British racing.' *Independent* racing writer, **Richard Edmondson**, October 1997.

'I'd love to do in racing what he (Tiger Woods) has done for black people in his sport.' Jockey **Rosyton Ffrench** (*Daily Express*, 15 August, 1997).

'Of course, the French, who eat horses, have not the same feeling for the sport as we have in these islands.' **Tim Fitzgeorge-Parker**.

'He was the man who christened me "Wop". I never minded because from him the nickname came with a smile.' **Luca Cumani** paying tribute to the late Alec Stewart in *Thoroughbred Owner & Breeder* magazine, September 2004.

Jockey John Reid.

'A good day for Wop Land.' Italian trainer **Luca Cumani** after he and fellow Italian, Frankie Dettori, had enjoyed a winner and Italian golfer Constantino Rocca had played a key role in winning the 1997 Ryder Cup.

'I was trying to kill the Cuban son of a bitch.' Unrepentant US jockey **Eddie Aracaro** after being banned for deliberately colliding with rival Vincent Nordarse during a race.

'A pioneering example of what an ambitious individual from an ethnic minority background could achieve in a white-dominated sport would set a path for others to follow.' **Department for Culture, Media and Sport report**, which recommended that, 'a concerted attempt to market the sports (greyhound racing, too) to ethnic minority groups is needed.' (*Racing Post*, 2 July, 2004).

'You see a great cross-section in betting shops that simply isn't replicated at the racecourse. Our (advertising) images were not encouraging non-whites to go racing, so we are now targeting urban databases as part of a campaign to attract a better mix.' BHB Marketing Director, **Chris John** (*The Times*, 24 June 2004).

'It's interesting that even today the racing establishment is not interested in black fans, which could be a tremendous source of support for a sport that is losing fans.' Journalist and historian **Ed Hotaling** in an Associated Press article by Linda B Blackford about black spectators at Keeneland and other US racecourses, in which black Keeneland racegoer, Gloria Walker, declared: 'To be honest, the only color they look at here is the color of your money.' However William 'Chuck' Hamilton, one of the few black trainers who runs horses at Keeneland, said, 'They treat me nicely when I'm here, but if I tried to get a box seat, I might have a problem.'

The legendary Champion Hurdle and Gold Cup winning mare Dawn Run won 21 times in her career – who rode her to victory for the first time at Tralee?

'I think the authorities were a little embarrassed.' Writer **Ed Hotaling**, at whose prompting a ceremony commemorating black jockey Jimmy Winkfield's 1902 Kentucky Derby victory took place at Churchill Downs, home of the race, in 2002, attracting over 200 African-American community leaders (*The Times*, 27 November 2004).

'His status brought other perks – protection from the Ku Klux Klan, for one.' **Mark MacKenzie** on turn-of-the-20th-century black jockey superstar, Jimmy Winkfield (*The Times*, 27 November 2004).

'Many people feel there was a prejudice against black jockeys but in my experience the only issue is, can he win, what can he do for me?' Veteran racing writer **Joe Hirsch**, who met Winkfield (*The Times*, 27 November 2004).

'I don't make it a colour thing, just work hard and ride hard.' Up-and-coming jockey **Kerwin John**, 29, from St Croix in the US Virgin Islands, who was making an impression on the racing scene in southern California and rode at the Breeders Cup (*The Times*, 27 November 2004).

'In Australia, even canters on a slow morning are timed which, to an Englishman abroad provides the greatest culture shock,' recalls former work rider **George Haine**, adding, 'First lot pulls out at 3.30a.m., which means the first three or four lots you ride are in darkness.'

'To the left I saw Lester Piggott. His uncle, Dragomanov told me, also used to race in Moscow at one time. He once made a bet with one of our jockeys that he could outride him, and then lost. He went straight off the scales to the jockey's toilet, and took poison.' Odd tale of racing in Russia by seventies champion jockey **Nikolai Nasibov**.

Her owner, 62-year-old Mrs Charmian Hill.

'I have never seen anything like it before and the atmosphere is great.' French jockey **Thomas Huet** rode Cabeza de Vaca to win a nine-furlong race run over more than four circuits of a specially laid, circular fibresand course at Paris' Stade de France on 18 September 2004.

'There are no ups and downs on the tracks in Brazil, they are all left-handed and the jockeys jump and go.' Brazilian jockey **Nelson de Souza**, who rode 32 winners over there before moving to ride for Paul Cole in 2004, explains the difference. He was backed up by countryman Leandro Gonçalves, who also made the move, 'In Brazil every track is the same. Here, every track is different.'

'The Euros take all the worst of it. They have done a hell of a job when they win on dirt. They have the shipping, then have to deal with quarantine, they have no experience on the dirt surfaces the way we do, they have to take on the speed-favouring horses we have over here, and if they pull it off, you must salute them.' **D Wayne Lukas** explaining why it is so difficult for Europeans to win at Breeders Cup, prior to the 2004 event.

'On the whole, French racing is very different to British. While most British races are run at a good gallop, French races tend to be run at a pace just faster than a trot.' **Marcus Armytage** (*Daily Telegraph*, 4 October 2004).

'There is a lot more camaraderie between the jockeys and trainers in the States. You move around together like a travelling circus. In England, people still tend to be in their own little world and there is a tendency to gloat when things go wrong.' Trainer **John Gosden** to racing journalist John Karter.

True or false – Lester Piggott rode Prince Charlemagne to win the 1955 Triumph Hurdle?

'Jockeys in Kenya celebrated 100 years of thoroughbred racing in their country with a running of the world's largest birds at a track in Nairobi.' Yes, with jockeys on their backs, a field of ostriches battled it out neck to neck (***Sports Illustrated***, 8 November 2004).

'At Saratoga in New York state there are two free seminars at each meeting at which experts educate newcomers about the sport, give their analysis of the day's races and take questions.' **Tony Paley** (*Racing Ahead*, December 2004). Customer service, or just information overload?

'Kenny McPeek...was breaking with the instinct of Americans to regard their own sport as the global template and away fixtures as a needless irrelevance.' Appreciation of the US handler bringing his Hard Buck to finish runner-up in the 2004 King George at Ascot by *Times* writer **Alan Lee**.

'What's there to be scared of? Why not go? It's not life or death – its just a horse race.' **Kenny McPeek** on why he decided to bring Hard Buck.

'Where he is building his parents' home, it's probably the only house with electricity and the only house with TV. That gives you an idea of where this kid has come from.' Friend **Willie Martinez** on 22-year-old sensation in US racing, jockey Rafael Bejarano, who was remembering his roots by creating a home in his native Peru for his Mum and Dad in July 2004.

'Is it any wonder why racing can't keep the public's interest when it cannot keep its stars running? And what good will stud fees be if a distracted public turns its back on the track entirely?' Lexington *Herald-Leader* writer **John Clay** criticises the retirement of America's 2004 top three-year-old Smarty Jones.

False – they won in 1954.

'Your horse springs away and you're in the saddle. Now it's up to you to control the power and speed. The first fence is looming. Press the jump button at exactly the right moment to judge take off. Apply the whip for a speed boost to cross the finish line first.' Just £34.99 would buy you the **Handheld Horse Racing Game** from www.DREAMdirect.co.uk for Christmas 2004.

'Did you ever wish you could recreate the great matchup between Seabiscuit and War Admiral? Would you like to see Smarty Jones run against the champions of the recent past like Empire Maker and Seattle Slew? All this can be yours with Horse Racing Fantasy, where champions never retire. You will be amazed at how accurately this computer game simulates a horse race. Our unique pace, running style, speed/stamina consumption and jockey intelligence algorithms cannot be found in other simulations.' Blimey, who needs the real thing, particularly when the **website** plugging the game also claims: 'We used it to pick the winner in 4 out of 6 Breeders Cup races on Oct 31!'

'Racing in England is of some importance to a section of the sporting community. In Ireland it remains a raison d'être.' Racing aficionado **Christopher Poole** in 1997.

'You have to have some years that aren't that good in order to recognise and enjoy the years when outstanding horses come around.' Senior Handicapper **Nigel Gray** reflecting on the 2004 flat scene in Europe (*The Times*, 19 January 2005). This comment may have struck a chord with some readers who remember his 20 September 2004 remark in the *Telegraph*, 'It is the sort of year that puts the star years into perspective.'

'A good handicap is the creative act of a good handicapper; a balancing of fine judgements; an appraisal of will o' the wisps; an array of intelligent guesses.' The late *Sporting Life* private handicapper, **Dick Whitford**.

Who is the Grand National winner named after a Channel Islands lighthouse?

'Racing is the only sport in which you are penalised for winning and, even worse, for finishing second. But that's handicapping for you and we all know the rules.' **Mick Channon**.

'You've got to grow several skins, but after prep school, public school, Sandhurst and the army, I couldn't give a damn what anyone said about me. You are inured to implications about your parentage, health and looks.' Former senior Jockey Club handicapper, **David Swannell**.

'I wouldn't say handicappers are necessarily any more respected than we were, but I think people are more accepting that we might be right.' Hold on; was that a well-handicapped pig flying past BHB senior jumps handicapper **Phil Smith** when he made this comment in November 2004?

'By using artificial lighting and a combination of hormones, we can now ensure that the vast majority of non-pregnant thoroughbred mares can ovulate between February 15 and February 28.' **Dr Twink Allen**, director of Equine Fertility Unit, Newmarket, on how the breeding industry assures that foals are born as soon as possible after the 1 January official birthday of all horses.

'The Queen Mother has asked me to write to thank you for your marvellous 100th birthday present of a unit in Fluffy the Super Horse which she is delighted to accept.' No joke, the Queen Mum's racing manager **Sir Michael Oswald** wrote in September 2000 to Aussie, Michael Pope, landlord of McGuires Hotel in North Queensland after he and fellow syndicate members bought £65,000 filly Fluffy The Superhorse and decided to give the Queen Mother one of the 80 shares. They were staggered when she accepted.

Corbiere.

'If absurdity be the object there ought to have been a tariff as follows; Gentlemen tattooing their faces after the fashion of the Esquimeux Indians allowed 9lbs. Gentlemen who between heats will grin through a horse collar for ten minutes, eat hot hasty pudding, climb up a greased pole or dip four pennies in a jar of treacle – 10lbs.' **Irate correspondent** to local press objecting that gentlemen wearing cocked hats should be allowed 7lbs in the Cocked Hat Stakes run at Oswestry in 1821.

'My worst was at the Cheltenham Festival when I fell at the first fence and the one coming behind put his hoof on my face. There were 32 stitches but I rode a winner two days later.' **Dick Francis**. (*Daily Telegraph*, 20 November 2004).

'Back in England you've got *Panorama* sticking a microphone in my face and telling me that I shouldn't be riding. You come here and they tell you that you're the best in the world. Where would you rather be?' **Kieren Fallon** tells the *Guardian's* Greg Wood why is he was riding in America in January 2005. He answered his own question by flying back in February.

'Too much puritanical purging and cleansing and child-proofing, however well intentioned, can seriously damage the allure of horse racing, which depends at least to some extent on the forbidden-fruit effect, the sense of indulgence in illicit pleasure.' Anthropologist **Kate Fox's** 1999 conclusion.

'People tend to get the wrong idea about our attitude to racing. We don't want to throw our weight about. We enjoy our horses. We do not bet. We run our horses fairly and we thoroughly enjoy British racing.' **Sheikh Mohammed Maktoum Al-Maktoum** (*International Turf*, 1998).

Who was the first lady to train a winner of an English Classic?

'One girl sent me a black latex thong which she asked me to wear the next time I was riding at Pontefract. I didn't wear it.' **Frankie Dettori** in *Loaded* magazine.

'Unlike other sporting types I have got no restraints on physical activity the night before a big race. How lucky the grateful Booby (his wife) is.' **John McCririck**.

'Sex the night before a race isn't going to do you any harm, although going out looking for it might.' **Jamie Osborne**.

'Versatile mare. Willing to go that extra mile.' Prostitute's calling card, reported by writer **Will Buckley**.

'I know some sportsmen abstain from sex before a major event – but I think I'm better for it.' Jockey **Tony Dobbin**.

'The Derby is a little like your first experience of sex – hectic, strenuous, memorably pleasant and over before you know it.' **Bill Bryson**.

'Not many people can claim to have ridden a winner on their honeymoon – at least, not on a horse.' Newly wed **Chris Maude** after riding a 1998 winner at Plumpton.

'Sex will be an anti-climax after that.' **Mick Fitzgerald** after riding Rough Quest to win the 1996 Grand National.

'Royal Ascot celebrates the noblest English obsessions. Class, animals, the monarchy and furtive sex.' **Tania Branigan** (*Guardian*, 18 June 2004).

Criquette Head trained Ma Biche in 1983, winning 1,000 Guineas.

'44 double D breasts.' **John McCririck**, one of several celebrities interviewed on camera by Channel 4, when asked, 'What is the best way to your heart?' in July 2004.

'Foreplay can be more fun than the real thing…where older horses take on the current Classic generation, I enjoy the parade-ring preliminaries nearly as much as the race.' **Robin Oakley** (*Spectator*, 31 July 2004).

'Mr and Mrs Butters belonged to a social circle in which the sex act is carried out in the dark by God-fearing people solely for the procreation of the species.' Writer **Quintin Gilbey** on the strait-laced Frank Butters, champion eight times and trainer of fifteen Classic winners.

'Isn't reducing the numbers in a big handicap a bit like having group sex – only without the group.' It must be me, but I'm still baffled about what **Jacky Paul** of Sale in Cheshire was getting at when she wrote to the *Racing Post* in August 2004 about proposals to restrict big field handicaps to 14 runners.

'If they were in season their reaction would vary from merely tolerating the "teaser" to throwing themselves against the board, squatting and peeing and "winking" at him with their vagina.' Writer **Rebecca Cassidy's** first-hand account of the stud process.

'I did ask the owner and he said it was named after one of the Ann Summers products.' Response from **Brian Meehan's stable** over the source of the name of their September 2004 Newmarket winner, Bunny Rabbit, running in the colours of Gold Group International Ltd, parent company of the Ann Summers shops.

Frankie Dettori rode all seven winners at Ascot in September 1996. Who, in October 1933, rode a world record 12 consecutive winners over three days?

'The former home of Grand National legend Red Rum has been turned into a brothel.' ***Sunday Mirror* 'Exclusive'** on 4 April 2004, which boasted the tasteful headline, 'Red Rumpy Pumpy.'

'A trainer I knew told me that a woman she knew had said she was having trouble with her horse because the horse wanted to have sex with her.' Yes, you can see how that might be a problem... **Jane Smiley** in her *A Year at the Races*.

'Chocolate can have a positive impact on a women's sexuality,' according to **Dr Andrea Salonia**, who carried out research for chocolate makers Thorntons. Frankie Dettori was given a chocolate rocking horse to give to wife Catherine. The couple have five children so seem to have done okay without the chocolate thus far (*Daily Star*, November 2004).

'People who think racing is not about gambling probably think that dancing is not about sex.' **Hugh McIlvanney** in 1999.

'An airship, suspended from which are a number of slings. These will be slipped around the bodies of the horses entered to race. When the bugle summons them to the post, the airship will sail to the paddock gate, receive the horses and float to the starting post. In order to prevent running away or fractiousness at the post, the horses are kept 18 inches above the ground. When everything is ready, the starter touches a button, the slings release their hold, the horses drop to the ground and off they go.' A **proposal** for a starting machine from *Turf, Field and Farm* magazine in 1896.

'Predicting whether a horse will stay is a lot more difficult than explaining why it hasn't.' **James Willoughby**, *Pacemaker*.

Gordon Richards.

'More modern forms of communication have erased the tic-tac man from the racecourse so if you see someone slap themselves on their shoulder now its more likely to be caused by an annoying insect rather than to indicate 7/4.' **Peter Levy** (who said this in *Racing Ahead* in July 2004), may be unaware that the art lives on at London's up-market RAC Club where sweet trolley waiter Robert, a Frenchman, greeted me during a July 2004 meal with a perfect demonstration of the tic-tac's art.

'Clive (Brittain) said Var got beat last time by coming too soon, so I should wait with him. I just nodded, then hit the gate running and "whoosh".' **Frankie Dettori** on not quite obeying his trainer's instructions when winning the 2004 Prix de l'Abbaye.

'I thought that racing was the meaning of life but I know now that Jesus is.' Aussie jockey **Darren Beadman**, when retiring in December 1997 to become a preacher.

'If you were my kid brother, and came to me for a tip about racing, my advice would be: "Don't back horses, but, if you must, never bet odds-on."' And **Steve Ahern**, whose *Riches From Horses* appeared in 1964, should know, as he was a professional punter who 'began backing horses at sixpence a time while still at school and went on to win half a million pounds tax free before retiring young to live in luxury'.

'People expect there to be skulduggery in horseracing and, over the centuries, the sport of monarchs, and scoundrels, has not failed them.' **David Ashforth** opens his *Ringers & Rascals*.

'If it be more grateful to an ingenuous mind to celebrate the praises of humanity, it is no less necessary to explore the vices that deform it. In enumerating the excellences of men, we present a model to imitate; in detecting their depravity, we hold out an

What is a rig?

example to deter.' The not surprisingly **anonymous author** of *The Jockey Club*, or *A Sketch of the Manners of the Age*, published in 1792, tore into thinly disguised targets such as The P—e of W—s and The D—e of Y—k, and Old D—k V—n-n who is, we read, 'notorious for denying bets, when the race has been decided against him'.

'Joe Mercer will go down in the annals of the turf as the best jockey never to have won the Epsom Derby.' The opening line to **Richard Baerlein's** *Joe Mercer* may have to be reconsidered if Frankie Dettori doesn't pull his finger out!

'Some people say I am a legend but I do not think that is true; I only know that the opportunity to make a living backing horses as I have will not come again.' The legendary gambler, **Alex Bird**, at the start of his *The Life and Secrets of a Professional Punter*.

'I remember I was just ten when I promised my mother I'd never smoke, never drink, never gamble and never mess about with women. Today, I'm thirty three and in Gamblers' Anonymous, Alcoholics' Anonymous, divorced and smoking like a trooper.' Admit it, you'd like to read more of top jump jockey **Barry Brogan's** *Story* wouldn't you?

'It was a happy childhood. When I was two years old, a bomb went off nearby and I went flying across the living room and crashed through the glass door into our shop.' The opening lines from *Lucky John* by **John Brown** (former William Hill chairman).

'Bob Champion looked remarkably healthy for a man who had just been given eight months to live.' The beginning of **Bob Champion** and **Jonathan Powell's** *Champion's Story*.

A male horse that has one testicle that has not descended properly.

'Looking back, I must have caused my parents many anxious moments. In my school reports and on Open Days, teachers would express their concern at my ability to turn anything competitive into a betting opportunity.' **Michael Church** in his *Ripping Gambling Yarns*, sub-titled 'Tales of a Misspent Youth'.

'There is no family tree in the Kinane household. Details of ancestors are passed on from one generation to the next by word of mouth. Those sufficiently interested remember what they have been told.' **Michael Clower** in *Mick Kinane: Big Race King*.

'This book begins at the happy ending, as the champion "retires to stud". Usually, those words are the last you ever read about a favourite horse... To many men, the phrase represents an unattainable ideal, like "assumed into heaven."' *$tud*, by **Kevin Conley**.

'It has been said that the true horseman is so born, not made, and that hereditary leanings are sure to manifest themselves during the up-bringing of the child.' **Harding Cox**'s racy intro to 1925s *Chasing and Racing*.

'For longer than I care to admit, my riding career was as keen to start as an ancient car on a winter's morning.' **Pat Eddery** wasn't always at the top, as he revealed in *To be a Champion*.

'King Athelstan, 924–40, the grandson of Alfred the Great, is the first English Sovereign who is recorded as owning racehorses.' **Arthur Fitzgerald's** *Royal Thoroughbreds* begs the question, why is it not known as the Sport of Athelstans?

'Johnny Murtagh, the Irish champion jockey, once said to me, 'Mick, if you want to do this job you've got to realise you are not a normal person.' *A Jump-Jockey's Life* by **Mick Fitzgerald**.

Who was the first South African to be a UK champion jockey?

'At fourteen Judith Johnson was quite simply the most beautiful creature I had ever seen. She had the face of an angel set on the body of a page three girl and moved on legs that seemed to end somewhere near her armpits. I fell in love with her the first time I saw her.' **John Francome** in *Born Lucky*.

'Funny things, horses. Dirty, dangerous, greedy beasts, they get into your blood like a virus, and once you've got it there's no cure.' **Susan Gallier**, who was *One of the Lads*.

'It is possible that among the crowd bathed in sunshine, enjoying the very first Cheltenham Gold Cup were Sir Edward Elgar and the child prodigy Yehudi Menuhin.' **Bob Harman's** *The Ultimate Dream*.

'The horse Arkle was first thought of in 1956 in an old grey house built rather like a boat, but squatting 700 feet up a hill in the north of County Dublin.' **Ivor Herbert's** *Arkle*.

'All the drama, heroics and horsemanship – humour even – that have epitomised the sport of steeplechasing for 250 years were crammed into the 11 minutes it took to run the 2001 Grand National. Run in pouring rain on ever deepening ground, it illustrated more than anything that the Corinthian spirit is alive and well, that man and horse can rise together in adversity.' *Steeplechasing* by **Anne Holland**.

'Since the first race was run at Ascot in Berkshire on Saturday, August 11, 1711, Royal Ascot has become a world symbol for all that is best in horse racing and elegant in fashion. Yet Ascot very nearly did not have a racecourse at all.' **Dorothy Laird's** *Royal Ascot*.

Michael Roberts, in 1992.

'Heroes are seldom what they seem. All too often, closer inspection reveals the feet of clay which destroy the illusions of idolatry. With Fred Winter, a hero to two generations of racing folk, there is no myth.' **Alan Lee** in *Fred*, the biography of Fred Winter.

'Dick Francis always wanted his wife Mary's name to appear as co-author on the covers of the Dick Francis racing thrillers because she played a much greater part in writing them than has ever been acknowledged, but she would never allow it.' *Dick Francis: A Racing Life* by **Graham Lord**.

'By the summer of 1711 Queen Anne had grown prodigiously fat.' **Sean Magee** gets to the bottom of things at the beginning of *Ascot: The History*.

'Tony McCoy's father Peadar never sat on a horse in his life, yet he bred a succession of top jumpers – and the human tornado McCoy Jnr.' Claude Duval, who co-wrote *The Real McCoy* with 'AP' McCoy himself.

'It is rare that the death of a racehorse is reported on the front page of the *New York Times*, but it happened on Wednesday, April 6, 1932 under the headline "Great Australian Race Horse Dies in West After First American Triumph."' *Great Horse Racing Mysteries* by **John McEvoy**.

'I know you! – you're the boogger who got tired before yer 'orse!' **John Oaksey's** autobiography *Mince Pies For Starters*.

'A racehorse's fate depends, often too closely for his own good, on the character, preferences and background of the human beings into whose hands he happens to fall.' **John Oaksey** in *The Story of Mill Reef*.

In 1903 Ard Patrick and Rock Sand, successive winners of the Derby, met in the Eclipse Stake. Which two Blue Riband winners lined up in similar circumstances in 1968?

'When Fairy and I galloped round Tattenham Corner some three months before the 1925 Derby winner, Manna, I had the sure conviction of a seven-year-old that I would be a jockey.' **Peter O'Sullevan** in his *Calling the Horses* autobiography.

'I remember how I pressed myself tight against the wing of the fence, halfway down the hill at Cheltenham where I had crept in over the railway line an hour before the first race – the place I found every time that I played truant from school.' **Richard Pitman** bunks off in *Good Horses Make Good Jockeys*.

'When first setting out on this voyage of discovery around Britain's lost racecourses, it appeared a pleasant, relaxing sort of ramble. I likened it to no more than a gentle climb up my local Clent Hills. I soon found that I was staring at the north face of the Eiger.' **Chris Pitt** in *A Long Time Gone*.

'The longest journey in Jonjo O'Neill's life started in October 1980 in an ambulance and, for thirteen and a half harrowing months, dragged him through four hospitals in Wales, England and Switzerland, in search of treatment for his shattered leg.' **Tim Richards**' *Jonjo*.

'The Irish Derby had an inauspicious beginning. The inaugural running of the classic took place at the Curragh on Wednesday 27 June 1866 and English trainer James Cockin had the honour of saddling the first winner, Selim, in a race which attracted only three runners.' **Daniel Roddy's** *The Irish Derby 1962–1995*.

'Danoli nearly killed me.' *Them and Us: The Irish at Cheltenham* by **John Scally**.

Royal Palace and Sir Ivor.

'At its worst, racing can seem like a minute of action followed by an age of talk. But when it gets it right there really is something to talk about.' **Brough Scott** in *On and Off the Rails*.

'The most certain aspect of a jump jockey's existence is that nothing is certain,' mused **Peter Scudamore** in *Scudamore on Steeplechasing*. 'Each day begins with a series of imponderables and ends, invariably, with a sequence of surprises upon which to reflect.'

'I must have been mad. Stark, staring mad. It was the morning of the Derby of 1939, I had the greatest chance ever of winning on Blue Peter, and there I was in the paddock at my father's farm, riding a hunter "over the sticks".' **Eph Smith** sets himself up for a fall in *Riding to Win*.

'The longer you are involved in horse racing, whether as journalist, owner, trainer, jockey or merely the smallest betting-shop follower, the more you realise there's never a time when you know as much as you need to know.' **Tony Stafford**, once of the *Daily Telegraph*, in his *Little Black Racing Book*.

'Since the dawn of civilisation, mankind has raced horses. Racing was an important event at the ancient Greek Olympiads, the Arabs have matched their steeds for centuries and a weekend in Rome was not complete without a sortie to the Circus Maximus in the days when the natives of yet unconquered Britain were matching shades of coloured earth and plant juice for woad whilst wondering why square cartwheels obstinately refused to rotate.' The late **John Tyrrel** in his *Running Racing*.

'The object of racing is to win; winning is everything, and second is nowhere. The essence of racing is uncertainty.' **Elizabeth Walton** in *A Slice of Glory*.

Who was the first horse to win three Ascot Gold Cups?

'Horse racing is a delightful bait for strange events. In 1935, for instance, a murder trial in the Bahamas was abandoned for the day at lunch-time – so that court officials, jury and lawyers could attend a Montagu Park race meeting.' **Andrew Ward's** *Horse Racing's Strangest Races.*

'The Classic Racehorse,' wrote **Peter Willett** in the opening line of *The Classic Racehorse,* 'is a phrase lacking official definition. "Classic" is not found in the list of Definitions in the British Rules of Racing or in the corresponding French rules, the Code des Courses.'

'If ever there was a golden age of betting, this is it. The choice is extraordinary, the opportunities are bountiful, and at last the betting man or woman has a real chance of earning money at the same time as enjoying the thrill of the chase.' **Prof Leighton Vaughan Williams** sees punting potential in *Betting to Win.*

'Lester Keith Piggott was born and bred to ride: there was no alternative. His pedigree is the human equivalent to that of the finest thoroughbred.' **Julian Wilson** in *Lester Piggott, The New Pictorial Biography.*

'It was 2.45 a.m. and the band were thinking about *Auld Lang Syne* and getting paid. I picked up my twelfth – or was it thirteenth? -- glass of champagne. Then came a familiar voice in my ear: "Are you going to take me home?" asked Suzanne.' *Some You Win* by commentator **Julian Wilson**.

'It is not a beautiful place. Frankly, it is above all that. What it has is a sense of purpose – more precious nowadays than beauty – unbroken and unchanged for more than three hundred years.' *Newmarket* by **Laura Thompson**.

Non-triers at the back.' Presumably apocryphal, yet oft-repeated, **instruction** of an unnamed starter.

Sagaro (1975–7).

Going Good?

The going at all-weather meetings virtually always seems to be described as 'standard', which is not a term used to indicate the state of the ground for turf meetings. The seven descriptions in common use here are hard, firm, good to firm, good, good to soft, soft and heavy.

The Irish don't believe that these seven are sufficient and chuck in 'yielding' as well. As for the French – well, how are we supposed to know what *sec, trés leger, assez souple, collant* and *lourd* might mean – *sacré bleu*! But they did blaze a trail by introducing the penetrometer.

Whether going reports are of any use whatsoever is a subject of continuous debate – often, different parts of the course have different going conditions. A variety of implements have been introduced in an effort to give a more accurate reading of the going – which is fine if you happen to understand what the readings indicate. Most clerks of the course seem to prefer the evidence of their shoe/boot heel or walking stick and can't be doing with new-fangled methods. Most jockeys and trainers seem to believe that going reports mean nothing other than that the course is anxious to persuade people that their meeting will go ahead and that it will be run in decent ground.

At St Moritz in Switzerland, for example, they race on ice. How do you reckon they describe the going there?

'A country where the boat race course would be considered good to firm.' This comment about Ireland has been attributed to Wisden editor and racing buff, journo **Matthew Engel**, by *Time Out's* Steve Grant.

Longchamp, Chantilly and Deauville are three of just four French courses to stage Group 1 races. What is the other?

'I love racing. I've been going since I was a kid.' Charlton striker **Francis Jeffers**, owner of useful hurdler, Frontier (*News of the World*, 17 October 2004).

'The racecourse is as level as a billiard ball.' **John Francome**, 1996.

'Don't firm-ground horses have rights, too?' **Paul Haigh**, wondering why Ascot was watered when seemingly not in need of it (*Racing Post*, 25 September 2004).

'Apart from natural sprinters, who can't do anything else, all horses are capable of contesting races over a variety of distances and trainers should be given every encouragement to exploit their versatility.' Breeding expert **Tony Morris**.

'If I ever had enough money I would love to have my own cinema.' *Morning Line* regular and racecourse commentator, **Simon Holt**.

'In a perfect world we'd all travel as sweetly as Danoli.' **Car advert tribute** to the great Irish jumper.

'I'd love to win a Gold Cup. Other than that, the ambition is to become solvent.' **Nigel Twiston-Davies** (*Independent*, 30 November 2004).

'All I want out of life is a cigar, to go see a bullfight and have the freedom to turn up the heating when I want to.' Easily pleased handler **Sir Mark Prescott's** wish-list.

'I've always had a passing interest in racing.' Ryder Cup skipper **Sam Torrance**, who in November 2004 went into ownership via the Favourites Racing set-up.

Saint-Cloud.

'For my wife Gill who has endured more than 25 years of my obsession with racing. Her 25th wedding anniversary was spent at the races this July and her wedding was delayed until 4pm because the Eclipse Stakes was being run that day at Sandown.' **Tony Stafford's** *Little Black Racing Book.*

'Pat, my wife whose forbearance has been matched only by that of our understanding, under-exercised poodle, Topo.' Dedication in **Peter O'Sullevan's** *Horse Racing Heroes.*

'Horses either jump the fence or they don't. There is no point worrying about it. They are not trying to fall on purpose.' **Ruby Walsh,** (*Observer Sport Monthly,* January 2005).

'Ivor Guft. The Grand National, ideally beating Hoof Hearted by a short head. Anybody who heard the commentary would never forget it.' The 2004 Betting Shop Manager of the Year Finalist **David Bennett** answers the question, 'If you owned a racehorse, what would you call it, and which race would you like to win?'

'Deirdre's wonderful leather trousers – which won the C4 best-turned out award before (and after) every race.' **Alastair Down** is smitten by Deirdre Johnston's dress sense at Newmarket's Champions Day in October 2004.

'Mumans was wearing green tinsel on his eyelashes,' noted *Racing Post* reporter **Colin Russell** as the horse won at Haydock on October 21, 2004.

'If you're winning races, you can go without shaving and wear any old thing you want. But if you're not winning races, you at least better look good.' US trainer **Richard Mandella**, (*Evening Standard*, 27 October 2004).

Which 1993 Arc de Triomphe winning jockey was emulating his father?

'Smart shorts and jeans are acceptable, but no bare tops, vests or tracksuits!' **Grandstand Enclosure Dress Code** at Newbury, 2004.

'There is no dress code – we recommend racegoers to dress for the weather.' **Cheltenham** leaves garb up to the individual – and the Met men – for the 2004 Open meeting.

'She rode side saddle, in purple jacket and cap, nankeen skirt, purple shoes and embroidered stockings' The high-fashion gear in which a Mrs Thornton rode against – and beat by half a neck – the great jockey of his day, Frank Buckle, in an 1805 match race over two miles at York. **C M Prior**, 1926.

'I'd got to 50 and I didn't even have a passport. I'd never even been to France. But he's had me over to Monte Carlo and Paris. It's magic.' **Howard Johnson** reflects on his change of situation since wealthy, private jet-owning Graham Wylie gave him a string of horses to train.

'I have this American habit of eating my sausage on a piece of toast and marmalade. One morning, as I cut my sausage it shot across the table. I had to mumble, "My apologies, Your Majesty". Dad just growled at me.' **Clare Balding** remembers an occasion when Dad, Ian, had one of his owners, The Queen, over for breakfast (*Sunday Times Magazine*, 19 September 2004).

'I've seen Kieren stop racecourse staff throwing away some of our left over food and insisting that it is offered to the valets. He's very thoughtful, you know.' **Kevin Darley** on his colleague Kieren Fallon (*The Times*, 2 October 2004).

'The first place I went after leaving Newcastle and returning from a break abroad was to watch one of our horses run at Catterick. That was an escape into that other world.' **Kevin Keegan**.

Eris Saint-Martin, son of Yves.

'Spark Off stormed home at a starting price of 12/1. Mick won more than £7000, which was big dough then, but all he could keep saying was how guilty he felt because he hadn't told the other lads that he fancied the horse.' Mick Channon's great mate **Bob 'Larry the Cab' Charles** on the then Southampton star's New Year's Day 1981 coup at Devon & Exeter, which he couldn't divulge, not only to preserve the price but, 'also, hand on heart, to save me the cringing embarrassment of having to apologise to all and sundry if I said I fancied them and then they went and got beaten'. Adds Channon – 'That rule still applies today. It stops me making enemies.' (Channon's *Authorised Biography*).

'Emlyn was a great chap and absolutely fanatical about racing. He was full of enthusiasm – so much so that he thought the horse would win, even before it had run.' **Martin Pipe**, who trained Maragun for the former Liverpool and England skipper Emlyn Hughes, who died on 9 November 2004.

'Every time you tell the racegoers that I was the last person to score a hat trick in the League at Highbury while my runner's on the way down to the post, it runs terribly.' Footballer turned trainer **Mick Quinn** facing the curse of Derek Thompson (*Talksport Radio*, 30 November 2004).

'Everybody talks about him as if he has found a cure for cancer, brought about complete peace on Earth, scored the winner in the Cup Final and dated Marilyn Monroe in his lifetime.' Now *Racing Post*, then *Sporting Life*, writer **Bruce Millington** on Peter O'Sullevan in April 1996.

'It's a very unusual conversation piece.' An **eBay seller** of droppings from 2004 Kentucky Derby winner Smarty Jones, available at $12.50 on the net in June of that year.

The great Derby winner Mill Reef won his first race in May 1970 at which course?

'There has never been a day lost to the rain on the Rowley Mile.' **Alastair Down** (*Racing Post*, 17 October 2004).

'After a big winner I'm overwhelmed by immense relief. Beforehand, I'm so nervous, I ask if I can still do it. When I do, it's similar to an orgasm. After one you want another.' Trainer **Ben Hanbury** (*Racing Post*, 31 July 1996).

'Racing is the only sport in the world in which you can participate, spectate and socialise all at the same time.' **Peter Savill**.

'Racing may have more right to be called the "national sport" than football, as it appeals to all ages, all social classes and a higher proportion of women.' **Kate Fox**, author of *The Racing Tribe*.

'Racing is the best fun you can have with your clothes on.' Jockey **Andy Orkney**.

'Racing is a game of make-believe. If people didn't think they had horses that were better than they really were national hunt racing would collapse.' Irish trainer **Mick O'Toole**.

'Racing is the iceberg sport. Only a tiny part of the story, the bit on the racecourse, is above the waterline.' Writer **John Scally**.

'I expect you'll be no worse than fourth coming off the bend and try to be on the outside, at that point you'll make your move. It was like following a road map.' US jock **Gary Stevens** recalls the Queen's instructions prior to his winning ride on Blueprint at Royal Ascot in 1999.

Bath.

'The fact that in an absolute maximum of 90 minutes he bridged the 127 miles that the National Trainers' Federation diary says lies between the two sets of weighing scales, on Saturday afternoon and through at least two sets of roadworks, is scary.' **Howard Wright** notes that jockey Shane Kelly rode at Doncaster in a race finishing at eleven minutes and 30 seconds past 2 p.m. on 31 July 2004, and got to Newmarket in time to be declared to ride in the 3.45 p.m.

'Sprinting in North America is as close to a street fight as racing ought to get, and it is so, so different to sprinting in England – where the turf is nice, straight and green, where there is seldom a bend to negotiate and where there is plenty of room for everyone.' **Geir Stabell**, who believes, 'There are no top-class sprinters in Europe' (*Pacemaker*, November 2004).

'Being Italian I have superstitions but not so many since my plane crash. Until then I carried a number of good luck charms. Now I just have one cross around my neck.' **Frankie Dettori**.

'How lucky I had been to see a load of straw that morning, as I left the yard. My superstition – "A load of straw you draw, a load of hay you pay" – had been proved right again.' **Henrietta Knight** on the day in 2003 when Best Mate won his second consecutive Cheltenham Gold Cup.

'It sent a small shiver down my spine – I prayed it would be lucky for Matey.' **Henrietta Knight**, trainer to by now triple Cheltenham Gold Cup winner Best Mate, had her 'superstitions aroused' when a fox crossed her path and looked at her as she was walking the course prior to the horse's seasonal debut at Exeter in November 2004, which he went on to win.

'I kept the hen as long as I could, but more really as a kind of lucky charm.' Russian champion jockey of the seventies, **Nikolai**

Marquee Universal won at Salisbury on 7 April 1979 – the first winner in Britain for which future champion jockey?

Nasibov, who used to eat a raw egg a day before riding, courtesy of the bird.

'With a filly named Ouija Board it follows that we are particularly superstitious. My wife Cazzie insists we can't change anything. We will be in clothes identical to those we were wearing for the Pretty Polly – and what we have had on every time she has run since.' **Lord Derby** explained why his get-up for the 2004 Breeders Cup might have looked somewhat familiar.

'In the catalogue of superstitious rituals that racing people resort to in order to come up with a winner, I personally think that consulting a horse-astrology site is practically mainstream.' Few would concur with author **Jane Smiley**, I suspect, who revealed her consultation of an Aussie website in *A Year at the Races*.

'I try to forget what the pain was like, but I wouldn't wish it on a rapist.' **Gee Armytage** on the back injury that ended her riding career.

'Sometimes I feel like I'm patching up the Christians to throw them back to the lions.' Jump jockey physio **Rabbit Slattery**.

'I saw Dr Parry and he told me I was incredibly fit for a man of 55.' So said 32-year-old **Lorcan Wyer**, coming back from a three-month injury lay-off in 1997.

'My left hand fell off my arm. There was nothing but skin holding it on.' **Jamie Osborne** on his 1997 Cheltenham fall.

'When you first start riding, falls are just great fun – you're unbreakable.' **Peter Scudamore** (*Between Ourselves*, Radio 4, August 2004).

Steve Cauthen.

'I can touch my toes for the first time in ten years.' A rejuvenated **Jimmy Fortune** after receiving relief via a back operation in South Africa (July 2004).

'I stopped counting the pieces when I got to twelve.' Jump jockey **Kenny Johnson**, who broke his shoulder in a fall at Uttoxeter in 2004.

'I scrambled off the mark and got a few runs but during the innings I damaged my Achilles.' **Michael Stoute's** love of cricket kept him busy struggling to get fit during the summer, autumn and winter of 2003 after sustaining an injury in a cricket match the day after he had won the Derby with Kris Kin.

'The horse jumped right on top of me at the second last, kicking my teeth out and breaking a collarbone and three ribs. My mother came to see me in hospital, took one look at my damaged face and promptly fainted. As she did so, she fell against the wall and cut her head open.' Jockey turned trainer **Gary Moore** on a fall from Jamie's Cottage at Plumpton in the mid-seventies.

'He tied some baler-twine round his arm as a tourniquet, pulled what remained of his finger out, recovered a few bits of flesh and drove home in the tractor.' **Marcus Armytage** relates the injury caused to John Taylor, husband/assistant of trainer Lavinia, when he tussled with one of their schooling fences, losing a finger in the process (*Daily Telegraph*, 26 October 2004).

'I thought about ringing my builder, but it looked such a simple job that I thought, why would I get someone else in to do it.' Minutes later top US jockey **Jerry Bailey** climbed up a ladder to fit new storm shutters on his windows, fell and broke his wrist in September 2004.

Whose racing colours were emerald green, royal blue sleeves, white cap and emerald green spots?

'I said I would give my right arm to be back in the weighing room. Realising what I had said, I smiled to myself. There was a good chance that if I'd stayed I would have had to give my right arm. Yet I'm still not sure I made the right decision.' **Richard Dunwoody** in 2000 after packing it in when the medics ruled that one more fall could literally cost him the use of a limb.

'I was out for about three months, three agonizing months. I had my jaw wired shut and I couldn't eat anything unless it was through a straw.' Texan jockey **Jerry Bailey** recalls the aftermath of what he rates his worst-ever injury, a broken jaw in 1978.

'I thought when I took my glove off, my thumb might be left inside it.' **Tony McCoy** on the digital injury he sustained in November 2004, which he was told would keep him out for six weeks. He was back in nine days.

'The steeplechase is a mode of racing which I do not recommend. It is attended by a vast amount of danger, calls too much on the energies of the horse, and causes the death of many a valuable animal.' Not a contemporary RSPCA view but taken from *The Sporting Review* in 1858.

'When you're a jump jockey your fingers are permanently crossed.' **Tony McCoy**, 1997.

'Jumps racing in Britain should be banned: consigned to the knacker's yard along with foxhunting and other relics of an earlier, coarser, bloodier sporting age.' **Michael Thompson-Noel**, in the *Financial Times*, January 1998, who also called jumping, 'Britain's greediest, moaniest and most over-subsidised big-time sport.'

Robert Sangster.

'What other activity allows you to smoke, drink, make money and watch giant animals jumping over fences all at the same time?' **Tom Hodgkinson** (*The Idler*, Winter 1997).

'He was prepared to do it his way and ignore precedent, while picking the brains of those he admired.' **Peter O'Sullevan** on Martin Pipe.

'I wish people could only understand the real thrill, the challenge of steeplechasing. It's part of the great British way of life, and none of the sports I've done bears any comparison.' **Prince Charles**.

'One of my owners said he wanted a three-mile chaser. My reply was that you cannot buy one – you try to create one and then you wait and hope.' **David Elsworth** in 1989.

'Flyingbolt was the second greatest steeplechaser of all time, being officially rated only one pound inferior to Arkle, but was totally overshadowed by his stablemate – hence his shameful neglect today.' **John Randall** (*Racing Post*, 11 July 2004).

'Arkle and Easter Hero were the most brilliant, but as the former was never asked to face the gruelling task of jumping Aintree, for me Easter Hero deserves the palm.' Much-respected **John Hislop** goes against conventional wisdom by picking the 1928–30 Gold Cup champion as 'the greatest'. Some of us – well, I for one – rate Golden Miller even more highly than this pair!

'National Hunt racing is National Hunt racing. It started in the hunting field. Why should anyone be ashamed of it?' **Ginger McCain** is not best pleased as the BHB consider dropping the words 'National Hunt' and changing the name of the sport to Jump Racing (May 2004).

Which is the US's oldest racecourse that is still in use?

'Edward Gillespie will tell you that even now there are people who don't come to Cheltenham because they think they'll see people chasing foxes around the place.' **Toby Balding** is not sure he agrees with McCain.

'He was a hard man and a great critic who would criticise you more when you rode a winner than when you did a loser.' Trainer **Fred Rimell** remembers his jockey mentor Gerry Wilson, who was champion six times in the thirties.

'You have to be slightly peculiar to seek profit from the sort of grotesque spectacle that ensues after two exhausted, mud-caked animals kick and slither across the final hurdle.' *Times* writer **Chris McGrath** is scathing about betting on jumpers.

'A jump jockey has to throw his heart over the fence – and then go over and catch it.' Jockey turned bestselling novelist, **Dick Francis**.

'The great joy of jump racing is that everyone with whom you rub shoulders in the stands in a bitter November rain is a true believer.' Former Foreign Secretary, **Robin Cook**, September 2004.

'A more thrilling, uplifting, glorious way of living has yet to be invented. It's even better than shagging.' **John Francome** on being a jump jockey (*Racing Ahead*, October 2004).

'You look at him and see only strength. Gaunt and famished he may be, but he is not like other men.' *Telegraph* writer **Paul Hayward** on A P McCoy, in October 2004. He concluded, 'His stomach is like his spirit. Eternally hungry.'

Saratoga, which opened in 1863.

'I believe that June and July should be devoted to Flat racing and that the turf on the jump courses should be rested and given a chance to recover from the caning it gets during the winter.' **Henrietta Knight**, (*Daily Telegraph*, 21 October 2004).

'Jumping's a sport within an industry and deserves its own governing body.' **Toby Balding** to Andrew Longmore (*Sunday Times*, 7 November 2004).

'Jump racing is essentially a local entertainment, of little or no interest to most of the rest of the world.' **Paul Haigh**.

'I've been at the bottom for 22 years. It's too late for me to do anything else now.' **Paddy Butler** after his Park Royal won a Lingfield seller in 1999 to break a run of 93 consecutive losers for the trainer.

'I'm now handling 200 horses better than the 50 I had ten years ago, so why not have 250 or even 300? I certainly don't feel intimidated by the numbers.' **Mark Johnston** (*Racing Ahead*, July 2004).

'Faucets for Grohe-Tec Automatic Taps and Urinal Controls Maiden Stakes.' **Lingfield's 2.20 p.m.** on 24 November 1998.

'Mrs R Soles.' Signature on a fax read out on air by unsuspecting **Clare Balding** in 1998, rumoured to have been sent by the retiring Julian Wilson. And at Royal Ascot 2004, Clare was almost hysterical when Willie Carson read out an email he attributed to Ann On, instead of 'Anon(ymous)'.

'He absolutely hates me. He criticises me for bad tips, bad clothes, what I drink – he must be someone who is on the racecourse very regularly.' Professional punter **Dave Nevison** on why

Why did Popham Down go down in Grand National folklore?

he named a horse General Haigh, after the pseudonym of a 'chat-room stalker' who is forever panning him.

'I won £250 on Rooster Booster a few years ago, but Rooster Booster didn't quite have the ring we were after for the group's name. Then, though, we shortened it to Rooster and all the boys were happy.' **Nick Atkinson**, leader of rock band Rooster, explains where they got their name, in September 2004, just a few weeks after Mercury Music Prize winners Franz Ferdinand confessed that they had taken their moniker from flat stayer, Archduke Ferdinand.

'Er, it ran at Chantilly in France on Wednesday. Er, its name is…Er.' The *Observer's* **Tattenham Corner column** claims to have found the shortest name in racing in September 2004.

'One of the greatest athletes I've seen.' **Tony McCoy** explaining in November 2003 why he named his boxer puppy Henry – after Arsenal's Thierry.

'She employs an animal communicator, who tells her that her horse doesn't like his name, Hornblower, but would prefer to be called Wowie.' **Simon Barnes**, reviewing a book by Jane Smiley, who had spent a year training in the States, called *A Year at the Races* (*The Times*, 23 October 2004).

'I suggested the name as my dad was in the grocery trade. I've had some interest in horses before but knowing my luck this could be the kiss of death for Lady Lloyd-Webber.' **Terry Wogan** teamed up with Madeleine, wife of Andrew Lloyd-Webber, to acquire Nicky Henderson-trained Grocer's Curate in November 2004.

'On the advice of his aunt, he decided to play up his famous name and now sends all his horses to train wearing saddlecloths

He was the horse who precipitated the infamous pile-up that enabled 100/1 outsider Foinavon to win.

bearing the 007 logo.' **New York Racing Guide 1996** on trainer Harold James Bond.

'They might be better off sticking a camera up a horse's backside to have a look for the non-triers.' Straight-talking trainer **Clive Brittain** reacting in 1997 to news that helmet-mounted TV cameras would be used by selected jockeys.

'Get a crowd of racing people together and they will talk horses for sure and with such extreme gravity that many parties forget that racing is a sport and sometimes confuse themselves with normal people.' Former jockey **Jack Leach** was reported to have said this in 1970 – and it holds good today.

'Wasting does get you down and I was fasting for two days and then eating. When you haven't eaten for two days, you suddenly eat too much. I want to get back to eating like normal people.' **Walter Swinburn**, reported by the *Sporting Life* in March 1997.

Three generations of which racing family competed in a 25 October 1998 charity race at Wincanton with the senior of the three winning it 32 years after his last victory?

Trainer Trivia

In my experience, trainers make lousy tipsters.

One of the best winners I've ever had was at Cagnes racecourse in the South of France. There on a racing holiday, the word came through from Horse Racing Abroad supremo, Ian Fry, that Sir Mark Prescott's English raider, Humoreuse, was well fancied. We few English folk sitting in the restaurant enjoying a leisurely meal decided to lump on with our euros, and were delighted to note that the prevailing odds on offer were 7/1. We were even more delighted when the horse put up a great display of front running to charge home to victory with our cheers ringing around the restaurant.

But it was only our table that was cheering, I soon noted – everyone else was looking a little subdued, and a somewhat shame-faced Ian Fry was issuing apologies all round. Apparently, he had got the word late on, shortly before the race, that the trainer didn't fancy the horse after all, because of the going, or a bad trip over or some such reason. So Ian had advised everyone not to risk their money. Everyone, that is, but me and my party – and we'd cleaned up.

But no thanks to the trainer.

'Whatever you do, don't become a trainer.' Trainer **Towser Gosden** to his son, John who, er, ignored the advice.

'When I get too old to have fun I'll start painting.' Trainer **Lydia Richards**.

'That's the way I remember it,' said follically-challenged trainer **Charlie 'Bald Eagle' Whittingham** when he was asked why he had

Scudamore.

listed his hair colour as 'brown' when applying to train in New York.

'With balls of steel.' That was how trainer **Eddie O'Grady** told jockey Charlie Swan to ride the 1994 Cheltenham Festival winner Time For A Run.

'Win or lose, we'll have a booze.' Motto of trainer **Ken 'Benign Bishop' Oliver**.

'I'm terrified of him and I had to have a large vodka and tonic before I saddled him up.' Trainer **Hughie Morrison** on his September 2004 winner, Pastoral Pursuits.

'What do you want me to do? Get a bucket and wash him down?' Trainer **Roger Charlton** loses his cool like Trade Fair, who, pointed out Clare Balding at Glorious Goodwood 2004, was beginning to sweat up.

'After two minutes listening to Paddy (Prendergast, trainer) talk about your horse for two minutes, you just had to feel sorry for the opposition.' **Bing Crosby**, whose Prendergast-trained Meadow Court won the Irish Sweeps Derby. This Crosby statement was recalled in 2004 by Peter O'Sullevan.

'The easiest owner I trained for was Elizabeth Taylor. She was so worried her horses would get injured she never wanted them to run.' **John Gosden** (*Sunday Times* 13 April 1997).

'If she was human you would want to marry her, wouldn't you?' A rhetorical – one hopes – question from trainer of August 2004 Newmarket winner Golden Island, **John Hills**.

To which betting price does the tic-tac related word 'Shoulder' refer?

'Claiming horses is like trying to make a living by going through garbage cans.' US trainer **Lefty Nickerson**.

'I didn't want to get back into racing, to be perfectly honest. I was like an ex-racechorse turned sour.' But the lure of training for equally comebacking owner, the legendary gambler Terry Ramsden (for whom he trained his very first winner), saw **Geoff Huffer** pick up the reins once more in 2004, having been imprisoned for five months for a contested duty fraud offence in 2001. Of this he said, 'I wasn't guilty… But I just thought I'd get it over and done with.'

'It is not without precedent for someone with a criminal record to train again.' Jockey Club spokesman **John Maxse** 'welcomes' back trainer Geoff Huffer, who served a jail sentence for tax evasion (*Mail on Sunday* 11 July 2004).

'I didn't know I could water divine until we had a big underground leak in the yard and it was a case of find the leak or dig up all the concrete. It would have cost me a fortune to dig the whole lot up, so I got a couple of metal rods and had a go.' Trainer **Peter Harris**, confessing to a rare talent in October 2004.

'When I took the earplugs out he was so shocked he whipped round as if someone had slapped him on the arse and I fell out the back.' Fortunately for remounted **Richard Hills**, Bandari got over his surprise at trainer Mark Johnston's cunning plan to prevent the horse becoming upset during the preliminaries for Newmarket's 2004 Princess of Wales's Stakes and went on to win by half a length at 12/1.

'At (James) Fanshawe's it is not the horses but the staff who need earplugs.' **Alastair Down** on the trainer who loves 'obscure rock bands…blasting out at 150 decibels'.

'I think more of this horse than my wife as I ride him all the time at home, rounding up the cows.' Trainer **John Manners'** 1996 tribute to either his good lady or his Taunton winner, Killeshin.

'Meeting a horse for the first time is quite similar to meeting a woman, because the eyes tell me everything I want to know.' Trainer **Ken Hogg**, 1996.

'The lovely thing about having older horses like Marlborough is that you get to know them so well, like reading a favourite book. He tells you if anything isn't quite right – he can nearly talk.' Trainer **Nicky Henderson**, November 2004.

'Exeter is one of my favourite tracks.' Trainer **Robert Alner**.

'He's a top trainer, a good boss and a smashing feller to work for.' Travelling head groom **Roy Thorpe** is a fan of trainer Michael Bell.

'The only vegetable the trainer will eat is processed marrowfat peas.' **Richard Edmondson** on Martin Pipe.

'British trainers tend to be suspicious of European styles. Even when top French jockeys like Adam Kondrat were riding lots of winners here, nobody wanted to put them up.' German trainer **Christian von der Recke** (*The Times*, 4 November 2004).

'When Affirmed breaks like that you can put the beans on the fire – you're gonna eat for sure.' Trainer **Laz Barrera** after US Triple Crown winner Affirmed won the 1979 Jockey Club Gold Cup.

Which Royal mistress owned racehorses under the name 'Mr Jersey'?

'Rival trainers would be thoroughly justified in employing delaying tactics of their own. If they do, the next Derby will be run by moonlight.' **Andrew Longmore** in the *Sunday Times* on Stoute-Fallon's device of taking subsequent 2004 Derby winner North Light down to post on his own at funereal pace.

'This horse has had more problems in the last six months than Bill Clinton – and this fellow's a gelding.' Trainer **Dr Jon Scargill** on Herr Trigger in 1998.

'I don't think there is such an animal as a racehorse that is not genuine. If they don't give their all you can bet your life there is something amiss with them, and as the trainer it's your job to find out what it is.' **Mick Channon** dispelling many handlers' favourite excuse for failure.

'They (owners) live up their trainer's noses and haunt them.' Trainer **Brian Gubby** whose nasal passages are apparently crowded with spectres.

'I'd say we made a bit of history today. I doubt very much if a horse trained in Galway had ever won a Listed race on the flat until now.' Trainer **Kevin McDonagh** after his Senor Benny won the 5f (five furlong) Abergwaun Stakes at Cork on 16 October 2004.

'An Eton and Sandhurst man who had a leg blown off in Korea, he is said to travel with three artificial legs: one for shooting, one for riding and one for dancing.' **Robin Oakley** writing about trainer Fergie Sutherland in 1996.

'The best day I ever had was when I found my ex-wife had run off with an amateur jockey. The worst was when I realised how much it was going to cost me.' Trainer **Les Eyre**.

Actress Lily Langtry, Edward VII's intimate friend.

'When I was ten I built my first motor-bike from spare parts.' Malton trainer, **John Parkes**, a self-confessed bike freak.

'I adore getting away to the sunshine with a few books, and love reading cynical people like Maugham and Hemingway.' Trainer **James Fanshawe**.

'Computer illiterate and proud of it.' **Julian Muscat** on trainer James Fanshawe.

'In my younger days, body surfing was very popular – now it's all boogie-boarding' Keen surfer, Cornwall-bred trainer **Mark Polglase**.

'The talent was a common nineteenth-century term for the betting public.' So says specialist in the derivation of racing terms, **Gerald Hammond**.

'We should remember when we are rollocking jockeys that it is a job where the ambulance follows you when you are working.' Trainer **Bill O'Gorman**.

'Owners want a first-class ticket for third-class money.' Retiring trainer **Bill Watts**, in December 1997.

'I'm not sure I can get my head around a woman running the country.' Trainer **Ian Balding** in 1979, discussing Margaret Thatcher with, er, The Queen.

Maxims, saying, proverbs, adages and mottos–not trivial at all!

'Racing is a magnificent triviality.'

The lead singer of which chart-topping pop group owned steeplechaser Gainsay, trained by Jenny Pitman?

'Follow a winning two-year-old until it gets beaten and then back the one that beats it.'

'Always back the outsider of three.'

'The bigger the field, the bigger the certainty.'

'Winter follows on the tail of the last horse in the Leger.'

'All men are equal on and under the turf.'

'Sell in May and go away, buy again St Leger day.' **Stockmarket investment adage**.

'Blood will tell.'

'Breed the best to the best and hope for the best.'

'Do we breed to race, or race to breed?'

'The best thing in the world is to win at the racetrack. The second best thing is to lose at the racetrack.' **American truism**.

'A race is not a beauty contest.'

'Take wisdom from wise people: not everyone who rides is a jockey.' Extract from poem attributed to **Sheikh Mohammed**.

Errol Brown of Hot Chocolate.

'You don't get surprises in racing, just disappointments.' **John Dunlop**, December 1997.

'Sharp minds Betfair:' It may be their current slogan, but I can't help thinking that they are having a pop at me – even if they are pretty poor spellers – but then so was my granddad, who put the "e" on the end because he thought it looked classier.

'Mark Johnston chose the logo "Always Trying" in the wry recognition that not everyone else is.' **Clare Balding** (*Observer*, 5 September 2004).

'You are following racing's best: Jack Berry.' Slogan on the back of **Jack Berry's horsebox**.

'Ask any trainer, and I'm sure they would prefer to train 30 top class horses than 80 average ones.' Er, and why wouldn't they, Willie? Former jockey **Willie Humphreys** with a pearl of wisdom from his *Gloucestershire Echo* column on 12 November 2004. In the same piece he revealed, probably exclusively, that, 'Having been second for a long time, Jonjo has slipped to fourth in the trainers' championship and he won't want to sink any further.'

'There is only one place worth being and that is at the top.' **Michael Stoute**, who, once asked if he had always known he would be champion trainer, replied, 'Sure, I always thought I'd be champion of Barbados.' He is the son of the commissioner of police in Barbados.

'I'm a bit of a late developer, really – I didn't walk until I was ten. My wife Gloria says I'm a bit of a Peter Pan character.' **Alan Jessop** had just sent out his first winner as a trainer, Moss Run, at Huntingdon in January 2005 – at the age of 65.

Which influential, widely-read racing institution survived from 1859–1998?

'The most common reason for horses getting beaten is trainer error, but, thank God, it is seldom reported.' Rare humility from a trainer – **Sir Mark Prescott** (*Sporting Life*, 30 August 1996). He also declared, 'A happy trainer is a bad trainer; the worse the trainer, the happier he is – because he hasn't noticed what's going wrong.'

'There are plenty of people who train horses who think they are saving the world rather than preparing beasts to run round a field.' *Independent* racing writer, **Richard Edmondson**.

'It's a bit like being a pimp. You provide individuals for people's pleasure and you take money for it.' Newmarket trainer **Dr Jon Scargill** on his profession.

'If a horse is owned by the Queen, or George Smith, or me, it does not matter, it is the trainer's name that is always going to be attached to the horse... The poor owner is not going to be mentioned at all in the whole story. He is only there to pay the bills and to be told where the horse will run... I tried and tried to alter this and, really, I just gave up.' **Sheik Mohammed** on why he set up Godolphin (*Sunday Times*, 24 March 1996).

'I hate going racing.' **Ted Powell**, trainer, 1997.

'Where I was born and bred, just outside Streatham, to be associated with horses was definitely not the done thing. Robbing the sweetshop on the corner was more acceptable.' **Rod Simpson**.

'Some people train week to week. Some people train day to day. We train minute to minute.' **D Wayne Lukas**.

Sporting Life.

'My ambition is to get a decent horse and not make too many cock-ups with it.' Trainer **David Barron**, July 2004.

'I used to think that if anyone wanted a horse trained by me they would ring up and ask, and that if I had to ask anyone to train their horse they probably weren't the people I wanted to have as owners. But I haven't had many people ringing me up recently.' **Henry Cecil**, June 2000.

'It's like if you have a favourite restaurant, you can't go and eat in another one – it's ridiculous.' **Milton Harris** hits back at fellow trainers who were miffed that he was offering to under-cut them to attract new business in May 2004.

'Most people in racing, especially trainers, are shamefully conservative and narrow-minded, which is why no jockey dares to grow a beard or moustache, let alone come out of the closet.' **John Randall** (*Racing Post*, 11 July 2004).

'Not all trainers are good men. Some of them – not being too controversial here, I think – are miserable, tight-fisted, self-centred, scheming, rotten swine.' **Paul Haigh** waits in vain for a howl of outraged protest from punters and owners (*Racing Post*, 31 July 2004).

'The all-time master of bluff and counter-bluff.' **Marten Julian** on the enigmatic Barney Curley, August 2004.

'He's the best at it. He's come from nowt to plenty. We all want to be that good.' William Haggas pays a July 2004 tribute to master trainer **Sir Michael Stoute**.

If a racehorse 'stales' what has he/she done?

'Soon.' Entry from fledgling trainer **Alan**, son of Jack, **Berry** in the *Directory of the Turf*, in answer to the query, 'Major races won?'

'Mark Johnston's stable motto is 'Always Trying'. Would that there were other trainers who could boast in a similar fashion. Indeed, it is hard to think of a handful of his fellow trainers whose horses are virtually all seen to be running on their merits.' **Tony Paley**, who also absolves Martin Pipe and Godolphin of blame (*Racing Ahead*, August 2004).

'Jenny explained to my father that she would pay for my digs and riding clothes, provided they (my parents) sent me some spending money.' Trainer **Bryan Smart** recalls his early days as a would-be jockey with Jenny Pitman (*Racing Ahead*, August 2004).

'I wouldn't be quite sure, Ms Paget, but I've a pretty shrewd idea he's on the top of the stand, cutting his throat.' **Sir Gordon Richards**, who had just been beaten on hotly fancied Colonel Payne at Royal Ascot in 1939, to fuming owner Dorothy Paget. She had just spent a small fortune on the horse and was demanding to know where trainer Fred Darling might be found.

'The greatest trainer of steeplechasers there has ever been.' **John Oaksey** on Fulke Walwyn.

'I've always been of the opinion that anyone can put a saddle on, and that you can do more good at home than you can at the races.' **Keith Reveley**, preparing to take over from his mother, Mary, in August 2004.

'Sorry to hear news – Australia 4 for 185.' Possibly apocryphal response of old-time Aussie trainer **Jack Brown**, who had received a telegram from a pal, saying, 'Things bad, send a score.'

Urinated.

'Since I stopped training, I've stopped betting, too. Why? It's obvious; you've got to be right in the game to have the faintest chance of making money.' Trainer turned writer **Ivor Herbert** in 2002.

'One morning, as I stood on the Heath with a scruffy trainer on his old hack a traditional trainer who had just won the Derby rode over and berated him for his appearance. When ignored, the traditional trainer found purchase in a hole in my friend's jodhpurs and tore them from hip to knee. He rode away saying "Get yourself some new jodhpurs. You're a disgrace to the Heath."' **Rebecca Cassidy** in her 2002 book, *The Sport of Kings*.

'Trainers, like tribal shamans, witch doctors and rain-makers, are regularly credited with performing miracles when they are successful, but very rarely blamed when they are unsuccessful.' **Kate Fox** in *The Racing Tribe*.

'Of course I listen to my staff and my jockeys. There would be no point in having them if I didn't. But in the final instance they have to do as I tell them, or leave.' The late jumps trainer, **Gordon Richards**, with views echoed by many a handler.

'The moment you start thinking that you've got where you wanted to be, that's when you'll go down.' Not a mistake **Jack Berry**, who said this in 1993, ever made.

'It's a fact of modern training life that you're more likely to win a war if you've got an army.' **Henry Cecil**, who, in 1993, certainly had the necessary ammo to fight with.

'Trainers are professionals. An owner should approach a trainer in the same way that he would go to an accountant, and put himself in their hands.' **Luca Cumani**, quoted by Andrew Sim in *English Racing Stables*.

Which Derby-winning jockey's party-piece was an imitation of a barking dog?

'My father and George Todd would lay out a horse for a year. Leaving aside the economics of doing nothing with a horse for a year you couldn't get the cash on today. All the big bookmakers are interested in is servicing an endless fruit machine of mug punters in the betting shops.' **John Gosden** in 1993 – well, bookies wouldn't make much profit taking once-a-year bets on winners, when all's said and done!

'I find the whole process of finding the right race for a horse that can only win off a mark of 55 endlessly fascinating.' **Sir Mark Prescott** first said this in 1993 and is still standing by his own words and continuing to wind people up in the process.

'Henry was like a God in racing, almost untouchable. Stoutey was one of those guys that you could approach.' **Kieren Fallon** on Messrs Cecil and Stoute (*Thoroughbred Owner & Breeder*, September 2004).

'I didn't want to be one of those people who profess to have the ability to do the job but don't put their neck on the block.' Jockey turned trainer **Paul D'Arcy**, September 2004.

'If they leave it to me, we don't do too bad – when the passenger tries to fly the plane, it's time for the pilot to bale out.' **Dandy Nicholls** on keeping owners happy over riding arrangements when a stable has more than one runner in a race. He was speaking after Funfair Wane came out top of his multiple entry for the 2004 Ayr Gold Cup.

'I'm a sick person. I do nothing but work. I have no balance in my life and I recognize that. I've gone through numerous marriages, because the horses are always a priority and I don't think that makes for a good marriage and I'll admit that openly.' US trainer **D Wayne Lukas** (*Pacemaker*, October 2004).

Greville Starkey.

'We live in a dream factory.' **Mick Channon** on trainers (*Daily Mail*, 2 October 2004).

'His tongue is the vocal equivalent of that windmill right arm which rotated maniacally when celebrating a goal.' **Alan Fraser** of footballer turned trainer Mick Channon. Of Channon's verbal technique he also noted, 'Quoting Channon requires the removal of swear words, the insertion of grammar and, often, the completion of sentences' (*Daily Mail*, 2 October 2004).

'If he was in the Olympic Games he'd probably be on drugs and get suspended for two years.' **Mick Channon** discussing, tongue in cheek, Mark Prescott's ability to disguise the true merits of a horse until the last possible moment, (Channel 4, 3 October 2004).

'The most reactionary bunch of people in the world are racehorse trainers. As far as they are concerned, the public are a damned nuisance.' **John McCririck** (*Sunday Telegraph*, 31 May 1998).

'He's eaten up well. But then my girlfriend left me this week and I'm still eating.' **Rod Simpson**, asked how his horse Nipper Read was after an Ascot race in 1998.

'If you asked me why Flat jockeys can't do training I'd have to say I just don't know.' **Walter Swinburn**, on the verge of doing it himself (*Independent*, 7 October 2004). He had quoted Sheikh Mohammed as telling him, 'Jockeys don't make good trainers.'

'He's single-minded to an unbelievable degree and the amazing thing is his horses run so gamely they somehow seem to have taken on his refusal to accept second best.' Former jockey **Jason Weaver** on Mark Johnston, October 2004.

When Silver Patriarch won the 1997 St Leger ridden by Pat Eddery
what milestone did the jockey reach?

'I've never done this for the money – I do it for the buzz and for my ego.' Trainer **Jamie Poulton**, October 2004.

'The bottom line is that we've got everything here bar an excuse.' **Jonjo O'Neill** admitting that his state-of-the-art yard brings pressures of its own. He added, in conversation with writer Paul Hayward, 'A good jockey doesn't need orders and a bad one forgets them.'

'It's a load of bollocks really, and I'll be doing it with my tongue in my cheek. You know my opinion – everything's gone soft. I don't want to be offensive but if that's my feelings, I can't help it.' **Ginger McCain**, who was preparing to write his autobiography (*Observer*, 24 October 2004).

'Line those bastards up, I love to take them on… You don't have much fun at the shallow end of the pool.' Veteran trainer **D Wayne Lukas** explained the decision to aim his six-year-old mare, Azeri, at the Breeders Cup Classic in 2004, where she was an outsider, instead of opting to contest the Distaff, for which she would have started odds-on favourite. She finished fifth. An anonymous American journalist covering the meeting described Lukas, the first trainer in US history to reach both $100 million and $200 million of prize money, as 'a megalomaniac sociopath. He has a set of rules that only apply to him.'

'Not posh, but different.' **Sue Smith** describing her and husband Harvey's yard – the phrase could equally have been applied to the pair of them – at Craiglands Farm in Yorkshire.

'Spent a small fortune keeping up with his wealthy friends and died worth a mere £383.' Comment on trainer to the Prince of Wales, lover of high life, and mover in elevated circles, Richard Marsh (1851–1933), whose horses won four Derbies, three 2,000

His 4,000th winner in Britain.

Guineas; two 1,000 Guineas; one Oaks and three St Legers. The comment was in **National Horse Racing Museum's 2004 newsletter**.

'I spent four months driving him to the races. He taught me everything I know.' English-born trainer **Graham Motion**, whose Better Talk Now won the 2004 Breeders Cup Turf, recalling his time as chauffeur to jumps trainer Charlie Brooks (*Daily Telegraph*, 2 November 2004).

'It might be patronising to suggest that Teeton Mill's victory signalled the coming of age of the grey's trainer Venetia Williams, but there is no doubt she is now in the Premier League.' The late **Graham Rock** recognised the significance of the 5/1 shot's victory in the 1998 Hennessy Gold Cup, which was only the second by a woman trainer.

'This is a fickle business. You're either hot or cold. When things aren't going well, it's as if you've got chicken pox. Nobody wants to know you.' **John Gosden**, 1997.

'I wouldn't have the first idea about life in the real world.' Trainer **James Ewart**, November 2004.

'You get a horse ready for a race and they start coughing, they bleed, they lose a shoe. The public don't know that. They only lose their money, not their minds.' US trainer **Bobby Frankel**, 1992.

'The man who shot Bambi.' Self-description by **James Fanshawe** after his Soviet Song had beaten the public's favourite filly, Attraction, in the Falmouth Stakes in July 2004.

'I think trainers can probably get away with one bad season, but two in a row and people will start to ask questions.' And why

Who was the only trainer of the 20th century to win a Classic in five successive seasons?

shouldn't they, you might wonder? Former Gloucestershire jockey **Willie Humphreys** (*Gloucestershire Echo*, 12 November 2004).

'Well done, Timothy. They wanted to hang you yesterday but today they want to knight you.' Irish trainer **Ted Walsh** to controversial jockey Timmy Murphy, who had just ridden four winners for Martin Pipe and owner David Johnson at Cheltenham on 13 November 2004. He had been criticised the day before for losing on Well Chief for the same combination.

'What you know for certain is that you don't know nothing for certain.' US Hall of Fame trainer **Allen Jerkens**.

'See, here's the deal: the horse doesn't know what it costs. He doesn't know. Owners put the price on horses, okay?' US trainer **Nick Zito**.

'What I won't become is a trainer. Not because it's hard to train horses – but because it can be near impossible to train some owners.' Jockey **Vince Slattery**, (*News of the World*, 21 November 2004).

'It was his merciless insistence that in racing only America counted, his dismissal of every European horseman as a fraud that made our meeting unforgettable.' **Hugh McIlvanney** on 5ft 7in, 18-stone trainer John Campo, who trained Pleasant Colony to win the 1981 Kentucky Derby. McIlvanney also dubbed Campo 'the Godfather of American insularity' (*Sunday Times*, 21 November 2004).

'Tell that bloke if he's so unhappy about the trophy we'll buy it back from him.' Brisbane Turf Club chief **Sir Clive Uhr** after Lester Piggott won a race at Doomben in Aussie and was unimpressed with his trophy, which was then swapped for a payment of 100 Aussie dollars.

Sir Michael Stoute (1985–9).

'I've only won one race as an owner, but I think one crystal decanter is one too many!' **Clare Balding** calls for more imagination where race trophies are concerned.

'We owe it to our members to point out that, should they win a race at Leicester, they will often be paying for the trophy they collect.' **Sadie Ryan** of the Racehorse Owners Association on a practice she calls 'archaic and unfair' and which 'is now almost a thing of the past'. She also pointed out that of the 48 occasions on which 'optional trophies' had been handed out in 2004, '40 of them have been held at Leicester' (**Throughbred Owner & Breeder**, September 2004).

'I never take the slightest notice of what jockeys or trainers say about the merits of their horses. They are too close to them and cannot possibly be objective.' Racing historian **John Randall's** June 2004 put-down.

'People might think I'm mad or a witch.' Ancient Japanese spiritual healing expert, **Charlotte Watt**, who treats racehorses without ever seeing them and who was told by one of trainer Paul Keane's horses when she asked him why he always sped off in front: 'So would you if you had several tons of horses chasing your arse' (*Racing Post*, 13 January 2005).

What happened in racing for the first time in Britain on 26 July 1992?

On The Hoof

Funny things, horses. They all have four legs and are of similar colour – well, apart from the grey ones, of course. But for some reason you take to some of them and don't want much to do with others. I suppose a lot of that is to do with whether they win when you back them, but not always.

I was in Sweden for a race meeting at Taby when I met a racehorse whose name I couldn't tell you and who became one of my favourite equines despite not even running that afternoon.

Well, how else could you regard a horse who tipped you a winning bet? He did just that.

Fellow racegoer John Gloak and I were watching this horse jog around a paddock when it came over to see us. For a bit of fun we asked it for a tip in the first race, whereupon the horse pawed the ground nine times. Would you believe it that number nine finished second in the first race at 12/1, landing us a nice profit on our out-of-the-ordinary each-way tip.

Then there is First Gold. I was at Auteuil in France back in 1997 when this horse was a four-year-old. Trained by François Doumen, he won in style that afternoon and so delighted was the debonair trainer that you could tell he felt the horse was something special. I followed him throughout his career, which has had its ups and downs, and just minutes before penning these very words First Gold, now a twelve-year-old, ran second in a decent handicap at Haydock, partnered by Tony McCoy and returning odds of 9/1 – which would have made for a nice winning each-way bet had I not, inevitably, backed him win only!

Of course, very few horses are blessed with scintillating conversational talent so you will not find many equine comments herein – although Mr Ed was asked to contribute but merely offered 'no comment', while Derek Thompson has been spotted attempting to interview big-race winners from time to time, but with little success!

The first Sunday race meeting under Jockey Club Rules.

'When we went back one of the stallions had broken through the front of the stall and was biting chunks out of the one next door.' 'Air groom' **Dave Johnston** of the National Stud, who oversees the flying of stallions across the world. He said his favourite equine flyer was Bahamian Bounty, 'so quiet he'd walk into the stall and put his own seat belt on'.

'I recall one occasion, I was down at the start for the two-mile chase when the race was held up by cattle walking across the track.' Jockey turned trainer **Jimmy Fitzgerald** remembering a ride at the now defunct Northumberland track, Rothbury.

'I can remember going there and having to jump a sheep that had strayed on to the track.' Former jockey turned trainer **Pat Mitchell** remembered riding at the now defunct Wye.

'It is the feeling of movement and electricity, and projecting your viewpoint into the middle of the action; an attempt to control and fix what cannot be controlled or fixed.' Artist **Chris Bruce** explains what painting racing scenes means to him.

'Several of his exhibits are on racecards and one is on the panel of an old armoire cupboard he found at his home in France.' **Marcus Armytage** on leading equine artist Hubert de Watrigant's exhibition in London (*Daily Telegraph*, 16 November 2004).

'European horsemen do not fight shy of throwing fillies to the colts. It is quite different in America, where the prospect denotes one of two things: an outstanding distaffer or a totally insane trainer.' **Julian Muscat** (*The Times*, 27 July 2004).

'I exhibit for my soul.' Equine artist **Katie O'Sullivan**.

Aintree stages the longest race in the calendar – the Grand National. At four miles and two furlongs which course boasts the second longest event of the season?

'I've never tasted whiskey. I'm a lager man. The colder the better.'
At The Races presenter **Gordon Brown** – a Scot!

'Where do you want this nag?' Richard Hannon's dad, **Henry**, a
jockey and trainer himself, reportedly acquired his first horse,
Carrabawn, after sharing a few pints with a man from whom,
while in is cups, he bought a nag. To Hannon's befuddled bemuse-
ment, the man turned up at his door the next morning, along with
his equine friend.

'The origin is rhyming slang: "carpet bag" = "drag", a nineteenth
century term for a prison sentence of three months' hard labour.'
English language expert **Gerald Hammond** explains the derivation
of the racecourse slang, 'carpet' meaning 'three'.

'What Alec Wildenstein does is remove them mid-race, but we
have stuck by the rules.' **Johnston's** subtle put-down of the French
owners' deliberate flouting of the rules by having his jockey
remove Westerner's ear-plugs during the Ascot Gold Cup.

'Rock of Gibraltar reminds me, in a strange way, of Marilyn
Monroe.' If you want to find out just how strange you'll have to
read **Martin Hannan's** *Rock of Gibraltar.*

'As we say in England, "Bonne chance."' **Derek 'Thommo'
Thompson** to French jockey Olivier Peslier in 1997.

'People said I could not win with this horse. If he fails I say, that's
because I'm a bricklayer. If he wins, its because I'm a farmer.'
Philosophical gibberish from Cwmbran trainer **Ivor Jones** after his
Tilt Tech Flyer won at Newton Abbot in May 1996.

Taunton.

'Why was it a slow time? Because we went too fast.' **Willie Carson**, explaining a Newmarket defeat in 1996.

'Could be even better with another summer's grass on his back.' **Mark Pitman** predicting improvement for his jumper Nahthen Lad.

'If he was a human being I bet he'd be the type you'd want at a dinner party.' **Jimmy Lindley** about racehorse Son Of Sharp Shot.

John Francome quizzed **Walter Swinburn** about his terrible accident in Hong Kong, which left him dangerously ill, 'Does it all seem a long time ago now?'

'Yes' replied the 'choirboy', 'it does, the time seems to have gone so quickly.'

'His head is on back to front, if you know what I mean.' **Jimmy Lindley** describing 1997 Royal Ascot runner Captain Collins to TV viewers.

'Further Flight seems to get better and better, although he's not as good as he was.' **Derek 'Thommo' Thompson** baffles viewers.

'It could be something do with the fact that Donna, who looks after him at home has got married since last season.' **Martin Pipe's** explanation for the improved behaviour of his hurdler Pridwell.

'Danoli is too good for me to say how good he is.' Irish trainer **Tom Foley**.

'They've got well under just over two circuits to go.' **Satellite Information Services commentator** on the January 1994 race.

Later known as the Thomas Pink Gold Cup and the Murphy's Gold Cup, what was it originally called?

'Pilsudski is out in front, but only by virtue of the fact that that's where he is.' *Radio 5 Live* **race commentary**.

'He's got everything to lose and nothing to gain and everything to gain as well.' **Commentary on Irish TV**, covering Tom Treacey riding Danoli to win the Irish Hennessy in 1997.

'Nice little horse – gelded him – made a man out of him.' Trainer **Bryan Smart** on Sky Sport in May 2004.

'If he doesn't win today my dick will be a kipper.' **Barry Hills** assessing the chance of his Doncaster runner My Branch in 1996.

'We all have our knockers, women in racing.' **Gay Kelleway**.

'She hasn't been at the races when Astrocharm has won and thought it would be best to stay away.' Less than convincing explanation from trainer **Mark Tompkins**, as to why the self-styled all-seeing, all-knowing tabloid astrologist 'Mystic Meg' failed to attend Goodwood to see her filly win there on 31 July 2004.

'This horse seems to have become disenfranchised with racing.' **James Willoughby**, July 2004.

'Get Stuck Into A Bit Of Fanny.' *Daily Sport* **tip** for August 2004 Ascot runner Fanny's Fancy.

'Did you see me on the radio?' Well, jockey **Tony Dobbin** was pretty excited after his first-ever Cheltenham winner.

The Mackeson Gold Cup.

'CAN YOU RIDE JOE'S GIRL WOORE?' In his autobiography, *Second Start*, top jump jockey **Bobby Beasley** remembered receiving a curious telegram message that left him embarrassed – until he discovered Joe's Girl was a horse and Woore a track.

'Ouija Board flew at the end – well, she didn't actually fly, only birds do that.' **Cornelius Lysaght**, making sure that listeners to *Five Live's* 2004 Arc de Triomphe coverage weren't under the misapprehension that the filly had literally sprouted wings.

'The brand is the vehicle by which we will deliver our vision, and it's a brand that's elegant and sophisticated and confident in line with our customers' expectations.' **Alan Randall**, Group marketing director for bookmakers Victor Chandler, talking about the company's new corporate look in October 2004.

'The last furlong was a long one.' Jockey **Jamie Spencer**, after winning on Conquistadores in October 2004 at Limerick.

'If you have a jones for jazzy ponies, it could still be one heck of a party.' I'm pretty sure that *Sports Illustrated's* **headline** was suggesting that those with a prediliction for observing the finest specimens of thoroughbred racehorses in action might enjoy a jolly good day's entertainment should they choose to attend the 2004 Breeders Cup meeting, but I couldn't be 100 per cent sure. They did go on to say that in the absence of retired, almost-Triple Crown winner Smarty Jones, 'the Breeders' Cup will barely register beyond the world of boots and saddles.'

'One can only speculate how an Icelandic or Zimbabwean visualises a selling hurdle at Plumpton.' Baffling stream of consciousness from **Edward Gillespie**, managing director of Cheltenham, in his racecard notes for the 2004 Paddy Power Gold Cup day.

'Tips' is betting slang for which price?

'A girl rider is a danger to everyone else. I am dead against them. They are simply not strong enough or big enough.' **Bob Champion**.

'Jump racing is as physically wrong for girls as boxing. I would deny them the equal right to cripple their limbs or disfigure their faces.' **Dick Francis**, 1972.

'There are a lot of people out there that are basically doing the same as me, not paying to gain entrance, and I was probably sin-gled out as a test case.' Bookie **Phil Taylor** appears to be in denial in July 2004 after being warned off until 1 July 2006 for using false identification to gain entry to racecourses.

'Polo has become the biggest source of second careers under the BHB-backed Retraining of Racehorses scheme, with around 1500 ex-racers in action.' **Howard Wright**, August 2004.

'We're not happy about it, but they felt like they had to do what they did and we felt like we did what we had to do.' **John Asher**, spokesman for US track, Churchill Downs, which, in November 2004, banned fifteen jockeys for the rest of a meeting after they refused to ride because of a dispute over health insurance cover.

'Darryll Holland asks him to spread his legs and show his class to the world.' **Derek Thompson** paraphrases a famous David Coleman commentary, when describing a Yarmouth August 2004 race in which two-year-old Juantorena, named after the Cuban Olympic Gold medallist, finished third.

'There are only two classes of people who are completely irra-tional on the subject of horses – (a) the people that own horses; (b) the people who do not own horses.' **Simon Barnes**.

11/10.

'I've never felt like this before. It's almost personal, as if one of my children was about to do a party piece in the school's Christmas show.' First-time owner, writer **Stan Hey**, as his debut runner, Rowley Lad, comes under orders – and finishes 20th of 21 in a bumper.

'Drinking had become my life. Every day was the same – drinking, collapsing and vomiting.' Owner of 11 Group 1 winners, **John Martin**, to journalist Neil Morrice in July 2004. One of his horses was called Jim And Tonic.

'All my family, since hundreds of years, owned horses.' Trainer **Saeed Bin Suroor**, adding, 'When I went to school I'd take a horse with me' (*Daily Telegraph*, 23 July 2004).

'Owning a racehorse is probably the most expensive way of getting on to a racecourse for nothing.' **Sir Clement Freud**.

'If he had turned out to be useless, I'd have looked a complete arsehole.' **Archie O'Leary** risked paying fifty grand for a horse which had won just one point to point but he never regretted it – the horse was Florida Pearl.

'When we put the tongue strap on Persian War, a few people said it was a pity we didn't put it on the owner.' **Colin Davies**, who trained Persian War to win three consecutive Champion Hurdles in the late sixties, suggests that he did not enjoy the best of relationships with owner Henry Alper.

'I've got a bloke who pays weekly – w-e-a-k-l-y.' Aussie trainer **Jack Nicholls** with a common lament about owners.

How many individual bets make up a Patent?

'That is the first time she has had 14 hands between her legs.' **John Francome's** observation while watching the Duchess of York contesting a 1996 marathon horse race in the Qatar Desert.

'We will not be done in by this, and will just keep on trying.' The **Queen Mother** to trainer Peter Cazalet following their Devon Loch's inexplicable collapse on the run-in when it was looking sure to win the 1956 Grand National.

'It was cool. I thought: "I like that dress. I want to wear it. I'm going to wear it." It was great fun.' **Zara Phillips** on wearing a dress slashed to the hip to Royal Ascot, 2003.

'My Government will continue to reform the National Hunt...' said **The Queen** during her state opening of parliament speech in 2003, only to correct herself immediately with the words, 'National Health Service'.

'One perhaps couldn't have used that title today.' **Dick Francis** at the 2004 Sir Peter O'Sullevan Awards lunch, musing on his first book, *The Sport of Queens*.

'They were a partisan crowd. I remember once when a top overseas jockey rode a horse for Rufus Beasley. He came round the turn into the straight but instead of sticking on the far rail he went up the stands side. Near the finish somebody slung a cow pat off a board and it hit him full on.' Jockey **Walter Bentley** recalled racing at the now defunct Bogside.

'Cows used to graze on the course and they were only moved the night before racing. If a horse galloped through a cow pat you'd come back covered in the stuff.' Former champion jumps jockey **Tim Brookshaw** reflecting on racing at now defunct track, Woore in Shropshire.

Seven.

'It was dangerous all the way round. You raced amid sheep droppings, which made it treacherous because your horse couldn't get a decent foothold.' Jump jockey **Joe Guest** on riding round Wye, which shut in 1974.

'Betting is the manure to which the enormous crop of horse-races and racehorse breeding in this and other countries is to a large extent due.' **Richard Black** in *The Jockey Club and its Founders,* 1891.

'Shovelling muck at 6 a.m. one freezing morning, with a broken finger and a strapped ankle, covered in horse secretions of various sorts, I pondered my place in the scheme of things that was my fieldwork. I was shaken from my reverie by a loud blast from "the boss": "Rebecca! Get your anthropological arse out here!"' **Rebecca Cassidy** on researching for her 2002 book, *The Sport of Kings.*

'I realised the other day, when I was forced to do a bit of mucking out, that I'd been shovelling shit for forty-five years.' When he said that to writer Andrew Sim in 1993, **Ginger McCain** may not have expected that he would still be hard at it a dozen years later.

'Funfair Wane's Ayr win was Dandy (Nicholls) all over – blazing off like shit out of a goose, ploughing a furrow nobody else had tried all week and saying "catch me if you can".' **Alastair Down** celebrates the trainer's fourth win in five runnings of the prestigious Ayr Gold Cup with Kevin Keegan's wife Jean's horse in September 2004.

'Racehorse owners the Queen Mum (bum), Clement Freud (haemorrhoid), and Australian jockey Edgar Britt (shit) have appeared in Cockney vocabulary.' *Racing Post* 'anorak', **John Randall**, on rhyming slang.

True or false – the William Tell Overture is used to signal the off races at San Sebastian's course in Northern Spain?

'Terry Warner is a shit.' was what jockey **Jimmy Frost** wrote in black marker ink on the back of Warner's silks, which were then worn by Tony McCoy when he rode at Hereford for that owner – who had dispensed with Frost's services shortly before.

'A flamboyant dresser who found Savile Row readily able to meet his demands, his hand-made shoes were but size one and a half. On occasions he would ask female company to try to wear his shoes and took delight from the unsuccessful attempts.' Turn-of-the-19th-century jockey sensation Tod Sloan, a controversial character who came to ride in England from the States and was eventually warned off. Described here by **Russell March** in *The Jockeys of Vanity Fair*.

'Nell Barrington Is Great!' Bridgwater solicitor **Ed Boyce** named a handicap chase at Taunton on 10 January 2005, in honour of his girlfriend.

'I am appalled at the sponsorship of the Derby, what I cannot understand is how they expect to sell more batteries – or whatever it is.' **Lord Howard de Walden**, 1984.

'The title "Ever Ready Derby" must be the prime example of bad taste in racing.' **Gerald Hammond**, in his 1992 work, *A Book of Words: Horse Racing*.

'The stream of which his brainchild was the source has now become a flood, surging all winter long and swelling National Hunt prize-money to a level which, without commercial sponsorship, it would never have achieved.' **John Oaksey** on the late Bill Whitbread, racing's first modern commercial sponsor, who, in 1957, masterminded the Whitbread Gold Cup sponsorship by the family brewery of which he was chairman.

True.

'Every man has his price. For Judas it was 30 pieces of silver; for Esau when he sold his birthright to Jacob, a mess of potage. The authorities at Cheltenham yesterday announced, with pride, that they have consigned the title of the Stayers Hurdle to the dustbin in exchange for a bookmaker-funded prize-money boost.' **Sue Montgomery** (*Independent,* 6 September 2004).

'The only thing wrong with Champions' Day is its name. It is a superb day's racing in its own right, but nowadays true champions are more likely to be found elsewhere.' **James Willoughby** on Newmarket's big October meeting (*Pacemaker,* September 2004).

'One of the great things about horse racing is that it is over quite quickly.' Chelsea supporter and one-time politician **David Mellor**.

'The Derby is only a race.' **Jimmy Greaves**.

'The hideous thing about horse racing is the people.' *Evening Standard* TV critic **Matthew Norman**.

'No American president, or even a candidate for the presidency, would dare show his face at a racetrack these days. It is just too politically incorrect an activity for a politician of national stature in which to engage himself.' American writer **Alan Shuback** in 1996.

'Racing is a world inhabited by monumentally insular people, loath to talk to someone outside their environment, still less listen to them.' Writer **Will Buckley**.

'I would happily miss every darts match, almost every horse race and most boxing matches.' Premiership referee **David Elleray**.

Uttoxeter racecourse – is it left- or right-handed?

'Horse racing? Yawn, yawn. I'd rather watch paint drying, or even Paris, Texas.' Sportswriter **Hunter Davies**.

'The best thing to do with horse racing is to get rid of it.' TV pundit **Michael Barratt**.

'Horse racing does not come high on the list of sports that sports-mad US advertisers like to sponsor. This is partly because of the demographics, the double whammy of older and lower-income. And its partly because gambling, unless it takes place in glitzy Las Vegas, still suffers from a dodgy image that deters many blue-chip marketers.' **Stuart Elliott**, writing from America for advertising 'bible', magazine *Campaign*.

'I have no intention of watching undersized Englishmen perched on horses with matchstick legs race along courses planned to amuse Nell Gwynn.' Mid-20th-century broadcaster **Gilbert Harding**.

'I think it's awful. The way they tear round those tight bends and go like hell, it seems no different from dog racing to me.' The late **Jeremy Tree's** opinion of all-weather flat meetings.

'Who loves a race horse? Are not too many fond of it? Does it not lead to many evils, and to frequent ruin? Never go to a horse race. Mr Nix had one child whom he called Irene; he also had a good farm, and some money. He went to the races with his child, dressed in black crepe for the loss of her mother. Here Mr Nix drank freely, and bet largely, and lost all he was worth. At night he went home a beggar; took a dose of brandy, and died before morning, leaving his child a penniless orphan. Never go to a horse race.' So, let that be a lesson to you! Taken from a standard **1830 American school textbook**, *The Clinton Reader*.

Left-handed.

'The sport of horse racing has a peculiar and irresistible charm for persons of unblemished probity. What a pity it is that it makes just as strong an appeal to the riff-raff of every town and city.' Classic-winning owner **Charles Greville**, whose Preserve won the 1835 1,000 Guineas.

What unique feat did the horse Threadbare achieve over a three con-secutive day spell in August 1973 at Newton Abbot and Wolverhampton?

Bets, Flutters and Wagers

People back horses for all sorts of reasons. A very good friend of mine, the *Sun*'s chief reporter John Kay, enjoyed one of his biggest ever wins when he bet on an outsider with a Spanish name in honour of his good lady wife from that country, Mercedes. The horse duly obliged. John was delighted, even more so when Mercedes asked him why he had backed a runner with an Italian name!

Everyone thinks it is easy being a bookmaker – 'Never see a poor bookie', they say, and, 'A licence to print money'. John McCririck, though, confesses to being a failed bookie, and one of my early attempts at the business was only saved from self-inflicted financial disaster by unexpected outside intervention.

As a pupil at Harrow County School for Boys, I had opened a book at the Amateur FA Cup Final (along with a certain Michael Xavier Portillo) during the mid 1960s. The lads plunged on local side Wealdstone (of which I would later become a director) and I wound up with a lop-sided book.

Wealdstone beat Hendon in the Final at Wembley Stadium, but before I was mobbed by wining punters demanding payment, the school's deputy headmaster, Mr Cowan, rumbled what was going on, confiscated my betting book and threatened to expel me.

What a relief! With the book gone I could no longer confirm who had placed what bets and so declared all of them off, and referred all complaints to the deputy head!

'You could put your entire savings on the 2.30 at Kemptown (*sic*) if you wanted.' **Prime Minister Tony Blair** being questioned about the proposed gambling bill at a press conference and revealing his in-depth knowledge of racecourses. He also claimed, 'I'm not a gambler myself, but people do gamble. There's no point in taking

He won a hurdle, a chase and a flat race.

a position which says all gambling is wrong. That would be daft.' 25 October 2004.

'Bet enough to hurt but not to do damage and never less and never more.' Respected punting pundit, **Mark Coton**.

'Don't back any horse who is going to fall.' *Racing Post* writer **David Ashforth**, who also helpfully recommends, 'Only take a board price if it is going to be longer than the starting price.'

'If you fancy a 33/1 shot as much as a 5/1 shot then have twice as much on the 33/1 shot.' Champion tipster, **Henry Rix**.

'If I could offer one piece of advice to punters generally, it would be that they should specialise. There's so much racing nowadays that you can't possibly hope to keep up with all the form lines and everything that's happening.' Pro punter **Alan Potts**.

'I know some people say you should specialise and stick to one particular kind of race but I've never agreed with that. You should bet on any race in which you can win.' So, fellow pro punter **Eddie Fremantle** doesn't accept Alan Potts' advice.

'Never drink and bet, and never take under the odds you have assessed. Bet mostly between May and September – when the going is relatively constant – and never chase losses.' Successful punter and former TV face of racing, **Julian Wilson**.

'I believe that punters who impose restrictions on themselves – never betting odds-on, for example – act against their own interest. The only limitation should be never bet beyond capacity to pay.' **Peter O'Sullevan**, 2004.

Which horse was the first non-Australasian trained winner of the Melbourne Cup?

'What do you do when you hit a losing streak? The answer is carry on – because there is no rationale for a losing streak. Know how much you're prepared to lose and carry on.' Gambling actor and owner (of Jellybean, Star of Ring and Woody's Boy) **Nathaniel Parker** (*Sunday Mirror*, 25 October 1998).

'You can analyse all the other factors – jockey, trainer, trip etc – but if the ground is wrong, none of it really matters. I've always remembered that.' **Jim McGrath** on the invaluable betting advice given to him by the late Timeform founder, Phil Bull (Sportsadviser.com, March 2001).

'Dressed in a squirrel suit and hanging around the parade ring, they'll get me,' said Scoop 6 £200,000 winning punter **Richard Brocklebank**. He was indeed disguised as such a beast, complete with bushy tail in an effort to meet up with two fellow winning ticket holders in order to cooperate over bonus selections, at Glorious Goodwood in July 2004.

'Anyone can predict the winner of the next race, as was neatly demonstrated a few years ago when a West Highland terrier called Steptoe out-tipstered a well known TV racing guru. Let's spare Derek Thompson's blushes by not naming him.' Racing journalist **Alex Hankin**.

'While those who bothered to look might have fancied they could see straight into the soul of a thoroughbred when they came across the study of Striking Ambitions, I could only see a name straight out of yellow-cornered copies of the *Racing Post*. My friend helpfully pointed out that if I'd saved up all those crumpled tenners I would have had the £1,200 for the framed photo and at least have something to cover my wall.' Punting writer **James Corrigan**, of *Independent on Sunday*, reviewing an exhibition of photographic studies of racehorses at Proud Central gallery in London in October 2004.

Vintage Crop, in 1993.

'Running betting shops is not a sexy job. It's boring, like painting the Forth Rail Bridge.' Funny, I don't remember **John Brown** ever telling me or his 1,500 shop managers that when he was William Hill boss – it must have slipped his mind, but he remembered when he wrote his *Lucky John* autobiography, published in 2004. He did also add, 'It is the most important job in the organisation, but it can be monotonous.'

'Those of us who predicted the demise of the betting shop because racing punters will seek the best terms for themselves as surely as water runs downhill are just plain wrong. Or maybe just right too soon.' *Racing Post* columnist **Paul Haigh**, never a flag-waver for bookies, mounts his 'betting shops are doomed' hobby-horse yet again, 28 August 2004.

'It will take about 25 years to get Sunday racing with betting on the course and in the betting shops.' Then Tote Chairman, **Lord Wyatt**, in 1993 with a wildly inaccurate prediction.

'The only way to beat the bookies, as every punter knows, is over the soft part of the skull with a crowbar.' Journalist **Matthew Norman** was always a sore loser.

'Racing is a circus and we are the clowns.' On course bookie **Ron Bolton**.

'Pickpockets who allow you to use your own hands.' **W C Fields** on bookies.

'A stigma attaches itself still to bookmaking, and for many people bookmakers remain a fairly disreputable and slightly shady lot.' Taken, perhaps from an anti-bookie tract? No, from the inside cover blurb to **Professor Carl Chinn's** (himself a bookmaker as

Which was the first horse to win Classics in consecutive years?

well as social historian) *Better Betting with a Decent Feller,* a social history of bookmaking.

'A rich bookie, a poor bookie and the tooth fairy are in a room with a £100 on the table when the light goes out. When the light comes back on the money is gone. So who took it? It's got to be the rich bookie, because the other two are figments of the imagination.' **John Scally**, author of the excellent *Them and Us: The Irish at Cheltenham.*

'Bookies perform a social function which is, in some respects, similar to that of the medieval "sin-eaters" – a person hired at funerals to take upon himself the sins of the deceased person... So successful has been the transfer of sin to this marginalized caste that punters can speak proudly of "beating the bookies" or "outsmarting the bookies", as though they were knights in shining armour doing battle against the forces of darkness.' Social anthropologist, **Kate Fox**.

'Never be afraid to win too much.' Advice for nervous punters from, er, a bookie – **Victor Chandler**.

'The truth of the matter is that there should be no bookmakers and hence no betting exchanges.' Trainer **John Manners**.

'It was backed from 66/1 to 4/1 favourite on the day. It was easier to get money on then. Bookmakers were bookmakers, not accountants like they are today.' Trainer turned professional gambler **Tony Ingham** in 1993, recalling the day when his dad Staff's Chantry landed a mega gamble in the 1953 Cesarewitch and wonders why bookies gave up standing around and falling for such stroke!

Vintage Crop, who won the Irish St Leger in 1993 and 1994.

'The belief that bookmakers are odious has a long lineage, but so too does the assertion that they are honourable and generous. However, this opinion has made but little impact on the media, which seems to prefer the deprecatory figure of the bookmaker to one that is more praiseworthy.' **Professor Carl Chinn** in his *Better Betting with a Decent Feller.*

'The only sensible conclusion is that God is a bookmaker – and he sends the odd rotten day to remind us he moves in mysterious ways.' Bookie **Barry Dennis** after losing £50,000 at Newmarket in September 2004 when all six favourites went in.

'I wasn't even supposed to bloody be there. I was actually on my way to Worcester but there was a monster traffic jam. I phoned my clerk and told him to turn around and head for Ascot instead.' When **Gary Wiltshire** got there he lost the best part of a million pounds courtesy of Frankie Dettori's 'Magnificent Seven' in Ascot 1996.

'Beaten favourite is a bookmaker's favourite phrase.' Writer and English language expert **Gerald Hammond** backs a winner with this 1992 comment.

'I was ten, and my grandmother was the street's bookie's runner. I used to pick one out virtually every day and come home to have the bet with my dinner money. It was quite a regular occurrence for me then to get back from school to find Nan being carted off in the Black Maria.' Soccer manager **Harry Redknapp**.

'Sir Edward Elgar, another keen racegoer, was a welcome client of racecourse bookmakers because of his uncanny ability to pick losers.' Racing historian **John Randall**.

What otherwise unique distinction do point-to-pointers, Rossa Prince and Mister Chippendale, share?

'Remember – Lady Godiva put all she had on a horse.' **W C Fields**.

'I did it for a while in about 1956/7. What I tried to do was win £100 in a week. Bet to win £100 then stop. For the first six or seven months it was fine…then I had a couple of losers and I tried to chase my losses and that's deadly. You're gone.' Charlie Slater of *Eastenders*, alias actor **Derek Martin**, recalls his brief spell as a professional punter.

'The greatest cricketer most of us will ever see is at last free to attend British race meetings again.' The **'Diary'** in *The Times* of 9 September 2004, revealing that the name of Gary Sobers had been removed from the Disqualified and Excluded Person's List, where it had apparently been as a result of an unpaid betting account dating back to the 1960s. Sobers was 68 and living in Barbados when the item appeared.

'Six bookies have closed down my accounts, leaving me with twelve others.' Actor and racehorse owner, **Nathaniel Parker**, who added, 'About eighty per cent of the money I bet goes on the horses'. *Daily Star* article of 8 December 1998 claiming the then star of *McCallum* and *Vanity Fair* boasted a gambling income of an unlikely sounding £75,000 which, in another article in the *Sunday Mirror*, had shrunk to 'around £7000'.

'I used to enjoy having a bet, but one of the things that being a horse owner has taught me is that even when they are fit, fancied and trying, they are animals not machines. That taught me a good lesson early on. When they run they haven't a penny of mine on them.' Former Snooker world champion **Peter Ebdon** (*Independent*, 19 April 1997).

'He reminisced about losing £2,000 on a horse whose name he couldn't remember ridden by a jockey he wouldn't forget, Walter Swinburn.' **Will Buckley** on Bernard Manning, April 1997.

They both managed to lose a Walkover – the former bolting at the start, the latter's rider failing to weigh in.

'It would not be uncommon for me to have up to a thousand small bets in a day.' Now that's what you call a keen punter! Actor **Jack Klugman** also revealed in a 1996 *Sporting Life Weekender* interview what he did after backing a sequence of losers, 'I shout for a while, I swear I will quit backing horses and then I'm back doing the same thing the next day.'

'We're still regular Scoop 6 players but I think I've given most of it back now!' Former England cricket skipper **Mike Atherton**, referring to August 2002 when he was among ten Scoop 6 winners who shared a £686,120 bonus fund, upon becoming president of the Racegoers Club in October 2004.

'I have to confess I'm a bit partial to the odd quid or so on the horses.' Sky TV presenter, **Helen Chamberlain** (*Daily Star*, 24 October 2004).

'I tend to go for horse's names rather than what I know about them. For instance, if there was a horse running called Television Set, I'd take it as an omen and back it.' **Sir David Frost** (*Daily Express*, 21 January 1999)

'I do take bets from women. I even take bets from the Welsh. But never from Welsh women cos I'm married to one and I know what they're like.' Outspoken racecourse bookie **Barry Dennis** (*Racing Ahead*, January 2005).

'Punters who always break even – neither do I!' Dedication in **Graham Sharpe's** book, *Odds, Sods and Racing Certs.*

'Johnny Foy, my confidant, who invested millions of pounds for me purely on word of mouth.' Gambler **Alex Bird**'s dedication in *The Life and Secrets of a Professional Punter.*

Who won the 1985 Warwick match race for charity between Lester Piggott on The Liquidator and John Francome on Shangoseer?

'To The Booby – So lucky to have hooked her wonderful boy out of the great fishtank of life.' Dedication in **John McCririck's** *World of Betting*.

'To the many betting and racing friends and associates whose touching faith in the punter's belief that "losses are only lent" helped to make it all possible.' **Jamie Reid**'s dedication in *A Licence To Print Money*.

'To the memory of my grandmother, Marie Tanner, and her book-maker, Charles Allen.' **Jamie Reid**'s *Emperors of the Turf*.

'Amanda. Be as nasty as possible. If you write one kind word, I'll spew up.' **John McCririck** dedication in the copy of his book, *World of Betting*, which he gave to journalist Amanda Mitchison.

'I was one of many that suffered when Frankie Dettori rode all seven winners at Ascot. In just over an hour, I lost £500,000.' Bookie **Gary Wiltshire**, who ended up selling Christmas wrapping paper in an effort to restore his lost fortunes and is now back on an even keel.

'You'll be able to bet on the horses while on board.' Ryanair boss **Michael O'Leary** predicts an interesting service on his planes in August 2004.

'The term originally described the footwear of some bookmakers who, needing to be seen by the crowds milling round the joint, would wear specially built-up boots.' University of Manchester Reader in English, **Gerald Hammond**, explains the derivation of the term 'betting boots'.

Lester, by three-quarters of a length.

'Most footballers I know like to have a bet. Not to the Paul Merson levels, like, but just for a laugh.' **Steve McManaman** (*Racing Post,* 27 December 1997).

'I might have many other vices, but gambling on machines, or on horses, which so many other players do, has not been one of them.' **Paul Gascoigne**, 2004.

'It was the biggest bet I'd ever had in my life...my stake was 2000 rand and it was something like two rand to the pound in those days. It went like greased lightning and won by about four lengths. When I went back to the bookie with my ticket I found out he couldn't pay me.' But **Malcolm 'Supermac' Macdonald** eventually got the 8,000 rand due to him after the 3/1 tip from a bookie called King Louis obliged in Cape Town in 1975.

'Yes, you can have a bad year on the horses, but I would never gamble to the extent of putting anyone else at risk... I quite accept that it's easy to chase your losses by upping the stakes... It's at that point that you have to take a look at yourself and impose some self-discipline. And that's precisely what I do.' **Michael Owen** puts his betting philosophy into the public domain in his 2004 autobiography *Off the Record.*

'Stupidity, I guess.' **Niall Quinn's** July 1997 answer to the question, 'Why do you bet?'

'They all bet on every horse as it's supposed to be lucky to close the season with the winning ticket.' Hong Kong racegoer **Nigel Clifford** on a strange local ritual when the season closes each year.

'I opened a no-limit account for the former Archbishop of Canterbury, but unfortunately there was no divine intervention

Place the following horses in correct order: Ashley House; Bregawn; Captain John; Silver Buck; Wayward Lad.

and the horse lost.' Former head of William Hill, **John Brown**, reveals how he obliged the late Lord Runcie when, at a charity meeting, that worthy 'spotted a horse with an ecclesiastical name and told me he'd like to have a bet on it'.

'Walk down Leeson Street in Dublin and there you'll find the shop. Emblazoned on its wall is the legend: "Joe Byrne bets here, est. 1917". That was the year betting shops were legalised in Ireland' (***BOS*** magazine, September 2004).

'Because of the money involved in the Breeder's Cup they are the roughest races of the whole year. Nobody gives you a shot, so it's ironic that we're riding for a million dollars and yet we are only covered up to $100,000.' **Gary Stevens** pulls out of the 2004 Breeders Cup due to concerns that insurance cover for possible injury is not high enough (*Evening Standard*, 20 October 2004).

'Although we had the best racing in the world when I arrived, we also had the weakest financial structure in the world. Now we've got money to invest in things.' Former BHB chief **Peter Savill** congratulates himself.

'Those trainers who are considered to be "characters" sustain the racing industry by attracting owners who wish to be part of a society that seems glamorous, secretive, exciting and successful, features a trainer must embody if he is to inspire confidence in his clients.' Writer **Rebecca Cassidy**, 2002.

'Though success provides emotional compensation for countless reverses, it has to be admitted that racehorse ownership in general represents the purest form of economic suicide.' **Peter O'Sullevan** (*International Turf*, 1998).

The five Michael Dickinson-trained runners who filled the first five places in the 1983 Cheltenham Gold Cup did so in this order – Bregawn, Captain John, Wayward Lad, Silver Buck, Ashley House.

'The problem of whether to give his caddy a tip of two shillings (10p) or half-a-crown (12 and a half pence) was one to which he gave careful thought.' ***Biographical Encyclopaedia of British Flat Racing*** on Aga Khan III (1877–1957), who owned seventeen Classic winners – including five in the Derby.

'There is an immutable rule in betting that if you beat the odds by more than half, the beast in question either falls over, contracts Green Monkey Disease, or is assassinated by some raving loon.' Racing broadcaster, **Alastair Down**.

'If only George Bush and Jacques Chirac had a tipping column, I think the world would be a safer place.' MP and racing writer, **Robin Cook**, on how tipping losers can puncture self-importance and self-aggrandisement.

'The bookie was wired into a cage surrounded by dubious characters. I remember he had a chamber pot on the floor. If he wanted to pee he had to do it in public.' Actor **Richard Griffiths** recalls his first visit to a particularly unusual betting shop.

'It is a very hard way to make easy money.' Pro punter **Dave Nevison**, once 'something' in the city (*Independent*, 1 March 2000).

'Bollocks to that. I have not got the balls to back horses.' **Barry Dennis**, who has laid (taken bets for) them for donkey's years, cannot ever see himself becoming a professional punter (*Racing Ahead*, January 2005).

'If I were a serious punter I would go racing wearing a Walkman, pick out and back the horses I fancied and in no circumstances whatsoever talk to a trainer.' Now-retired trainer **Jack Berry**.

Why was the start of the 1987 Cheltenham Gold Cup delayed by one and a half hours?

'If you want to be a professional gambler you need deep pockets, and if you've got them, why the hell be a gambler.' So wondered actor **Richard Griffiths** in 1996.

'Christ, I'm not embarrassed. I don't drink, don't smoke, don't do drugs. I like a bit of a punt. You know, big deal.' Golfer **Laura Davies** responding to 1996 reports that she had lost half a million indulging her love of a flutter.

'I don't follow particular horses, although the horses I back seem to.' Soccer pundit **Tommy Docherty**.

'The considerations of the punter come second. It's the owner who pays my wages.' Trainer **Lynda Ramsden**, (*Evening Standard*, 23 October 1997).

'He just said, "I've the price of a good Rolls Royce on him". A good Rolls Royce was worth £50,000 to £60,000 then!' **Ted Walsh**, then a jockey, was shocked when Barney Curley told him how much he had invested on his mount – which lost.

'Every time I leave the racecourse at the end of a day's work, with a profit tucked into my zipped pocket, I offer a silent thank you to the mugs who make it possible – my fellow punters. Overall, I regard the rest of the crowd with contempt.' Pro punter, **Alan Potts**, in his *Against the Crowd*.

'Without betting, racing would be showjumping.' *Observer* writer **Will Buckley**.

'Many punters go to the races only incidentally for the racing. They go to have fun, to eat and drink and flirt and flutter.' **Will Buckley** (*Observer*, 26 September 2004).

There was a blizzard.

'When a non-favourite wins a race bookmakers are said to skin the lamb.' ***1864 Dictionary of Slang.***

'I've never seen anything like it in all my years coming racing. It's incredible that there were only four starting prices, 12/1; 14/1; 16/1 and 20/1.' Chief starting price reporter **Paul Finegan** after no fewer than 11 horses started as 12/1 co-favourites for a 23 runner Apprentice Handicap at The Curragh, 6 November 1998.

'It matters more when there's money on it.' Skybet's inspired, innovative, inventive 2004 **slogan**, or, some might say (me included), a statement of the bleeding obvious. I'm not sure that Victor Chandler's newly introduced 'Get more on – get more back' was much better. And from a 1966 *Ruffs Guide to the Turf* we bring you this bookie gem: 'You Win When You Lose With Margolis & Ridley' or, in the same publication, 'Never A Quarrel – Bet With Coral'.

'It's just sad that people who aren't racing people have brought it about to have racing seven days a week. The days when a man sat down with his wife and the kids for Sunday lunch have gone by the wayside. When I saw that next year I'd got to do 47 Sundays I said, I've had enough of this.' **Roger Smith** explains why he packed up running Turner & Kendrick credit bookmaker in November 2003 at the age of 63 (*BOS* magazine, April 2004).

'Only your experienced turfite comprehends the enormity of the idiocy of backing horses by systems.' As true today as it was in 1903 when **Arthur Binstead** made the observation in his *Pitcher In Paradise*.

'It appears that the racing lobby has succeeded in stitching up the taxpayer.' Economist **Keith Boyfield**, suggesting that only a 'racing trust' may be permitted to bid for the Tote, enabling it to bid well under the commercial rate (*Independent*, 15 July 2004).

Wetherby – is this a left- or right-handed course?

'No rider shall place a wager, cause a wager to be placed on his or her behalf or accept any ticket or winnings from a wager except on his or her own mount and except through the owner or trainer of the horse he or she is riding. The owner or trainer placing wagers for his or her rider shall maintain a precise and complete record of all such wagers, and the record shall be available for examination by the Stewards at all times.' **State Regulations** governing the 2004 Breeders Cup meeting, run at Lone Star Park, Texas, that seem to allow jockeys to bet.

'If you like to bet in France you cannot have friends. Because if you have friends and you tell them to back your horse, the price is spoilt. And if you don't tell them, well, you don't have friends any more.' **François Doumen**.

'If somebody is telling me their horse has a good chance, it's because they ain't trying. If they really think its going to win, they don't tell nobody.' Trainer **Dai Burchell**.

'I could have an each-way chance in the first and I may win the third.' **Frankie Dettori** before going out to ride all seven winners at Ascot on 28 September 1996 at odds of 25,095/1 – just so that I could write a book about it, *The Magnificent Seven*!

'When I was writing this column, my father rang and said "Did you know that Richard Rufus (best defender ever to wear the red and white of Charlton Athletic) wants to become a priest?" Just two minutes earlier I'd written down the words Vicar's Destiny for tomorrow's sportingoptions.co.uk Handicap at Pontefract. Scary, eh?' **Richard Birch's** spooky *Racing Post* tip in August 2004 duly produced an each-way winner, finishing third at 7/1.

'Take it from me: most tips are trash and racecourse rumours are usually rubbish. Have faith in your own instincts and your own

Left-handed.

observations and you will back more winners, and enjoy them more.' Channel 4's ace commentator, **Simon Holt** (*Counter Attack*, 2002).

'The only useful tip is to ignore tips.' Racing journalist **John Sexton**.

'For Sale – A "ready-made winner" at Wolverhampton this weekend – Silver Socks. Contact – without delay – Michael Easterby.' After this **advert** in the *Racing Post* on 15 February 2001, Silver Socks duly obliged days later, next time up, at Wolverhampton.

'I have to admit that I availed myself of 33/1 about (Ryan) Moore to win next season's jockeys' championship.' **Eddie Fremantle** in the *Observer* in September 2004.

'Her final pick, Capote Bell in the eighth race at Saratoga on July 27, came home a winner.' *Sports Illustrated* **report** on the final tip from *New York Post* racing pundit 'Gamblin' Rose Hamburger, before she died in 1996 – aged 105.

'I asked him about football then he asked me about art. But he gave me some lousy horse tips.' Scottish artist **Jack Vettriano** on meeting Sir Alex Ferguson, (*Daily Record*, 26 October 2004).

'My advice is to take the 14/1 now!' Rare tip from **Martin Pipe** in October 2004 about his Comply Or Die, for the Royal & Sun Alliance Chase at the 2005 Cheltenham Festival.

'I've helped myself to 20/1 this morning and I would recommend you have a go as well.' **Nigel Twiston-Davies** pushing the chances of his Redemption for the 2004 Paddy Power Gold Cup at Cheltenham in November 2004. It was a non-runner.

Which Champion Hurdle winner was killed in the 1977 Cheltenham Gold Cup?

'Alex's tip knackered us.' Soccer boss **Jim Smith**. He and Portsmouth manager Harry Redknapp picked a winner, Race The Ace, at Newmarket in late October 2004, but backed it in a double with beaten 9/4 shot Joseph Henry – a tip given to them by Sir Alex Ferguson.

'I've got such faith in the horse – he was 100/1 to win the Cheltenham Gold Cup within five years and I've taken some of it.' Owner and *Attheraces* presenter **Matt Chapman** on his November 2004 Newton Abbot winner, Geton, named after Chapman's show. Trainer Martin Pipe quipped, 'I was hoping they'd call the horse Getoff so I wouldn't have to put up with Matt every day.'

'As a railway shunter you always remember horses who get you out of the smelly stuff and I was doing my absolutes a few Saturdays ago until Royal Prince put some much needed folding stuff back in my sky rocket when bolting up in the last race of the night.' **Mark 'The Counch' Winstanley** waxes lyrical in his *Weekender* column, 14 July 2004.

'It is not winning that beguiles the gambler, but the thrill of waiting for a result.' **Milton Shulman**.

'How many jockeys could honestly say they have never had a bet? Not many, if any. I'm sure of that.' **Lord Huntingdon** (*Sporting Life*, 24 October 1997).

'Obsessive workaholics with nerves of steel who can walk away after a major loss.' *Daily Star* racing editor **Tony Lewis** on why we can't all be pro gamblers.

'Never bet odds-on. If you could buy money, they would sell it at the shop down the road.' Trainer **Barry Hills**.

Lanzarote.

'There's a big difference between a punter and a gambler. I've been backing horses all my life but I'm not a gambler.' **Peter O'Sullevan**.

'The most successful gamblers are the ones that are able to go racing for two or three days and not have a bet.' Trainer **John Gosden**.

'Women love gamblers when they're winning, but can't hack it when they're losing.' Pro gambler **Alan Poots** explaining in 1997 why he was still single aged 50.

'Akin to moving straight from sharing an occasional joint with friends to a full blown crack habit.' **Greg Woods** on the difference between fixed odds and spread betting.

'There is no quarrel with gambling. Life's a gamble, isn't it?' The racing reverend, Canadian pastor **Rev Shawn Kennedy**, trainer turned jockey.

'A foolproof system is the stuff of dreams and dodgy small ads.' **Greg Woods**.

'There was talk of a steward's inquiry because some punters swore it was really pale blue.' **Paul Weaver** of the *Guardian* on controversy at Royal Ascot 2004 over the colour of the Queen's Hat for Ladies Day when 10/1 outsider White was ruled the winner.

'Sometimes I think there are punters who have either got an awful lot of money or have taken a grudge against the money they've got, but I'm not there to look after them – as long as the money's not mine I couldn't care less.' Trainer **David Barron**, who admits to having the occasional flutter ('I'm quite selective, though'), on

Which jumps course staged its last flat meeting on 20 August 1966?

times when, 'I see ones of mine going off shorter than they should because somebody has put two and two together and come up with all sorts of figures' (*Racing Post*, 2 July 2004).

'One minute it's titles and royalty, the next minute it's Bob the Builder. Toffs and spivs all rolling up their sleeves together, trying to take down the bookie's trousers.' **Peter Beaton-Brown**, nephew of bookie Victor Chandler, on the clientele of their Mayfair betting shop (*Financial Times*, July 2004).

'I don't want to waste it. I shall have a bet and buy some yearlings.' Former William Hill chief executive **John Brown** on the £5.7m he made by selling company shares.

'As soon as you think "that horse can't win" you're dead as a bookmaker. When "faces" want it, even if you think it can't win, not only can it win, it probably will.' **John Brown** on the lesson all bookies learn fast unless they want to become ex-bookies.

'It has to be said of the "sport of kings" that, so long as it is surrounded by that army of gamblers which now so fatly flourishes on all our racecourses, it will continue to be what it has long since become, a monstrous game of speculation.' **L H Curzon**, *A Mirror of the Turf*, 1892.

'No employer I ever knew offered me a five-pound note for guessing the name of a horse. Yet that is what every bookmaker, even the humblest of them, does daily. If I guessed West Countryman the fault cannot be imputed to the bookmakers. They were perfectly willing to pay out if I guessed Grandcourt.' Irish journalist and racegoer **Robert Lynd** (1879–1949).

'I decided I'd have two grand on. I woke up the night before with sweat pouring off me. I dreamt he'd got beat. I thought I'd halve

Worcester.

my bet. When I woke up again I decided I was off my head betting a grand, I'd have £500 instead. At the races I heard various trainers fancied their horses. I ended up betting fifty quid and he won by 30 lengths. That's how bad a punter I am.' **Mick Easterby** remembers backing his 6/4 1976 Royal Ascot winner, Lochnager.

'It was widely known in racing that the vast majority of jockeys had their own "punter". I find it inconceivable that the Jockey Club do not know of this practice.' Former trainer **Charlie Brooks** at warned-off former jockey Graham Bradley's July 2004 Appeal Court hearing.

'At the moment, I'm £135,000 up. That's since 1983 and a lot of it was won when there were 9 per cent deductions.' Bookie cum punter **John Brown**, former William Hill supremo, in his 2004 autobiography, *Lucky John*.

'Anyone who can't take tough luck doesn't, or shouldn't, bet.' *Racing Post* columnist **Tony Morris**.

'The average betting shop punter is guided far more by habit and distance from his front door than he is by percentage overrounds and five places each-way.' **Peter Thomas** (*Racing Post*, 22 July 2004).

'By combining exchanges, bookies, spread firms and the Tote odds, you will rarely find a race that isn't very close to overbroke and, when offered that sort of opportunity, only the mugs will pass it up and go for glory with one runner.' Punting advice from pro **Dave Nevison** (*Racing & Football Outlook*, August 2004).

'There's a mug born every minute of the day, and thank God, some of them live.' Bookie **Fred Swindell**.

Which is the only horse to have finished second three times in the Grand National without ever winning it?

'I don't do a lot of research or take a long time going through the form, I just decide what I fancy and go with that.' Well, so do a lot of us – but WE don't then win £104,000 for a two-quid Scoop 6 bet like **Alan Snow** did in August 2004.

'Do we really care if we get 11/4 or 3/1 about a 5/2 shot? The answer, unless you're J P McManus and betting in hundreds of thousands, is no. Do we care if we get 20/1 about a horse that has a 10/1 chance of winning? Of course we do and that is basically all that value betting is.' 'Pricewise' tipster, **Tom Segal** in 2002 book, *Counter Attack*.

'Betting is one of two things in life that everyone thinks they can do well without training – and I've learned (from women) that most men are rubbish at both.' Pro punter **Alan Potts**.

'If you're losing and you don't chase, then you'll never get out of trouble. A punter who can't have a bet is like a golfer with the yips or a darts player who can't let go of the dart. It's the worst way to be.' Long-time pro punter **Eddie 'The Shoe' Fremantle** challenges conventional wisdom.

'There is little doubt that upwards of one million guineas has already been laid.' The ***Sporting Magazine*** estimating the money staked on the 1806 St Leger.

'In the unwritten etiquette of betting, £2 is a "lady's bet" and anything below a fiver casts serious doubt on the masculinity of the punter.' Anthropologist **Kate Fox** observing the betting ring at racecourses in the early 21st century.

'One of the principal residents (of Epsom), the Rev Madan, was successful in using his magisterial authority in repressing gaming

Wyndburgh.

in the town during race week, at which some of the inhabitants were so indignant that they burned him in effigy near the spot where the pump now stands.' **A History of Surrey** reporting a 1760 incident.

'A gambler can't be professional by definition. I still stand by that. They're not professional gamblers, they're people that are very well informed. They're not so much gambling, they're getting very good value; in some cases too good value. And there's a lot of them out there that can beat the bookmakers. An awful lot more than I ever thought there was!' Irish bookie **David Byrne** (*BOS* magazine, Sept 2004).

'People used to say to me, "I can tell what you've backed". And I'm glad to say 90 per cent of the time they were wrong. Which pleased me. I tried to keep my bias to myself. Even when I was haemorrhaging fiscally, they couldn't spot it.' **Peter O'Sullevan,** (*Daily Telegraph*, 25 September, 2004).

'This study has recognised the positive function betting shops play in punters' lives. For pensioners the visit commonly gives structure to workless days. For lunch time punters, the visit is time out from work and the bet provides hope of change in often changeless circumstances. For non-routine workers the shop commonly provides a forum for companionship and banter. For the homeless, the betting shop provides a refuge from the public arena, and structure and companionship in lives that can lack both.' **Dr Mark Neal** of the University of Reading in his 1998 article, 'You Lucky Punters!', the result of a three-year study.

'Addictive gambling is number one on the media's hit list. The truth is different. If anything the statistics show that Britain is a nation of boozers, not gamblers, but there are elements in the media who want the public to believe something else.' **Warwick Bartlett** of the Association of British Bookmakers in the face of an

The first-ever sponsored flat race in Britain was run at Ascot in which year: 1846, 1886 or 1926?

unprecedented stream of anti-gambling articles – mostly aimed at casino gambling – in the media in October 2004.

'Any punter will tell you, there's no such thing as a free hunch.' **James Corrigan** (*Independent on Sunday*, 24 October 2004).

'I've little doubt New World was my best actual training perform- ance. He was also my last serious punt. You just don't get time to gamble when you're training.' **Toby Balding** recalls the 1959 Portland Handicap winner that landed him a bet of £200 at 33/1 (*Racing Post*, 5 November 2004).

'To all those gallopers, fast and slow, genuine and dubious, I am grateful. Without their help, I might never have learned that get- ting poorer by the minute can be marvellous fun.' **Hugh McIlvanney**, 1995.

'We know him as Ken and he is a once-a-week punter who usu- ally comes in, puts his bets on and then goes out.' Betfred betting shop manager **Judith Blaney** on the customer who, in November 2004, won £1,132,657 – the biggest-ever betting shop payout and the biggest ever dividend in Tote history, on the £2 per line Scoop 6 on which he invested £480 in a perm.

'Without gambling there would be no horse racing... Astonishingly this aspect of the sport is regarded with distaste not only by America's legions of bluenoses and the ignorant general public, which regards all horseplayers as the comical, slightly sin- ister clowns immortalized by Damon Runyan, but also by seg- ments of the racing establishment itself.' US writer **William Murray's** viewpoint would not be out of place in the UK (*The Wrong Horse*, 1992).

1846, and it was sponsored by the Great Western Railway.

'Taking a bad mood to the betting windows is risky business. Prior to some horse racing, an hour at the gym or swimming pool or jogging path does wonders for a person's emotional composition and handicapping skills.' Interesting theory from US writer **Jay Cronley** of ESPN.com

'The *Racing Post* operates a policy prohibiting staff from using any inside information considered to provide an unfair advantage for betting purposes.' **Howard Wright**, 22 October 2004.

What is the longest continuously sponsored flat race in the calendar?

Courses of Action

All racegoers have a favourite course they are quite happy to tell you about, and a least favourite which they seem to be more reticent to reveal.

My favourite racecourse is at San Sebastian in Spain – because they begin each race there with a loud blast of the *William Tell Overture*. My least favourite is Cheltenham during the Festival, because the one time I ever went there during that great event it was so crowded that I couldn't get a drink, a bet or a view of anything more than the rear end of a horse or two. Cheltenham did go back up in my estimation when I went along in much more relaxed circumstances in November 2004, backed a winner or two then got to see sixties band, the Foundations, in the Centaur auditorium after racing. What more could one want from a day at the sports?

The man who left a note in the Warwick racecourse suggestion box, pleading 'Never let me in here again', left few in doubt of his feelings.

Dr Michael Turner, at the time Jockey Club medical adviser, offered an unusual definition of the ideal quality for a track, 'A racecourse should be a place where you would be happy to have a heart attack.'

'A few years ago on the Monday after the Arc an irate wife rang me and said "what have you done with my husband?". I had to tell her I hadn't a clue where he was. She soon found out when she checked their bank balance. The husband had used the Arc to do a runner and has never been seen since.' **Ian Fry**, owner of travel agents Horse Racing Abroad, who has taken over 70,000 racegoers to the Arc at Longchamp over the years.

The John Smith's Cup at York, first sponsored in 1960 (as the Magnet Cup) and still going strong.

'Longchamp on Arc day is a mix of French chic, British blazers and the green-and-red shades of autumn in the Bois de Boulogne, and it is also one of the last habitats of the bowler hat.' **Marcus Armytage** (*Daily Telegraph*, 4 October 2004).

'Israeli Yael Bartana's DVD projection in the mock-up, old-fashioned cinema in the Museum of Liverpool Life is a deftly edited wander through the crowds at Aintree, during the Grand National. All human and equine life is here, even a man wearing a joke horse's head. Bartana cuts from horse's hooves to high heels, from preposterous hats to plaited manes. A punch-up erupts by the toilets. You can almost smell the money and the lack of it, the booze, the scent and the horseshit.' **Adrian Searle** (*Guardian*, September 2004).

'We can't stop fashion. As long as the girls look smart its OK. We are not even checking for bare legs any more.' An **Ascot official** at the 2004 Royal meeting admits that the dress code has now vanished as ladies exposing navels, wearing micro-minis and 'strappy dresses' were all allowed in.

'The Melbourne Cup is a race of no great significance and should be called by its proper name – the Australian Cesarewitch.' **John Randall** (*Racing Post*, 11 July 2004).

'Alcohol has a role in all of the significant relationships in Newmarket; lads drink with each other, trainers drink with owners, successful punters drink their winnings with losers and racegoers slurp gin and tonics and champagne.' **Rebecca Cassidy**, *The Sport of Kings*, 2002.

'The simple fact is that John Smith's drinkers love their racing and there's a perfect fit between the Grand National and the No Nonsense Pint.' The simple fact is that **Tim Seager**, Marketing Director of Scottish & Newcastle, who had just been announced

York's Ebor Stand was opened in which year?

as 2005 sponsors of the Grand National via their John Smith's brand was talking tosh, particularly when he added: 'We have made a long term commitment that will see John Smith's Grand National, and racing in general, brought to life in pubs, clubs, supermarkets and off-licences.' Yes, I can just visualise horses jumping round the course set up in the aisles and bars.

'Was it a coincidence that the Dettori's Italian Ice Cream Challenge Stakes at Newmarket was part of the Scoop 6 programme?' asked *Racing Post* letter writer **Ian Mackenzie** of Bury St Edmunds in August 2004.

'There are too many courses everywhere. I'd love to have around ten main courses and use them. It would make the sport more centralised and more concentrated.' **Frankie Dettori** (*Daily Telegraph*, 23 November 2004).

'Short of engines.' **Excuse** for leaving racegoers on the way to Epsom for the Derby stranded on the platform at Nine Elms Station, Battersea. No, not a recent renewal – but the 1838 race. Some things never change.

'I understand that Milton's "Paradise Lost" is being revived and will appear in Derby Week and will be published under the title "Paradox Lost" by Melton.' Telegram sent by **Oscar Wilde** to celebrate Melton's 1885 Derby triumph, brilliantly ridden by Fred Archer, beating Paradox into second. Melton was owned by Wilde's close friend the 20th Baron Hastings.

'Poor fellow, how damned hot he will be.' Last words of Derby winning trainer **Matthew Dawson**, who died in a 1897 heatwave, having just been told his secretary had departed on honeymoon.

2003.

'Not a one, they have all migrated over here.' American trainer **John Higgins**, who sent out Volodyovski to win the 1901 Derby, asked whether there were many crooks on the US racing scene.

'He was a horse that seemed to enjoy being admired and would lean nonchalantly against a wall with his front legs crossed, looking extremely pleased with himself.' **Roger Mortimer** on 1935 Derby winner, Bahram.

'I felt I couldn't go far wrong at that price.' Trainer **Fred Darling** who unsuccessfully offered a friend's two year old, Pont l'Eveque, to several would-be owners, so bought the colt himself for just £500 – he went on to win the 1940 Derby.

'I was driven home by my parents, spent an hour mowing the lawn and, as usual, was in bed soon after 9 p.m.' **Lester Piggott** on winning his first Derby in 1954 on Never Say Die.

'The general opinion of the jockeys was that too many horses were falling back after six furlongs, and the remainder closed up, and in the general scrimmage some horse was brought down, the rest falling over that horse.' **Official enquiry** into the 1962 Derby in which 7 of the 26 runners, including the favourite, fell.

'The name of the greatest racehorse of the 20th century was officially registered as Sea-Bird – not Sea Bird and definitely not Sea Bird II.' **John Randall** on the 1965 Derby winner.

'Quite frankly we can see nothing to stop him from winning both the 2000 Guineas and the Derby. We have not seen a two year old as promising as this for years.' Glowing praise from ***Timeform's Racehorses of 1973*** for Vincent O'Brien-trained Apalachee who started 4/9 for the Guineas, finished third and never raced again.

Name the venue for the 2005 Royal Ascot meeting.

'I feel more about this race than any other race in the world.' **Frankie Dettori**, yet to win the race, prior to the 2004 Derby, which he didn't win.

'The Derby, with its hundreds of years of tradition kowtowed to an uncompetitive kick-around between England and, heaven help us, Iceland. Such deference verges on the pathetic.' **Will Buckley** on the timing of the 2004 Derby to be run at half time of a football international friendly.

'Lester Piggott appeared in the Queen's role as guest of honour, thereby notching up an unlikely double, having gone on from spending time in one of her jails to acting as her stand-in.' **Will Buckley** on the 2004 Derby.

'The notion that the Derby is the ultimate test of a thoroughbred is nonsense. It is run on the unfairest course in Britain and if the race were devised from scratch, Epsom is the very last place we would choose as the venue.' **John Randall** (*Racing Post*, 11 July 2004).

'This Kentucky Derby, whatever it is – a race, an emotion, a turbulence, an explosion – is one of the most beautiful and satisfying things I have ever experienced.' Novelist **John Steinbeck**.

'When Funny Cide won the (2003) Kentucky Derby, he triumphed in a world that was essentially indifferent. In the 1930s, when Seabiscuit triumphed, racing was a national passion.' **Laura Thomson**.

'The All-England Club is a place of grace and serenity. It is very commercial but not ruthlessly so. It has, unlike Epsom, which in seeking to popularise the Derby has simply destroyed it, resisted turning Wimbledon into a mass day out for drunks and brawlers.' **Jason Cowley** (*New Statesman*, 12 July 2004).

York.

'Anyone who has ever won the Kentucky Derby knows that the feeling you get only increases each time you do it. I guess it's like being addicted to a drug: once you have experienced it, you want it even more. It's better the second time, and the third time is even better than the earlier one.' **Gary Stevens**.

'When all is said and done, Lukas, Baffert and Zito are the three guys who know how to pick 'em out, weed 'em out and send 'em out loaded for bear (*sic*) on the first Saturday in May.' US writer **Steve Haskin** on three of the most successful contemporary Kentucky Derby trainers.

'If Stanley (her horse Casual Lies) is the lightning in the bottle, my greatest fear is that if the bottle breaks, the lightning may escape and the chance of a lifetime will pass me by.' Unknown trainer **Shelley Riley**, based at the tiny Pomona track in northern California, came to the Kentucky Derby with her horse of a lifetime, which finished second to Lil E Tee – hours before huge bolts of lightning lit up the racecourse.

'Owners who come to the (Kentucky) Derby with their marketing hat on and start handing out souvenir shirts, pens, notepads, socks, dishes, or anything with their horse's name and picture on it are in grave danger of offending the Derby gods, who frown upon such commercialistic endeavors.' US writer **Steve Haskin**.

'Maker and sole inventor of the chronograph by which the Derby and all other great races are timed.' Advert in the 1880 *Ruff's Guide to the Turf* by a proud **Mr J W Benson**, 'of London's Ludgate Hill and Old Bond Street'.

'When the race starts you don't blink, you don't even breathe for the whole two and a half minutes of the race. It is so intense.' **Frankie Dettori** on the Derby.

The Autumn Double includes which two races?

'The Kentucky, French and Irish Derby – they all come second to the Epsom Derby. The passion, the setting and the undulations of the track make it the world's greatest race.' Trainer **Terry Mills**.

'I thought that Epsom wouldn't really suit him. So I took him out of our Derby and I put him in at Chantilly instead.' And it was just as well that Michael Stoute then persuaded owner **Saeed Suhail** to shell out ninety grand to get Kris Kin back into the 2003 race – which he went on to win – after landing Chester's Dee Stakes.

'On Derby day, a population rolls and scrambles through the place that may be counted in millions.' **Charles Dickens**.

'The ultimate test for any human or equine athlete.' **Pat Eddery** on riding in the Epsom Derby.

'At thirteen I memorised all the Derby winners from 1780 and I still have them off pat as a foolproof cure for insomnia.' Keep away from **Tony Morris** at parties! (*Pacemaker*, September 2004).

'You can't beat Derby day for atmosphere. Within seconds of arriving on Epsom Downs you can bet your life on being pursued by a "lucky heather" salesperson. I still have a sprig I bought at immense expense in 1981, just a few hours before Shergar galloped his way into turf history. I've used the same piece every year since, saving £23 so far.' **Robert Cooper** (*In The Know*, June 2004).

'That is how I came to be standing at the winning post when Shaamit won the 1996 Derby. I didn't actually *see* Shaamit win the Derby, of course: at Epsom, as at every other race meeting I was facing the other way, watching the audience.' Well, **Kate Fox** *is* an anthropologist.

Cambridgeshire and Cesarewitch.

'Forfeiting the media monopoly that the Wednesday Derby enjoyed was a serious mistake, because on a Saturday the coverage available, and even the off-time of the race, are dictated by other interests.' Trainer **Bill O'Gorman**.

'The "Wednesday was better" argument is dead. It's a red herring and not worth talking about. It's not coming back.' Epsom MD, **Stephen Wallis**, September 2004.

'I would recommend dropping the English Derby back to a mile and a quarter, and the St Leger to a mile and a half.' Controversial suggestion by former BHB Chairman, **Peter Savill**, made in September 2004 following French moves to reduce the distance of the Prix du Jockey Club.

'I can say with certainty we have no plans even to consider reducing the race from a mile and a half to a mile and a quarter, but we have to make sure a mile and a half remains fashionable.' Response to the idea, from Epsom MD **Stephen Wallis**.

'Perhaps the desire to reduce the distance is more a reflection of the inability of some trainers to produce middle distance champions, and their efforts ought to be directed to this rather than to calls to undermine our sporting heritage.' Concerned *Racing Post* letter writer, **Steve Prior** of Walton-on-Thames, who also wondered whether reducing the number of sets would help Tim Henman at Wimbledon and the number of holes Monty at The Open!

'Nothing matters more to a trainer than winning the Derby.' **Sir Michael Stoute** – a four-time winner so, perhaps, he would say that, wouldn't he, in a conversation with Rishi Persad (*Thoroughbred Owner & Breeder*, September 2004).

In which year were betting shops first permitted to stay open for evening racing?

'This year's Derby has seven runners facing the starter, four geldings, two mares and a filly.' Don't panic, the **preview** by *The Post* was for the 2004 Carling Jersey Derby.

'Having a dance band on a racecourse is a bit like having a snooker table on a boat,' declared **David Elsworth** at Goodwood's charity day meeting on 30 September 2004, not convinced that the accompanying sounds made for a perfect blend.

'Quick, they've just announced that the Foundations are playing in the centre of the course.' My good friend **Mike Bishop** alerting us that the sixties band were performing at Cheltenham on Paddy Power Gold Cup day, 2004 – we found them at the course's Centaur arena.

'A roistering party at a country house founded two races, and named them gratefully after their host and his house, the Derby and the Oaks. Seldom has a carouse had more permanent effect.' The **5th Earl of Rosebery** on the naming of two of the Classics planned during a party at the 12th Earl of Derby's house, The Oaks.

'Soon after its inception, the Derby was attracting tens of thousands. Most would never see the big race itself, coming for the sideshows and entertainments and, above all, the gambling that was part of the occasion. Pickpockets, prostitutes, shady bookmakers and con-artists no doubt abounded, and there were hideous freak shows, but, by all accounts, Derby Day was an occasion without equal in the sporting year.' **Nigel Townson** in *The British At Play – A Social History of British Sport From 1600 to the Present.*

'Reputations have been established, repaired or shattered more frequently in the roughly two and a half minutes taken to run the

1993.

Derby than in any other single race.' And that's an American admitting that – **Timothy T Capps**, writing in the glorious 1997 book, *Crown Jewels of Thoroughbred Racing.*

'The *Racing Post* referred to Lester Piggott as being the most successful Derby jockey. The crucial word "Epsom" was omitted. There are numerous Derbys in the world, not forgetting England's oldest horserace, the Kiplingcotes Derby, run every year since 1519. I should point out that Ken Holmes has won the Kiplingcotes Derby ten times and been second five times and therefore in my book is the most successful Derby jockey.' Letter writer **Moira Emmett**, not being at all pedantic in her correspondence of 5 November 2004.

'We've had a bunch of horses, all of us, that started up the road, but they never quite made it. They got on the wrong elevator. They never got to the penthouse.' US trainer **John Ward**, whose Monarchos won the 2000 Kentucky Derby.

'It is conventional for ambulances to follow every horse race in case of an accident. This year the ambulances will have to follow the punters as well.' **Peter Oborne** warns that an extra Cheltenham Festival day may prove a step too far for punters already having to endure, 'marathon drinking sessions or all-night card games, only to emerge in time for the first race the following day' (*Observer Sports Magazine*, January 2005).

'If it's good for the industry we have to support it, but it won't be very good for the liver.' **Jim Old** greets the idea of an extended Cheltenham Festival.

'The English–Irish thing is absolutely vital to the Festival meeting…without that it would just be an ordinary meeting. That's what gives it its bite.' Trainer **Jim Dreaper**.

In which year did Frankie Dettori achieve his Magnificent Seven winners at Ascot?

'Let me see my hoss – he's the only reason I came back to this country.' Old Etonian war hero turned trainer **Fergie Sutherland**, who moved to Ireland during the 1960s, tries to clear enthusiastic well-wishers out of the way after his Imperial Call won the 1996 Gold Cup.

'To win at Cheltenham you need brains. Some horses that have won there are a long way from the brightest. The brains have to come from the men on top. Those guys have plenty of them. They are not the sort of men to follow standards. They set them. They have given the Festival a form of immortality.' **Peter O'Sullevan**.

'Cheltenham is about excellence. It is the place to win for any fella involved in the national hunt game. To win there is unbelievable because of the fantastic reception you get in the winners' enclosure.' **Ted Walsh**.

'Cheltenham is huge to us. There are two types of racing days for us: ordinary days and Cheltenham days. I'd say our business goes up about 500 per cent for those three days.' **Ian Marimon**, Paddy Power bookies.

'Cheltenham's popularity is as difficult to explain to those who have never experienced it as the lbw rule in cricket.' **John Scally**.

'I long to be able to sponsor the Cheltenham Festival, giving me the opportunity to insist that my favourite comedian, the brilliant Joe Pasquale, carry out all the commentary there.' Interesting suggestion from **Johnnie Mack** of Tottenham in an October 2004 letter to the *Racing Post*.

'I would be a most unpatriotic judge if I did not accede to this request.' **Judge Esmonde Smyth** postponed a hearing at his Irish civil court so that witnesses could attend the 1996 Cheltenham Festival.

1996.

'Newmarket is the smallest population in Britain capable of supporting a Waitrose, and its stock reflects its place in racing life as a source of food for racing families who have to entertain visiting owners at short notice.' **Rebecca Cassidy** in *The Sport of Kings*.

'It transpired that a meal packed in coolers was being airlifted to Heathrow and thence to New York for a celebrity dinner.' **Alan Lee** of *The Times* reveals why a helicopter landed at Lingfield Park racecourse to collect a curry in November 2004.

'In Britain, the best example of a town which is intimately identified with sport and owes its raison d'etre and visual character to it, is, in my view, Newmarket, home of British horse racing... My own impressions are that it is somewhat more "horsy" than Saratoga, New York.' **J Bale** in 1994's *Landscapes of Modern Sport*.

'I couldn't live in Newmarket: Far too many one-dimensional people who can't talk about anything other than racing.' Telescombe, near Brighton-based trainer **Jamie Poulton**, October 2004.

'Locos por los caballos.' How ***El Diario Vasco***, the paper of northern Spain's San Sebastián, reported the news in April 2004 that I, my wife, Sheila, and a couple of dozen other intrepid travelling racing fans were in town to attend the local racecourse on a trip organised by travel company Horse Racing Abroad.

'National Hunt Jockeys Oppose Hunting Ban. Will Blair Ban Racing Next?' **Banner** displayed during protest at Stratford racecourse in September 2004.

'The earliest English horse race of which we know, took place, not at Newmarket, but at Weatherby in Yorkshire, in the reign of the

'Carpet' is the racecourse name for which betting price?

Roman Emperor Severus Alexander (ad 210).' So says **R Lyle** in his 1945 book *Royal Newmarket*.

'They don't hang about in America. They don't even bother hearing evidence from the jockeys involved. They watch the replays from different angles, make their decision, take down the offending horse's number, amend the result, end of message. Next race please.' **Tony O'Hehir** on the US way of dispensing racecourse justice, August 2004.

'The fittest horse wins the Guineas; the luckiest horse wins the Derby, but the best horse wins the St Leger.' Old **horse-racing proverb**.

'As racing maxims go, the one about the Guineas being the best guide to the Derby ranks high on the list of the most nonsensical...the best guide to the Derby is the horse that Kieren Fallon rides.' **James Willoughby** (*Pacemaker*, July 2004).

'The racetrack is an inherently amazing place, rich in language and personality, sometimes beautiful and sometimes sordid, always unpredictable. Racing is a business, an art, an athletic contest, a moral and a spiritual test.' Writer **Jane Smiley** in *A Year at the Races*, 2004.

'We are keen to encourage more racegoers to share their journeys and we are working on setting up our own car sharing network.' Perhaps owners could travel with their horses to help **Cheltenham's 2004 initiative**.

'We wanted to bury the treasure at a prominent north-east location. In hindsight, it would have been better to ask permission from Sedgefield first.' Reaction from radio station **Galaxy** 105–106

in November 2004 after their marketing manager Andy Saxon was discovered digging a hole in the course's main straight, burying £25,000 of gold treasure – the prize for a competition.

'I suspect that when couples are engaging in passion in the cars on Warren Hill they throw their McDonalds or KFC cartons out of the window.' Trainer **James Fanshawe** bemoaning litter on Newmarket Heath.

'The course may lack many members these days but it now has a mascot called Sir Willy Winnit.' Journalist **Andrew King** on Chepstow racecourse, 31 August 2004.

'Miles and miles of bugger all.' Description of Newmarket recalled by **Robin Oakley** in the *Spectator*.

'The most uncomfortable, expensive – and successful – sardine convention in the world.' **Alastair Down** on the Cheltenham Festival, to which I can only say, 'Hear, hear.'

'There's no dress code here. It's fun and relaxed. Lots of tits and bare legs.' A 1997 description of Yarmouth by Clerk of Course **David Hansen**.

'Glorious Goodwood, racing's most applied and accurate alliteration.' **Cornelius Lysaght**, July 2004. Alan Lee of *The Times* agrees: 'They have even removed the line in the dress code that banned hotpants from the Richmond Enclosure.'

'The man in the wheelchair who used to spend the afternoon wheeling himself over people's toes has also disappeared.' **David Ashforth** detailing recent improvements to Brighton racecourse in

What was notable about Garden Path's 1944 2,000 Guineas victory?

August 2004. **Greg Wood** noted at around the same time, 'A man on stilts at a racetrack is hardly a novel idea, particularly during the school holidays. Only at Brighton, though, you suspect, would he stroll around the enclosures clutching a glass of red wine.' Bookie **Tony Styles** had his own damning with faint praise take on the improvements: 'It's not very good, but they're trying hard to make it better and it is getting better.'

'There's something about Ascot that makes you want to dress up as Wonder Woman,' said IT worker, '**Richard from Kent**' who was there on August 7, doing just that.

'If you had been beaten on an odds-on favourite, some of those fellas were ready to dig your mother up out of the grave and throw her at you.' **Ted Walsh** recalls riding at Leopardstown.

'Although nowadays the entertainment is confined to the track, time was when an afternoon's jollification would be prefaced by a hanging. Most notably, Dick Turpin met his end at the Tyburn in 1739. Nowadays it is horses who must deliver, though (obviously) not while standing.' **Sue Montgomery** on York (*Independent*, 17 August, 2004).

'Redcar, Wetherby, Sedgefield, Newcastle and Kelso.' Role call of trainer **Mary Reveley's** favourite courses, as she retired in August 2004.

'If Balcarmo is Samantha Fox, then Bogside is the Elephant Man.' Wry comparison of Scottish point-to-point courses Balcormo and Bogside, ***Point To Point Hunter Chase Formbook 1987***.

'If a green creature appeared from outer space and asked me to show it a "good day out" I would, without a moment of hesitation,

---

She was, at the time of writing, the last filly to win the Classic.

take it unswervingly to the Newmarket July course.' **Robert Cooper** (*In The Know* magazine)

'Santa Anita, probably my favourite racecourse in the world.' **Kieren Fallon**, September 2004.

'I've always thought of Ascot as a man's track. I'll keep my fingers crossed the new Ascot will be as kind to me as the old Ascot.' **Frankie Dettori**, awaiting the 2006 return of his favourite course.

'Kelso, which may be in the Scottish borders but draws a big gate of lifelong punters from Geordieland. It still provides real, living fires and the best tea of any racecourse, courtesy of the home baking of the W.I.' **Robin Cook**.

'I just felt so confident there. Maybe I was Clerk of the Course in an earlier life.' **Frankie Dettori** on Ascot.

'This is the nicest racecourse in England. If I have a day off, Sandown is where I'll come.' **Toby Balding's** opinion may have been influenced by the fact that when he said this that very course was celebrating his November 2004 retirement.

'People who love Del Mar say it isn't just a racetrack; it's a way of life.' **William Murray**, US writer, on the California course, 1997.

'The American Longchamp.' Writer **Paul Moran** on Belmont Park in New York, 1997

'The sprawling track is a magic place whether it's the first Saturday in May or any other day.' US writer **Jennie Rees** on the home of the Kentucky Derby, Churchill Downs, 1997.

Name the last filly to win a 20th-century Derby?

'For a little country track in Hot Springs, Arkansas, on a two-lane road between nowhere and no place, Oaklawn has made quite an impact on the racing world.' **Randy Moss** on Arkansas course, Oaklawn Park, also described as, 'one big party', 1997.

Fifinella in 1916. The race was moved from Epsom to Newmarket during the First World War.

Turf Wars

They have quite a war – a war against sand – over the turf for the racetrack at Nad Al Sheba. It is in Dubai where they hold a World Cup of sorts, which is primarily, well, desert. Yet, as Alan Lee, the respected 'Course Inspector' of *The Times*, who gives the courses he visits a tough time, says, 'No grass will grow naturally here, yet the place has a turf racetrack'. Pretty impressive, huh, and a real tribute to the groundsman. Him and the wealthy Sheikhs.

A real war on the turf broke out in 1892 when racegoers, jockeys and officials at Garfield Park, Chicago, raced for cover while the course was raided by armed police as part of a turf war between rival tracks raged. Garfield's owner, James M Browne killed two cops before being shot himself.

The track was closed down for good.

Newbury has real turf and it got involved in wars – real ones. A prisoner of war camp, a hay dispersal centre, a tank testing ground, a munitions depot and a troop camp – these were among the uses to which Newbury racecourse was put during World War I. It was in demand again during World War II when the US armed forces took it over as a supply depot – burying the turf under 35 miles of railway lines and concrete roads. After extensive repair work the course was able to reopen for racing in April 1949.

How does the old song go... 'War...bom, bom, bom...bom, bom... What is it good for?... Absolutely turf-all!' .

'You are a sarcastic ***** and I'll poke your ****ing eyes out.' Conversation opener from **Cash Asmussen** to journalist Richard Evans during a discussion of riding tactics at Longchamp in September 1997.

Which two racecourses dropped jump racing during 1998–9?

'Perhaps his behaviour says more about a jockey whose best years are behind him.' **Richard Evans'** neat put-down riposte.

'Like eating haggis, reading Dick Francis is something that must be done once but never again.' *Sunday Times* critic **Guy Walters**.

'Mrs Jenny Pitman is one of the more unpleasant people I have met in racing and reminds me of a manatee who employs a blind milliner.' **Jeffrey Bernard** (*Spectator*, 15 April 1997).

'She's about as cuddly as a dead hedgehog. The Alsatians in her yard would go around in pairs for protection.' **John Francome** on Jenny Pitman (*The Times*, 31 December 1999).

'I would sooner kiss Garrison Savannah's arse than speak to Julian Wilson.' **Jenny Pitman**.

'He don't talk to me and I don't talk to him, other than that we get along real fine.' US trainer **Sonny Hine** on 'colleague' Bob Baffert.

'He said "Francome, you're the worst f***ing jockey in the entire world." I looked him up and down and said, "nah...that's too much of a coincidence."' **John Francome's** riposte when Ginger McCain was not best pleased with the ride he gave one of his horses (*Racing Ahead*, October 2004).

'I detest all-weather racing.' **Toby Balding** to Claude Duval, 6 November 2004.

'Jamie Spencer's continued determination to ride like his name-sake Frank.' **Tony Paley** (*Racing Ahead*, December 2004).

Nottingham and Windsor.

'That Elsworth is on a real roll and I shall have to try and stop him somehow. Maybe I'll shoot him.' **Richard Hannon** after one of his runners had been turned over by a David Elsworth representative at Newmarket on Friday, 15 October 2004.

'If you have six runners and they all come last, you can't wear purple check trousers and pink shoes, can you? You'll just look like a clown.' **Henry Cecil** ponders a little-realised knock-on effect of a downturn in fortunes (*The Times*, 27 June 2004).

'Dress Code; Smart Casual. No Sports Shorts; no ripped, cut or torn Denim; no Football Shirts.' **Dress requirements for Sandown Park** on 4 December 2004 –so, that'll be no shorts for this depth of winter meeting, then? And, no 'Football Shirts' – so, what about Rugby, then? Or Hockey? Or…okay, okay, there must be 'standards', I suppose.

'An unprecedented act of ethnic cleansing that will wipe 15 per cent of older horses off the map.' Writer **Michael Clower** is not best pleased by Horse Racing Ireland's edict that no horse rated below 36 will be allowed to run on the Flat in Ireland in 2005. (*Racing Post*, 12 November 2004).

'This encourages betting with unlicensed and anonymous individuals and opens the floodgates for illegal betting.' Ladbrokes top man, **Chris Bell**, was not happy in 2003 when the Levy Board allowed on-course bookies to hedge with betting exchanges.

'This is the million-dollar question with exchanges: do they invite malpractice or shed a light on what already existed?' **Lydia Hislop** (*The Times*, 24 June 2004).

'I am personally convinced by what I have read and listened to that at least one race a day, if not more, is being corrupted by the

Phantom Bridge and Resistance earned their place in racing history at Doncaster in October 1947. How?

availability of laying horses to lose.' Hugely controversial anti-betting exchanges comment by Ladbrokes' boss, **Chris Bell**, on BBC TV's *The Money Programme* in June 2004.

'The flawed thinking behind it is that the good name of the sport is secondary to a misguided attempt to dirty the exchanges' reputation.' **Rob Hartnett**, MD of Betdaq.

'I'm just too angry and need to calm down. I laid two bets to win a total of £410 against a very big ante-post wager, many, many times more.' Owner **Darren Mercer**, warned off for six months after laying one of his horses, Joss Naylor, to lose on a betting exchange when, it was alleged, he knew the horse to be a non-runner (8 July 2004).

'I'm fundamentally opposed to the concept of betting exchanges because I think sport is about winning. To have people cheering on a racecourse because a horse is getting beaten is anathema to the whole concept of what sport is about.' **Peter Savill**, former BHB Chairman (*Daily Telegraph*, 10 July 2004).

'I am now satisfied that one in seven races is corrupted… I'm finding that well fancied runners are performing way below their ratings, which leaves me with no other explanation than they are being bet to lose on exchanges.' **Clive Reams**, announcing that he had closed his Racefax service, which monitored 'suspect' races (*Sunday Mirror*, 11 July 2004).

'Exchanges are so information-orientated that it no longer behoves us to rail against bookmaker cynicism when horses about which they offer the best ante-post prices are withdrawn or revealed to be behind in their preparation… If individuals can profit from information it is churlish to demand moral restraint from bookmakers.' Racing writer **Julian Muscat**, July 2004.

They were the two horses involved in the first dead-heat decided by a photo-finish.

'Some will tell you that this rule is out of order because it stops owners from hedging to offset their expenses. I would argue this inconvenience is a small price to pay for a public image of openness and integrity.' *Racing Post's* **Peter Thomas** on the rule prohibiting owners from laying their own horses on exchanges, 12 July 2004.

'There is, however, every reason to believe that owners should not lay their own horses, even if it is to hedge their position, having backed their horse elsewhere.' Former trainer **Charlie Brooks** (*Daily Telegraph*, July 2004).

'To me it is an electronic bookmaker and to pretend it should not exist is fine in a country where bookmakers don't exist and there is a pool monopoly. But if you are in a country where you have bookmakers running alongside the Tote, to me it is a smart new modern form of bookmaking. I don't think it is a question of banning it, but of regulating and managing it, and making sure it pays a fair share to racing.' BHB Chairman, **Martin Broughton** (*Daily Telegraph*, 2 August 2004).

'Betting exchanges present the greatest threat to Australian racing as we know it in the 170-year history of our sport.' Australian Racing Board chairman **Andrew Ramsden**, reported on 19 August 2004. Not surprisingly Mark Davies of Betfair retaliated by calling Ramsden's stance 'Canute-like'.

'Betting exchanges make nothing out of corruption because they draw their commission no matter who wins. As anything that damages confidence reduces their turnover they have every incentive to stamp it out.' **Paul Haigh** (*Racing Post*, 4 September 2004).

'We are all in agreement that ever since the betting exchanges started they've thrown the integrity of the sport into doubt… Every

Who was the first horse to complete the Derby-Arc de Triomphe double and when did this happen?

professional in the sport is totally against the exchanges because they do cast that doubt about a horse running bad should it be fancied – they're not good for the sport.' Former champion jockey **Kevin Darley**, joint president of the Jockeys' Association on BBC *Grandstand*, 4 September 2004.

'People who are suggesting that betting exchanges are somehow responsible for corruption in racing are wrong. Their argument is the equivalent of saying that roadside cameras are the cause of speeding.' Betfair spokesman **Mark Davies**.

'If opportunities are created for people to benefit from horses losing, then you shouldn't be surprised if those opportunities are taken up.' William Hill chief executive **David Harding**.

'The authorities should act and stop betting exchanges. They are carte blanche for skulduggery.' Trainer **Richard Hannon** (*Racing Post*, 5 September 2004).

'Talk at such gatherings naturally centres on the fact that it is acceptable to back horses to lose. Many outsiders remain astonished, even appalled by this.' The *Times* racing writer **Alan Lee** considers the subject matter of conversations at 'the average Saturday night bar or dinner party' in September 2004.

'The exchanges have initiated a culture of suspicion about the conduct of wagering on horseracing that, whether or not it is justified, does the sport no good at all. And it is quite disingenuous of their spokesmen to deny the fact.' **Tony Morris**, who added, 'The exchanges brag about snitching on their clients, almost to the extent of flaunting that unethical practice as justification for their existence.' (*Racing Post*, 10 September 2004).

Sea Bird II – in 1965.

'Exchanges have allowed punters to bet with virtually no margin against them. Almost every price offered by bookmakers can be beaten by exchanges, albeit sometimes for small stakes.' Channel 4 racing guru **Tanya Stevenson** in September 2004.

'By facilitating the laying of horses, exchanges have provided further and easier opportunities for people to cheat other punters. Yet the voluntary co-operation of exchanges to identify and monitor betting patterns of particular accounts had proved an invaluable tool to the regulator in investigating alleged malpractice and bringing corrupters to account.' **Christopher Foster**, Jockey Club executive director at the conference, 'The Evolving Landscape of British Horseracing', 13 September 2004.

'When betting exchanges first arrived on the scene, the big bookmakers ignored them. Fresh from having their fingers singed by trying their luck at spread betting, they thought Betfair was another niche betting product. It was an error of judgement which the likes of Chris Bell at Ladbrokes, John Brown of William Hill and Tom Kelly, the betting industry's spin doctor, will take to their graves.' The apparently all-seeing, all-knowing, **Richard Evans** (*Thoroughbred Owner & Breeder*, September 2004).

'Betting exchanges encourage the professional punter to cheat small punters, and they are a definite threat to integrity. We will do everything we can to stop them coming into France. We prefer to get nothing from them by way of payment to keep them out.' France-Galop director-general, **Louis Romanet**, speaking at the 2004 International Federation of Horseracing Authorities.

'If it meant getting rid of Betfair I would shut down the Spring Carnival.' **Robert Nason**, chief executive of Racing Victoria, which hosts the Melbourne Cup in its Spring Carnival, confirmed his opposition to the Exchanges in October 2004.

Fujiyama Crest is famous as the last horse in Frankie Dettori's 1996 Magnificent Seven at Ascot. The horse had won the same race a year previously, too, beating which Champion Hurdler-to-be in the process?

'What betting exchanges do provide is the facility for jockeys and their intermediaries to lay the horses they are riding anonymously and without any fear of discovery. They also allow unscrupulous owners and trainers to send unfit horses to race to lose in order to lay them.' **John Pegley** of West Sussex in a letter to the *Racing Post,* (24 November 2004).

'I have still yet to meet anyone who loses on Betfair.' And isn't that just the case? I can only assume that there is just one poor, unfortunate punter who is subsidising everybody else who is playing on the Exchanges, because **Dave Nevison** put his finger right on the button when he identified this bizarre truth that absolutely no one ever admits to doing anything other than winning copiously. The comment appeared in his *Racing & Football Outlook* column for 30 November–6 December 2004.

'Is this not a place of work?' **Jim Bolger** is not happy on spotting a press hack smoking in the winner's enclosure at The Curragh in July 2004. Smoking in the workplace is illegal in Ireland.

'Because of who you are, a Scouse ex-footballer, if you ever did anything wrong the racing hierarchy would come down on you like a ton of bricks.' Warning to **Mick Quinn** from Mick Channon when the former announced he was to join the training ranks. In 2001 he was accused of allowing the condition of three horses to fall 'below that expected of a licensed trainer' and had his licence withdrawn for two and a half years.

'Thousands of ex-racehorses have had happy retirements in the hunting field or point to pointing. If those avenues are closed, to where are those horses going to retire? The plate of a ravenous Frenchman?' Pro hunting, former trainer **Charlie Brooks**, (*Daily Telegraph*, 25 October 2004).

Istabraq.

'The *Racing Post* is neutral, although individual contributors have strong views both for and against.' **David Ashforth** sets out his paper's stance on the hunting issue, 27 October 2004.

'Over the years I've been very lucky.' **Brendan Powell** overlooks: a ruptured stomach; broken left leg; internal bleeding; broken left leg (again); broken arm; broken wrist, (several) broken collar bones.

'It is part of a jockey's job to get on to the best horses, and if that involves ruffling a few feathers, so be it.' **Lester Piggott** on the controversial practice of 'jocking off'.

'The form book should be written in braille for the benefit of Jockey Club stewards.' Racing writer, the late **Clive Graham**.

'I think Tony Blair would do well to employ John Maxse – he's so good at bailing out all the military types who sit around making up rules they don't have to implement.' Trainer **Paul D'Arcy**, September 2004.

'Dubai's Crown Price believes he knows as much about horses as many of his trainers, while (Henry) Cecil thinks the only words he should hear from his owners are "the money is in your bank account, O Great One".' Writer **Richard Edmondson** on the differences that led to the eventual split between Sheikh Mohammed and Henry Cecil (*Independent*, 22 April 1996).

'No business that is closed down, as racing was at Sandown Park last year, by a group of its participants (the jockeys) striking for the dubious human right of ringing their punters from the weighing room, can see itself as very far from a laughing stock.' **Brough Scott** (*Sunday Telegraph*, 5 September 2004).

Where do the winners of the Lincolnshire Handicap race each other?

'I soon learned it doesn't matter who you vote for, they all tell lies. If I was to follow the politicans' example I'd offer money back on all losers and double odds on all winners. I would just fail to cough up when people came for their money.' Bookie **Barry Dennis**, 6 November 2004.

'I'm very happy for the race to continue to be called the Foxhunter. Lots of things that are illegal are still referred to, and to ban the use of the word based on political legislation would be taking things to the extreme.' Chairman of Christie's auction house, **Dermot Chichester**, was not best pleased at suggestions that the name of the Cheltenham race he sponsored should be changed in the light of anti-foxhunting legislation, November 2004.

'I don't care which side they're on – I think you have to take half of what they say, cut that in half and believe the bit that's left. Perhaps.' **Clive Brittain** on politicians (*Racing Post*, 10 September 2004).

'One thing led to another and I ended up losing it and hitting out at him.' **Eddie Ahern** admitting coming to blows with fellow jockey Declan McDonogh, who ended up with a cut nose, after a race at The Curragh on 2 October 2004. He was banned for 21 days.

'I have met some wonderful people, but I've also met some first-class prats.' Retiring trainer **Charles Booth** in January 2005.

'It's becoming increasingly embarrassing to witness the lewd comments towards the ladies each week. For example, 'the best job in television is being the person who fits Emma Ramsden's microphone.' *Raceform Update* correspondent **Robert Chisleworth** slams Channel 4's *Morning Line*, 7 July 2004.

On a Totopoly board.

'She doesn't look like a girl when riding a finish.' Trainer **Michael Bell** on jockey Hayley Turner (*Racing & Football Outlook*, 7–13 September 2004).

'The judge who heard Mrs Nagle's submission said with undisguised scorn that refusing someone a licence because of their sex is akin to doing so because of the colour of their hair.' **George Ennor** on the 1966 case involving Mrs Florence Nagle, which forced the Jockey Club to permit the fairer sex to train horses officially as they had been doing undercover for many years.

'I'll be horrified if my sister Hayley rides over jumps, hopefully Dad won't let her.' Up-and-coming flat jockey **Ryan Moore**, 19 September 2004.

'F— off.' Former female jockey **Gee Armytage**, taken by surprise while broadcasting live on Sky from Cheltenham in March 1997, after her then boss, trainer Oliver Sherwood, goosed her. 'I've never had my backside pinched so hard before,' she said. 'I was so shocked the swear word just shot out.'

'Bookmaking may not have always been a woman's game, but look about now and you see them more than ever.' Larger-than-life bookie **Gary Wiltshire**, who works on the course with Pam Sharman, December 2004.

'Not their proper sphere,' said Australia's Victoria Racing Club Chairman, **LKS Mackinnon**, justifying its early 1930s ban on female trainers.

'Horse racing used to be an entirely male world, and on a scale of one to ten, its masculinity quotient remains about an eight.' US owner/writer, **Jane Smiley** (*A Year at the Races*, 2004).

Which Daily Express *Triumph Hurdle winner was named as 'Best Horse Ridden' by three different jockeys – Chris Leonard, Robert Hughes and Roger Wernham, in the* Directory of the Turf?

'You've got to want success every day, and when you get it that makes you greedy for some more.' **Tony McCoy**, 1997.

'The only Tory worth backing to win is Frankie Dettori.' Deputy PM **John Prescott**.

'John Prescott would be a bookmaker par excellence. Its no insult to say you can imagine him standing on a box at Doncaster and shouting the odds.' **Jamie Reid** of the *Guardian*, who said of Prescott's boss, Tony Blair, 'He's a little too saintly to be mistaken for a bookie of the old school, although with his shiny black suits and gleaming smile he could easily be a representative from Hills or Ladbrokes.'

'I've never come across a horse that wanted to talk politics.' **Robin Cook** explains his love of racing.

'We'd drain all the lakes on racecourses and replace the water with wine.' Loony Party vote winner from late **Screaming Lord Sutch**.

'You see the dregs of humanity there in a way I've never seen in a bingo hall.' Portsmouth MP **David Martin's** controversial comment on betting shops just before the 1997 General Election – after which he found himself a former MP.

'As long as I can look back and say I've ridden more winners than anyone else, I'm happy.' (*Sunday Times*, 28 November 2004). So why doesn't **Tony McCoy** ever look it? He was quoted two days later by Patrick Weaver in the *Daily Express* as saying: 'If you sat me down and said you can have £5million or ride 250 winners this season, I'd take the winners.'

Peter O'Sullevan's Attivo.

'Yearlings, the teenagers of racing, are like pop idols who would be stars. Most will prove no better than pub singers, but that does not stop investors.' **Carl Evans** (*Pacemaker*, September 2004).

'Yearlings and foals can be prepared by masters of disguise, some of whom can transform ugly ducklings with crooked legs and lack of athleticism into swans worth millions of dollars. Surgery may be performed, feet totally reshaped, muscle developed by unaccustomed exercise, body weight increased by mysterious potions, skin colour and texture improved and a gangling gait developed dramatically to mimic the swagger of an Olympic hopeful.' Renowned bloodstock adviser **Grant Pritchard-Gordon** with a warning prospective purchasers would be well advised to heed (*Pacemaker*, September 2004).

'These needle matches are a Texas equine junkies' jamboree. How we all yell "cheat" over Olympic athletes found using drugs and then stand by and see horses pumped with similar pain-killers and performance enhancers beats me.' **Claude Duval** doesn't pull his punches about the 2004 Breeders Cup meeting, 'where drugs are openly used to enhance horses' performances.' (*Sun*, 30 October 2004).

'The worst thing was I didn't even enjoy the ice cream. It was a horrible flavour.' **John McCririck** after a racegoer shoved ice cream into his face on screen at Newmarket in 1997.

'He even wears that hat in the shower.' **Mrs Jenny McCririck**, alias The Booby (*Sun*, 2 October 2004).

'If everyone in racing was as passionate as he is, this would be Britain's number one sport.' **John 'Greatest Jockey' Francome** sticks up for Big Mac, aka John McCririck.

Why was the trainer known as 'Frenchie' Nicholson?

'He says something different and some people don't like him for that.' *Talk Sport* presenter **Graham Beacroft** on the same man, 11 January 2005.

'I'm not a pleasant man. I have very few friends, if any. I don't go to parties.' **John McCririck** on Channel 4's *Celebrity Big Brother*.

'A cantankerous cross between Jimmy Edwards and a Turkish pasha, John McCririck is the reason why we had an empire – and the reason why we lost it.' **Allison Pearson** (*Evening Standard*, 19 January 2005).

'What racing doesn't need to boost its public image is a bloated, hectoring ex-public schoolboy with serious hygiene issues snivelling to a collection of fellow D-list "celebs" about the injustice of life without Diet Coke.' **Graham Cunningham** on McCririck (*Evening Standard*, 14 January 2005).

'In the 24 years I have known him he has been right about the great issues in racing on the vast majority of occasions.' **Alastair Down** on McCririck.

'Having had the misfortune of seeing the "face of racing" picking his nose and eating it on national television, ensuring I watch no more of this particular programme, I find it very depressing if this is indeed the image of racing it is desirable to promote.' *Racing Post* correspondent Patricia Morgan from Kent on McCririck, 16 January 2005.

'Racing should not underestimate the impact of Mac being in the house. The Tolworth Hurdle got three name checks to my knowledge and greyhound racing has been mentioned too.' **Tanya Stevenson**, Mac's (McCririck) Channel 4 racing colleague, who

He was apprenticed in 1925 to Charles Clout in France for three years.

says 'his chauvinism doesn't faze me as much as my disregard for anything other than sport doesn't faze him.'

'"Come racing" is McCririck's battle cry but will anyone want to come racing after viewing him? John's performances have entertained many but the potential damage he has done is immeasurable.' Former champion jump jockey turned trainer/pundit, **Peter Scudamore**.

'He spotted some kids playing marbles and began to stare at them. I gave him his head and he got his nose to the floor and started playing marbles with them.' **Sir Gordon Richards** on his mount Abernant, voted Britain's greatest sprinter of the century – who won 14 of his 17 races in the late forties/early fifties.

'The greatest sin at Heath House is to be late in the morning. It happened just the once. It was only by five minutes. But Sir Mark's reaction was…well, unprintable. It'll never, never happen again.' **Seb Sanders** on clocking in for duty with Sir Mark Prescott.

'Against all the odds, Bob [Champion] fought his way back from cancer, not just to ride again but to win the world's greatest steeplechase on a horse who a couple of years earlier the vets said should be put down. No argument – the Greatest Race has to be the 1981 National.' **Derek Thompson**.

'The League (Against Cruel Sports) also takes the view that the Grand National, in its current form, is unacceptable. Too many horses are entered and run, thus causing collisions. We also consider the length of the course and height of the obstacles too gruelling for many horses.' **Douglas Batchelor**, chief executive of the League in an October 2004 letter to the *Racing Post* that perpetuated the 'turf war' between the organisers and antis.

How old was the legendary champion jockey Fred Archer when he took his own life in 1886?

'I dreamt twice last night I saw the race run. The second dream I saw the Liverpool run. He won by four lengths and you rode him.' Owner **Lord Poulet** in a letter to jockey Tommy Pickernell, urging him to ride The Lamb for him in the 1871 Grand National. The jockey agreed and duly won, but by two lengths.

'Casse Tete looked as though she were in training for an anatomical museum instead of the Grand National,' wrote **The Times** after the horse ran third in Croydon's Great Metropolitan Chase, only to go on to win the 1872 National at 20/1.

'Last year it was a blooming Lord (Manners) won the National; this year it's a furring Count (Kinsky) and next year it'll be an old woman, most likely.' Professional jockey **Jimmy Adams** complaining at gentlemen riders' success in the 1882 and three Nationals, to which Kinsky, fresh from victory on Zoedone at 100/7, riposted, 'Yes, Jimmy, and I hope this old woman will be yourself.' It wasn't.

'His head is preserved in the Museum.' Unusual boast by Newmarket-based National Horse-racing Museum in their 2004 **Newsletter** 3, referring to 1893 National winner, Cloister.

'I direct the Corporation shall prefer a man who is a sportsman and not a total abstainer from alcohol and tobacco.' **Ambrose Gorham**, owner of 1902 National winner, Shannon Lass, who with his winnings restored the church and parish at Telscombe near Brighton and left instructions for its incumbent in his will.

'To keep our spirits up, Frank described his ride around the Grand National course in Reynoldstown. Again and again. By the time we were rescued I could have ridden the race blindfold.' Fellow RAF man **John Hoare** on how he and 1935 National winning rider Frank Furlong survived when they ditched their plane into the North Atlantic in 1941. Sadly, Furlong was killed in September 1944 while testing a prototype plane.

'If I get through this without a disaster even, I'll never do it again.' **Peter O'Sullevan's** unkept vow as he waited to carry out his first Grand National commentary in 1949.

'A few minutes later I was a rich little five-year-old; my one penny punt having yielded a staggering 2s4d.' **Alastair Down** recalls his first ever bet, at a tender age, on Nicolaus Silver to win the 1961 Grand National, for which his Dad had to cough up the winnings.

'An experience that will last me to my grave.' **Richard Pitman** after he and gallant front-running Crisp were collared almost on the line in 1973 by the then little-known Red Rum.

'I even had a dream that I might be in a position of having to interview myself after the race if by some miracle the veteran Another Duke could have won. I had leased the horse to run in my colours.' **Des Lynam's** runner didn't win the 1986 National. The 200/1 shot fell.

'Keep remounting.' Pre-race instructions from trainer **Tim Forster** to Charlie Fenwick who won the 1980 Grand National on Ben Nevis.

'*Athletics Weekly* has regularly likened the Olympic marathon to the Grand National horse race. Every April, the toughest course on the jumps calendar turns a thoroughbred line-up into a donkey derby. Usually, betting on the race is a complete lottery.' *Athletics Weekly* Editor, **Jason Henderson**, September 2004.

'There aren't enough Grand Nationals in a lifetime.' **Dick Francis** should know, having ridden in eight and had the race at his mercy on Devon Loch only to miss out as the horse inexplicably collapsed on the run in.

In 1875 which racecourse, still flourishing today, became the first to be properly enclosed?

'I had a burning ambition to win the National but I never got remotely near achieving it. Nonetheless, the thrill of riding a horse over those fences will always stay with me. It is simply the world's greatest steeplechase.' **Jonjo O'Neill**.

'Not bad for a bloody taxi driver.' **Ginger McCain**, accepting the trophy from the Princess Royal after Amberleigh House won him the 2004 National.

'Shows you what real Grand National jockeys face during the race – including Becher's Brook.' **National Horse-racing Museum** in 2004, plugging its Grand National Ride simulator, which presumably doesn't feature false starts or bomb scares.

'I only ever bet on the Grand National but the one I back always seems to die,' **Davina McCall** told Bruce Millington, author of 2004's *Definitive Guide to Betting On Sport.*

'It's like a battlefield when the battle's over – there's been forty brave horses and brave men doing battle round there – it just makes my hair stand on end.' **Ginger McCain** on Aintree after the National had been run (BBC TV, 21 November 2004).

'Hi! We will begin attack on your site soon. Our team needs money. Your website has the large incomes. We want that you paid to us. We think that the normal amount is 30,000 USD. If you don't pay, we will attack your site for a long time. We not make of evil to anybody, it is only our work. Good luck!' **Sinister blackmail threat** made to Internet bookies Blue Square and Capital Sports in June 2004, after which both were subjected to a three-hour distributed denial of service attack, badly affecting their sites. Neither they nor the several other bookies similarly targeted are believed to have paid any ransom.

Sandown Park.

'Along the way, we were the victims of a deliberate, £800,000 fraud, most of which we later recovered in court.' William Hill boss **John Brown** reveals that their fledgling Internet business didn't always run smoothly (*Lucky John*, 2004).

'I think Goodwood is a hard track to ride… I've been very open in saying out loud I don't especially like riding there.' Serial champion jockey **Kieren Fallon**, August 2004.

'Nottingham is home to Robin Hood, the Goose Fair and, above all, the worst set of on-course bookmakers in England.' Richard Birch of the *Racing Post* is Nott impressed.

'If Great Yarmouth was a birthday present, I'm not sure I'd bother to tear off the wrapping paper.' **Stephen Cartmel**, after visiting every course in the country for a book. He was a little keener on the course bearing his name: 'Racing at Cartmel is pure madness, an eccentric pursuit, wonderful and completely irrational.'

'A little worrying to see a place which once oozed class allow droves of one-man mobile "hoses" to sell cheap lager more rapidly and in public areas away from bars. Good business, certainly, but will punters pay increased admission prices if the social standing falls?' *Racing Post* greyhound correspondent **Jim Cremin** fears an Ascot dumbing down when visiting in July 2004. He also worried about the re-vamp: 'There is something different about the shabby charm of Ascot's current stands. There's nowhere in the world like it.' Certainly there isn't now!

'You can't run the horse at Salisbury, the lunch there is terrible.' Owner **Lady Beaverbrook** to her trainer, Dick Hern.

Name the first female to train a Breeders Cup winner.

'If someone gave me a tractor I'd plough it up today.' Jump jock **Ian Lawrence's** 1996 verdict on Taunton.

'I woke up and didn't fancy going to Plumpton.' **Mark Perrett** on what decided him to quit as a jockey in 1996.

'You have to play "spot the grass". It is the worst course in the world and I was beaten on every favourite I rode there.' That may explain jockey turned trainer **Sean Woods'** opinion of Catterick.

'It struck me as a god-forsaken place at the end of the earth.' So, we'll take it that Newton Abbot is not *Racing UK* presenter **Nick Luck's** favourite racecourse, shall we?

'What are the four racecourses beginning with F? Fakenham, Folkestone, Fontwell and f*****g Plumpton.' Trainer **Richard Philips** (*Horse & Hound*, September 1989).

'Directly beneath me was a group of males all dressed up as Widow Twankey, being urged on by members of the fairer sex with their cameras to expose themselves by "mooning". With no shame they duly obliged.' **M A J Rodgers** of Scarborough was 'quite shocked' by this distressing experience at Beverley on 28 August 2004, so wrote to the media to share the details.

'Epsom has sat on its laurels with its ostrich head stuck in the sand of the 1970s,' believes *Racing Post* letter writer **Alan Procter** of Carshalton in Surrey.

'This stand should have been replaced years ago and I regard it as the worst owners' and trainers' facility I've come across in my visits to all but five of Britain's flat tracks.' Syndicate owner **Ken Wilson** from Leicester on that very course, in September 2004.

Jenine Sahadi with Lit de Justice in the 1996 Sprint.

'I met an old chap the other day who told me he rode there 35 years ago and the place hadn't changed.' Jockeys' valet, **Chris Maude**, on Fakenham, the 'worst track to work', September 2004.

'The paddock at Epsom is the worst in the world, an absolute disgrace. It is little more than a glorified car park.' **John McCririck** (*Sunday Telegraph*, 31 May 1998).

'Hopefully they will leave those bastards with the bowler hats in place when they commence the demolition.' Pro punter **Dave Nevison** is not a fan, then, judging by his comments as they prepared to pull Ascot down (*Racing & Football Outlook*, October 2004).

'Why did thousands of people waste their time and money by travelling to Newmarket on Saturday? Nobody had a clue what was happening as the horses invariably split into two, sometimes three, groups, and apart from the chosen few who enjoy watching animals race a mile away from each other, the whole day was a complete joke.' **Mark Winstanley** is scathing about Newmarket's Cambridgeshire day, 2004, asking, 'Why the clerk of the course didn't put a running rail down the middle of the track beggars belief.'

'A track that begins somewhere out there and gives punters, by way of entertainment, pictures of distant brutes' heads getting ever closer – never close enough to identify.' **Sir Clement Freud** on Newmarket, 20 October 2004.

'I didn't like it – getting here was a terrible journey, and Peter Cazalet seemed to run all his bad horses here.' **Dick Francis**, looking happy at Plumpton in October 2004, recalling what he thought of the place as a jockey.

Only one jockey rode in every one of the first 20 Breeders Cup meetings. Who?

'I wasn't disappointed when it closed. Even though I rode the last winner there I wish it had closed before I started riding. Quite a few of us jockeys fell off there and we weren't sorry to see it go.' On 18 October1977 **John Lowe** rode Bird of Fortune to win the last-ever race at the less than lamented Lanark.

'They're not bothered about trainers and owners there, all they're bothered about is beer-swillers and lager louts.' Trainer **Howard Johnson** was not best pleased with Sedgefield when the course refused to let him pop his Transcend over a fence or two to prepare him for the Hennessy in November 2004.

Nothing to Tout About

'I gotta horse' was the catch-phrase of the legendary tipster Prince Ras Monolulu, who would ply his trade around the racecourses in the 1920s and 30s. A flamboyantly clad, exotic looking self-publicist who demanded attention, it is difficult to believe that he does not share a distant ancestor with a similar contemporary figure who astonished the nation when he entered the *Celebrity Big Brother* house in January 2005 – John, 'I'm a deeply unpleasant man', McCririck, who has made his racing reputation by shouting his opinions from the sport's rooftops.

The Prince, born in Abyssinia in 1880, and The Old Harrovian are just two of the multitude of personalities who populate racing and who are always out to prove –generally at a price – that they know better than you do when it comes to what's going on, and, more importantly for the punter in the street, what's going to win. They don't, of course, but from the TV pundits to the newspaper tipsters, it seems to suit everyone to pretend that maybe, just maybe, they do. Which is why I was only too happy to accommodate the computer genius who, so I had been told by his local paper, was going to revolutionise the world of betting and probably bankrupt my company by tipping winners on his machine. Not only did I offer him the freedom of one of our betting shops to set up his equipment and come up with his tips, I also gave him a supply of free bets with which to do his worst, or best, as the media looked on. After two of his selections fell and another ran off the course halfway round he gave up the ghost, packed up his computer and left, never to be heard from again.

It doesn't score heavily in terms of advertising and as such it's very hard to make it stack up commercially.' Channel 4 Head of Sport **David Kerr** on how difficult is to screen racing profitably (*Evening Standard*, 22 November 2004).

Philip G Johnson, whose Volponi won the Breeders Cup Classic in 2002, became the oldest winning trainer in the event. How old was he – 71, 77 or 79?

'Races for amateur riders of either sex are generally contested by poor, unreliable individuals of very doubtful stamina – and, sadly, the horses are even worse.' **Greg Wood** (*Independent*, December 1997).

'Betting shops are not allowed to sell alcohol on their premises, so why should you be allowed to walk up to a bookmaker on a race-course carrying a pint of beer and place a bet? It is time that the Jockey Club took the lead and ordered racecourses not to allow anybody to remove alcohol from the bars.' Racegoer **Neville Kent** from Crewe, outraged by people, 'who had absolutely no interest in horse racing whatsoever and merely attended with the intention of not leaving until they had spent all their money on alcohol,' at Haydock on 4 September 2004.

'The poorest horses, whose owners have already been duped into wasting tens of millions of pounds, must be phased out, but in as sympathetic a way as is practicable.' **Bill O'Gorman** is not keen on the surfeit of moderate beasts in training (*Racing Post*, 16 January 2005).

'If you pay peanuts, you get Monkees.' Journalist **Peter Corrigan** after former pop star Davy Jones won a race worth under £3,000 on Digpast in February 1996, while trainer Roland O'Sullivan got in on the act, commenting, 'I warned him Digpast can be a bit of a monkey'.

'They're all the same until they race – dangerous at both ends and uncomfortable in the middle.' Owner/commentator **Des Lynam**.

'Brian Potter, of course, is in a wheelchair – and the horse was about that fast.' Trainer **Alan Berry** after his five times beaten 2003 two year old, named after Peter Kay's fictitious nightclub owner in *Phoenix Nights*, failed to get his head in front.

'Somebody told me to think of myself as a racehorse and put the blinders (blinkers) on.' Comedienne **Joan Rivers** during August 2004 TV programme *What I Wish I'd Known When I Was 20,* reviewed by *Times* critic Hugo Rifkind who observed: 'It certainly helps to explain the look she has been aiming for all this time.'

'This keen golfer is more the Vijay Singh than the Tiger Woods of the weighing room.' **Graham Cunningham** on Seb Sanders (*Evening Standard*, 9 August 2004).

'I hate to end this piece praising Derek Thompson but just about the only time he has said anything useful on Channel Four was when he interrupted his guest and told him to forget about the value and just "tell us the winner".' Pro punter **Dave Nevison** in an article doubting the concept of 'value' in betting. Poor old Thommo takes a lot of unwarranted stick in my opinion.

'I am so pleased to meet you. I have always enjoyed your cricket writing. Such a shame you gave it up and started writing about racing.' Arc winning trainer **Jonathan Pease** to *Times* writer Alan Lee (3 October 2004).

'If regional racing is allowed to continue it should be branded in a way that indicates it is not a part of the proper racing product. As it stands, regional racing is devaluing the sport as a whole.' *Guardian* racing writer **Tony Paley** doesn't think much of the BHB 2004 initiative.

'I think if you have a mature three-year-old that stays a mile and a half well, then you are a bit of a wanker if you worry about the handicap mark.' Trainer **John Gosden** (*Observer*, May 2004).

Champion two-year-old of 1994, Celtic Swing, was named after a musical track by which rock star?

'It's a stupid idea that smacks of creators – the Football Furlong Co – who don't like racing and won't understand how insulting it is to those who do, nor how pathetic it makes us look again to hang on football's coat-tails.' **Lydia Hislop** (*The Times*, 14 July 2004), is not impressed with Haydock's Football Furlong in which jockeys wore silks representing Premiership football clubs.

'Take his balls off, Rishi.' **Andrew Balding's** straight-talking answer to BBC TV reporter Rishi Persad's request for elucidation of the term 'cut' in relation to the trainer's 20/1 July 2004 Ascot winner Prince of Thebes.

'A piece of piss.' **Kieren Fallon's** verdict on Ouija Board's 2004 Irish Oaks victory.

'The system is stupid, it's crazy and there's no common sense. Situations like this just make our industry a laughing stock... What's the point in having reserves if the reserve can't get in the race at 10 a.m. when normal declarations are finished?' **Mick Channon** berates the deadline for inserting reserve runners into major races, 26 July 2004.

'I can't think of anything more uncomfortable for a horse.' **John Francome** on being informed by fellow Channel 4 pundit Jim McGrath that Godolphin's horses run with tongue ties, used to prevent tongue swallowing, or getting over the bit, causing problems with breathing and steering (*Pacemaker*, August 2004).

'People have talked so much horlicks with a capital B about this horse.' **David Elsworth** defends his Norse Dancer in August 2004.

'He has appeared to win races at both Nottingham and Windsor this season, but lost out each time – because he has a short neck.' **Stan Mellor's** explanation for dual 1996 runner-up Court Nap.

Van Morrison.

'I had the race won and then he saw the lights and then boom.' **Frankie Dettori's** rather dubious reason for Swain's Breeders Cup defeat at Churchill Downs.

'For the last four years I've had my head bald. I've always shaved the rest.' Great US jockey **Patrick Valenzuela**, who had previously served a six-month drugs ban, only to receive another after failing to take a hair follicle test, which requires ten strands of hair to test for substance abuse, in July 2004.

'I got head-butted in the stomach by a deer.' **Paul Carberry** explains why he missed his rides at a 2003 Cartmel meeting.

'Apparently, it was the ground that scuppered him, ground that we were told might be ideal by his previous winning rider.' Pro punter **Dave Nevison** reflects on the defeat of his Willie Supple-ridden Otago at Pontefract in October 2004.

'In a sixteen runner race there will be one winner and fifteen excuses.' Writer **Gerald Hammond** in 1992.

'The long grass.' Excuse put forward by trainer **Victor Dartnall** to explain Lord Sam's poor jumping display at Wetherby in November 2004.

'The reason given for Golden Nun swerving markedly left and losing a race she looked to have in the bag at Nottingham was that she was spooked by the sight of a bouncy castle.' (**'Tattenham Corner' column**, *Observer*, 28 November 2004)

'A foal and his money are soon parted.' *Evening Standard* **headline** as Satish Sanan paid 2.5m Guineas for 10-month-old Generous offspring in late 1997.

What is French trainer Criquette Head's real first name?

'We go in one of the roughest pubs in Brixham and you can see him there singing along with all these hairy trawlermen.' **Chester Barnes** reveals a hidden side to Martin Pipe.

'Racing, unlike many other sports, rarely features beyond the back pages of newspapers. It makes the national news only when connected to corruption or adultery.' Sophie Topley, (*Sunday Telegraph*, 24 October 2004).

'Nose patches that are meant to help free the airways are an example of a new product patently not staying the trip. Not only have trainers cut down on using them, so have the few jockeys who tried them.' **George Haine** (*Pacemaker*, August 2004).

'It seems that eight out of ten copies go straight to the smallest room in the house.' *Racing & Football Outlook's* **'Off The Bit' column** reflects on news that, according to an NOP survey, 83 per cent of male readers' favourite time for reading is 'when sitting on the bog', August 2004.

'I still find it very hard to understand the Duchess's (of Westminster) decision to have Arkle disinterred and "reconstructed". I have not seen the result and do not intend to.' **John Oaksey**, uneasy that the skeleton of Arkle is displayed at the Irish Horse Museum in County Kildare.

'It is very cool to have access to this animal's actual skeleton.' **Dr Alan Wilson** of the Royal Veterinary College in London, who is using scanners and high-tech computer equipment to analyse the skeleton of the first great racehorse, Eclipse, whose unbeaten career ended in 1770.

'My muscular skeleton has changed, so I'm nothing like Marvin Hagler or Jonny Wilkinson, but hopefully I'm not like Mr Bean

Christianne.

either.' Twenty-three-year-old amateur jockey **David Dunsdon** on training to take on the pros in the 2004 Hennessy. He was to partner Joly Bey, who had been purchased especially for him – only for the horse to miss the race through injury.

'Only a handful of the 9000 races run in a year have anything wrong with them. This idea that racing is institutionally corrupt is incorrect.' One hopes that Jockey Club Director of Security **Paul Scotney** is a man with very small hands (*BBC 5 Live*, 5 January 2005).

'That the French filly was beaten on her merits no one who saw her when she returned to the enclosure for one moment believes. For my part I think a grosser robbery was never perpetrated upon the Turf.' Not mincing his words, **'Harkaway'** of the *Standard* was in no doubt what had gone on when 5/2 favourite for the 1864 2,000 Guineas finished last, partnered by jockey Arthur Edwards – who was rumoured not to be the straightest of riders. When the combination subsequently won The Oaks the crowd was so enraged that Edwards' life was endangered by angry spectators and trainer Tom Jennings had to be locked in a room below the stands for his own safety.

'It's like finding your best friend in bed with your wife.' **Hong Kong Jockey Club member** after 50 people were arrested over the 1997 betting scandal.

'I think racing would lose its appeal to the vast majority if they thought it was 110 per cent squeaky clean.' BHB Senior Handicapper **Nigel Gray** in a 1997 *Evening Standard* interview.

'If you get this horse beat today there will be six grand sat in a brown paper bag waiting for you at Leicester services.' Anonymous phone caller to **Mick Fitzgerald**. The mystery man never rang back for an answer (*Between Ourselves*, Radio 4, August 2004).

Name the only flat jockey to finish runner-up to three different champions in the title race.

'I was rung up late at night. An Irish voice said, 'If you win on that horse you'll be shot.' I just went to bed and laughed because Jimmy Duggan was riding the horse – and he deserved to be shot.' **Peter Scudamore** (*Between Ourselves*, Radio 4, August 2004).

'We have before had occasion to compliment the sagacity and intelligence displayed by Mr Cartwright's horses. They never win when they are favourites, but always when long odds are to be obtained about them. The public ought to be grateful to him.' The most subtle of put-downs by the *Sporting Life* in 1865.

'A large foreign substance was sneezed out by my horse. It was like a fibresand plastic-type substance.' **Paul Dixon**, owner of Milk It Mick, who ran poorly after drifting from 11/8 to 2/1 at Chester in August 2004, is suspicious after the horse expelled a 'golf-ball' sized mystery substance from his nose.

'Listen, you had better go and back this horse, because it is going to win.' **Fred Winter's** comment to an owner who told him not to win on a horse. Reported by trainer Ryan Price.

'Of course an element of chicanery clings to the Turf. That's one of its main selling points.' Racing writer **Jamie Reid**.

'I was attacked by all the ignoramuses of Seestu, and upbraided for being bribed and behaving like a thief. How they came to say this I know not, but this I can say, that I did all in my power to win the different races, and took the turns of the course like a compass. In doing so I tore my breeches and cut my leg severely. I was also struck to the effusion of my blood by a cowardly person, in consequence of his having been told by the owner of the mare that I rode that I had been bribed. All I can say to the said owner is that he knows as much about horse racing as a cow.' Jockey

Richard Quinn – Eddery 1996; Fallon 1999; Darley 2000.

Robert Brown indignantly defends himself in the local *Advertiser* against accusations of 'taking a pull' at Paisley races in 1830.

'He was crossed at a bank by Delme Davies-Evans and vowed he would get his revenge. This he most certainly did by jumping off his horse on to the back of Davies-Evans and, dragging him out of the saddle, proceeded to give him a real going over.' **Brian Lee**, author of *The Races Came Off*, recalls racecourse justice, early 20th-century style, at Pembroke, by club-footed jockey Gwynne Anthony.

'I think for rowdyism, welchers and general uncontrolled villainy, the old Scarborough racecourse was the worst I was ever on. I remember on one occasion a whole trainload of some two or three hundred known crooks, boys, welchers and violent black-mailers being collected before racing commenced, marched to the station and sent off by train.' Owner cum bookmaker **Tom Devereux** reminiscing in 1927.

'People will be asking: was that race crooked and was that horse trying? That has been the cry down the centuries about horserac-ing, but now it has been brought into these lurid headlines once again.' **John McCririck** on *Sky News* after the arrests of 16 people, including 3 jockeys and a trainer, in September 2004.

'Anyone who thinks skulduggery didn't exist before Betfair et al is living in cloud-cuckoo land.' **Nicholas Godfrey** (*Racing Post*, 5 September 2004).

'Corruption in racing is like a snake that will always slither in if it gets the chance. It is much easier to scotch it than to kill it.' **Brough Scott**, September 2004.

What was the highest position Greville Starkey – and he did it six times – managed to finish in the jockey championship during his career?

'If you are a pin-sticker, whether or not a race is fixed does not affect your chances of picking a winner. It is yet another unpredictable factor in an alphabet soup of unpredictable factors.' **Will Buckley** (*Observer*, 5 September 2004). He added, 'That one out of ten races might be bent is no more surprising than the news that one out of 10 trains might be late.'

'I repeatedly came across the idea that the leading bookmakers employ a "ray gun" that they use on the favourite over the last fence in order to prevent a big pay out.' **Rebecca Cassidy** on researching for her book, *The Sport of Kings*. I wonder whether she spoke to Paul Haigh?

'One poor fellow, who was the possessor of a fine pair of whiskers, had them completely torn off.' Don't feel too sorry for the chap, who was a bookmaker, referred to in **J Snowy's** 1896 work, *The Stanley of the Turf*. He refused to pay out after a winner was disqualified at Pakenham, near Melbourne, Australia.

'There are plenty of people in racing whom I would trust with my building-society account, rather fewer whom I would trust with my daughter, and I am comforted to find some with a lifetime's experience in the sport like former trainer Ian Balding, who insist they have never encountered skulduggery.' **Robin Oakley** (*Spectator*, 11 September 2004).

'Horseracing has always been vulnerable to corruption. Whatever the form of betting, whether it be with traditional bookmakers, totalisators, exchanges or spread-betting firms, there are those who will seek to gain an unfair advantage over other punters. This is the experience worldwide.' **Christopher Foster** of the Jockey Club, September 2004.

Fourth.

'It's time for racing to come to terms with the fact it is now associated in the public mind with wrongdoing.' **Jim Cremin** of the *Racing Post*, 15 September 2004.

'I am a bit thick and I didn't recognise the implications of it all.' Trainer **Alan Berry** after being cleared of a charge of conspiracy to defraud in September 2004, over the running of his horse, Hillside Girl.

'This has major implications for competitive equine sports, including racing, where large numbers of drugs and chemicals are banned. More work still needs to be done, but the studies give a strong indication that retrospective hair analysis could prove invaluable in the battle to ensure the highest standards in racing.' A **spokesman for the Royal Veterinary College** indicating that hairs of a horse's tail could soon provide crucial evidence in the battle against skulduggery (*Observer*, 19 September 2004).

'I was involved in the mid fifties scandal of Peaceful William, a three year old that ran as a two year old. The horse had a star on its forehead that was covered up – otherwise it was identical to another juvenile in the stable. It won at Ayr, Yarmouth and Nottingham and I was the person who put the money on, not knowing it was a ringer. The only bet I had for myself was £30 to £9. An 86-year-old tic tac man, **Mickey 'Hokey' Stuart** (*Guardian*, 5 December 1998).

'Probably the worst level of integrity management of any racing administration anywhere in the world.' **Robert Nason**, chief executive of Australia's Racing Victoria, which hosts the Melbourne Cup, is critical of British standards, 20 October 2004.

'It is tiresome to hear people who blindly defend racing's integrity. Yes, the sport is probably far less corrupt than the man

Which is the only jumps track in Great Britain on which Richard Dunwoody failed to ride a winner?

on the street might suspect, but those who make their livelihood in the racing industry should stop and ask themselves whether something untoward has actually taken place before automatically jumping to its defence every time a whiff of skulduggery wafts across the sport.' **Bruce Millington** in his 2004 book, *Betting On Sport.*

'I stopped gambling on horseracing when the number of bent races topped 98 per cent, in my estimation. There are too many people in racing who can make too much money from horses running too badly to be true.' Cynical 'Betting Guru', **Derek McGovern** (*Daily Mirror*, 23 October 2004).

'I was introduced to a boy in a wheelchair. He was a former jockey. I asked if he'd had a fall and it all went quiet. Later, someone told me that he'd won on a horse he wasn't meant to win on. They snipped the back of his tendons. He never rode again.' **Walter Swinburn** on his time in Hong Kong in 1986 (*Guardian*, 1 November 2004).

'If a horse wins, then pulls up, it is highly unlikely that I'll drop that horse. If I did that on a regular basis it would be an incentive to trainers to run their horses dishonestly.' BHB Senior Jumps Handicapper, **Phil Smith** (*Racing Post*, 17 November 2004).

'The life is halfway between appalling and so enviable, you wonder why everybody doesn't do it.' **Simon Barnes** on stable lads.

'Here is a multi-million pound industry that has developed from a gentleman's sport and still treats staff as if it was a hobby.' **Baroness Mallalieu**, BHB director and chairman of the Stable and Stud Steering Group, who also warned in August 2004: 'The workforce is largely female and discrimination and harassment are common in racing yards. I am not against banter and joking, but times have

Catterick.

moved on and, unless there is a major change, it is only a matter of time before there will be some extremely embarrassing litigation.'

'Racing today is not a married man's job. During the summer it is a full commitment, seven days a week. My daughter is 15. I missed a lot of her growing up and won't make the same mistake again with my five year old son.' Stable lad for 26 years to Paul Cole, **Chris Sharp** explains why he now drives tankers for a living (*Observer*, 26 September 2004).

'An old-fashioned industry with low rewards and high job satisfaction but where staff are sometimes not treated with the respect they deserve and need.' **Lord Donoghue**, who chaired a commission looking into the lot of stable staff (*Observer*, 26 September 2004).

'She has a shocker of a job. In short, she has to use her hands to make sure the right things go in the right places, ensure that the right result occurs and give the relevant parts a wash afterwards – and all of it darting beneath a ton of precarious, living horseflesh.' **Robert Hardman** admires the professionalism of Shade Oak Stud stable girl Sue Titley, who oversees top National Hunt stallion Alflora's activities (*Daily Mail*, 3 July 2004).

'Horse biographies have two obvious but screamingly crucial problems. Their subjects are only half of a child's age and do not even have a toddler's vocabulary.' **Brough Scott**.

'I've forgotten my false teeth so don't ask me many questions.' Trainer **John Manners** following a 1996 winner at Taunton.

'Do you know, I'm 73 and I've no teeth. It's why I like soup so much.' **Mick Easterby** imparts dental details to Alan Lee in *The Times* in July 2004.

Richard Dunwoody won most races on which horse? And how many did they win?

'A set of false teeth has been found in the paddock; will anyone who has lost a top-set please see the clerk of the course.' Chepstow PA announcer **Charlie Parkin** had an unusual message at the 5 August 2004 meeting.

'I started from scratch and built up the business through word of mouth.' Well, how else would an equine dentist like **Dean Crossman** expect to make an impression?

'He popped in the teeth, not realising that the man's pocket was full of horse hair, cigarette ash and God knows what else. When he met the Queen Mother again he almost puked on her.' Irish racing legend **Ted Walsh** recalls the time, 'an Irish jockey friend of mine, who shall remain nameless', had given his false teeth to someone for safe keeping before a race that he duly won for the Queen Mum. He then had to grab them quickly and put them back in as she came to speak to him.

'I was testing cattle and one of them charged through the crush and hit a gate. The gate came off on top of me and caught my face, and my teeth have gone right through my lips. I'm in a hell of a state.' Trainer **Howard Johnson**, who doubles as a farmer, explains why he is not feeling photogenic in August 2004.

'There were two things he hated – physic or any form of medicine, and having his teeth attended to.' His **lad** on 1933 Derby winner, Hyperion.

'Tim (Brookshaw) and I had been having a few words and I went past him at the second last absolutely cantering. As I did so I over-did my laugh, and my dentures fell back down my throat. I was choking. It was a frightening experience and as a result Tim got up to win. I always rode without my teeth after that.' **Josh Gifford** remembers riding over jumps at Birmingham.

Waterloo Boy, fifteen races.

'I was drawn right on the inside. I only weighed 5st 7lb then and knew I wouldn't be able to hold him. He rushed forward and grabbed the tapes just as the starter had let the gate go and it pulled two of The Shah's teeth out. He lost a good six lengths but he came down the inside rail and won comfortably.' Jockey **Herbert Jones** on a late 1940's winner at Stockton.

'You are snatching a hard guy when you snatch Bookie Bob. A very hard guy, indeed. "In fact" I say, "I hear the softest thing about him is his front teeth."' **Damon Runyan** in his story *The Snatching of Bookie Bob.*

Name the first woman to train the winner of the Arc.

Triumph, Tragedy, Temptation and Taboo

Tragedy in sport could be a striker missing an open goal, a slip fielder dropping a catch, a rugby kicker slicing his effort wide. In racing, tragedy is often just that – a fatal happening. I was at Ascot when the marvellous, hugely popular Persian Punch collapsed towards the end of his race and, within seconds, was dead. The whole atmosphere of the racecourse changed instantly, from celebratory to sombre. The eerie silence that descended was most affecting, and lingered for the remainder of the afternoon.

Tragedy is part of racing because it is a dangerous sport – for the jockeys, who by and large choose to face up to that reality, and for the horses, who have no choice about being there, but who for the most part enjoy a life far more fulfilling and cosseted than they otherwise would. In fact, but for racing and its inherent dangers, the thoroughbred racehorse would very soon become an endangered species.

The triumphant element of racing is far more frequently visible – at the climax of every single race for starters. This takes place in the winners' enclosure when back-slapping connections are celebrating with the jockey and trainer, champagne often erupting into the air. It is this kind of ecstatic reaction that underpins the appeal of the entire turf experience. Who could ever forget Frankie Dettori's triumphant celebrations after winning all seven races at Ascot in September 1996?

A couple of the racing calendar's great races revel in triumph – the Cheltenham Festival's Triumph Hurdle, one of the most open and spectacular races of the entire meeting; and, of course, the Prix de l'Arc de Triomphe, France's fantastic feature race, which attracts thousands of English racegoers to Paris each autumn.

Criquette Head – she trained Three Troikas in 1979.

In racing, winners celebrate all the more wildly when triumph pays a rare visit, in the certain knowledge that, ultimately, tragedy will regain the upper hand.

'Rooboy!' Greeting to Aussie race starter Paul Didham on arrival at a 2004 meeting in Geelong – on his way home on 5 June from carrying out starting duties at Bendigo he had hit a kangaroo with his car. 'His car still bears the battle wounds,' commented writer **Bradley Thomas** – who made no mention of the fate of the Roo.

'On pulling up, Jack Anthony, who'd ridden Old Tay Bridge, asked me where I'd finished. "I've won" I replied. "Don't talk rubbish, I won," said Jack. He hadn't seen me, probably because he'd drunk a ginger beer bottle full of port before he went out to ride.' **Keith Piggott** after winning the 1925 Welsh Grand National on Vaulx.

'There was a match between Mr T Walker's hackney gelding and Capt A Hay's road mare, to ride from London to York. Mr Walker rode his own horse and Capt Mulcaster Capt Hay's. Mulcaster arrived with the winning mare at Ouse Bridge, York in 40 hours and 35 minutes. Mr Walker's horse tired and died. The mare drank 12 bottles of wine during her journey and was so well on the following Thursday as to take her exercise on Knavesmire.' *Sporting Magazine* **account** of a 1773 match race that failed to record how much Mulcaster himself quaffed *en route*.

'German Derby winner Alchimist became an unusual casualty of World War II. The grooms at Gradiz, where the highly valued stallion was at stud, fled the advancing Russian troops who relieved their starvation by tucking into what must be one of the most expensive meals ever consumed!' **Graham Sharpe** – oh, that's me, then – in his *Turf Accounts*.

Which is the latest date on which the Derby has ever been run – 30 June, 17 July or 31 July?

'My favourite big name horse was Never Say Die. It was a great Derby when we first saw the genius of Lester Piggott and I'll never forget that race or horse.' Rolling Stone, **Ronnie Wood**, in 1997.

'Dad, can you speak? Neither can I.' Not a dry eye in the house as **Clare Balding** attempts to interview her emotional Dad, Ian, after brother Andrew's 2003 Oaks victory with Casual Look.

'His admirers are convinced that had he been on the rails at Balaclava he would have kept pace with the Charge of the Light Brigade, listing the fallers in precise order and describing the riders' injuries before they hit the ground.' **Hugh McIlvanney** on Peter O'Sullevan (*Observer*, December 1973).

'The Game Spirit Chase, named after Game Spirit, a lovely horse, owned by the Queen Mother, who dropped dead here after a long and distinguished career.' Gaffe attributed to BBC commentator **Peter Bromley**.

'It was the lowest point in my life, barring family tragedies. I cried. I sat down and cried. I was probably close to a nervous breakdown.' Trainer **Graham Margarson** on the aftermath of the demotion of his Barathea Guest after winning Longchamp's Grand Criterium in 1999 (*Racing Post*, 8 November 2004).

'Orpen Wide won his third race on the trot since we had him gelded – making us wonder what to cut off next to keep him winning.' **Sir Clement Freud** celebrates his hat-trick achiever (*Racing Post*, 19 January 2005).

'Don't ride the brute, George, he'll kill you.' Jockey **Arthur Yates** to friend and fellow rider George Ede upon hearing that the latter was to ride Chippenham in the 1870 Sefton Chase at Aintree. Ede,

31 July, in 1917.

who rode as Mr Edwards, and who won the National on The Lamb two years earlier, fell heavily and was killed.

'I put "dead" by the wrong horse.' Trainer **Rodney Baker** explains how his Coochie, officially expired, managed to finish sixth in a 1994 Newton Abbot race.

'When I go to meet my maker at the Pearly gates, he'll ask what I did in life and when I answer "racehorse trainer, sir" he'll say, "a *what* for pete's sake? I've got the likes of Mother Teresa in here".' **Sir Mark Prescott** reckons he's odds-on to go downstairs.

'Colonel Bill (Whitbread) died in November 1994, and so he will not be at Sandown this year.' A 1996 **Whitbread Gold Cup press release**.

'I'm burying my husband this afternoon, but I just had to have a little bet before the funeral.' Response to London cabbie who asked **betting shop patron** why she was dressed all in black, as reported by the *Evening Standard* in February 1996.

'A lot of trainers – up to 20 – were phoning on the day he died trying to get the horses.' Henry's nephew **Ben Cecil**, reflecting in 1996 on the dog eat dog nature of US training after Rodney Rash, for whom he had been working in California, died.

'I don't want a 69-gun salute or a day of mourning when I go, just Booby (his wife) – very quietly – and ashes strewn at the furlong pole.' **John McCririck** on his own demise and the ceremony to be held at the former site of Alexandra Park racecourse.

Of Martin Pipe's seven starters in the 2004 Grand National, how many completed the course?

'We're dead, mate, this is it, we're gone.' **Frankie Dettori** to Ray Cochrane moments before their 2000 plane crash.

'I said that if he won a race I'd die happy. Now he has won three, I'll have to start looking over my shoulder.' Irish trainer **Gerry Stack** when his Bahao won at Tramore in January 1998.

'On a horse in a race.' **Frankie Dettori's** reply, when asked in 1996, 'How would you like to die?'

'It is sad, but there again, he is a horse, and there are worse things in life.' **Criquette Head-Mararek** after her colt Millemix shattered a leg and was put down (*Pacemaker*, July 2004).

'I've decided I don't want to be cremated. I'm going to be buried, there's a slight chance I might get out again.' **Mick Easterby** (*The Times*, 10 July 2004).

'It was that awful you could have heard a pin drop. Absolutely shocking. I've never experienced anything like it. So we said goodbye to him there and then, and left the track as soon as we possibly could.' Persian Punch's owner **Jeff Smith** evocatively recalling the day in spring 2004 when the great Punch dropped dead at the end of a race at Ascot. I was there and shared one of the eeriest sensations I have ever encountered on a racecourse, which was struck dumb for several minutes.

'My father, James died yesterday. He would have been 97 today and he would have approved of me being at the races rather than moping around at home.' **Ken Wilson**, part owner of 25/1 Haydock winner Smokin Beau on 7 August 2004.

One.

'The first thing that came to mind as I was pulling up was that I had lost my brother… The next morning I caught a flight to Perth for his funeral.' Top Aussie jockey, **Damien Oliver**, recalls winning the 2002 Melbourne Cup just days after the death of his elder brother, Jason, also a rider.

'We'll refund all stakes.' **Graham Sharpe**. Well, what else could I say when it was pointed out to me that the horse Mounamara, quoted in William Hill's ante post list for the 1992 Champion Hurdle at a generous 33/1, was actually dead.

'On the flight from Dubai he committed suicide.' Bloodstock agent **Luke Lillingston** on his 'worst deal', Raah Algharb.

'When the (stable) lads called him up on an Ouija board, Fred told them to back Unblest the following day – he won at 6/4 – where his grave was, and where he committed suicide.' **Marcus Armytage** reporting on a Newmarket séance that purported to raise the spirit of former champion jockey Fred Archer (*Daily Telegraph*, 27 July 1997).

'The public dismay that greeted his suicide by all accounts must have been similar to the reaction to the news of the sudden death of Princess Diana in 1997.' **Alex Tosetti** discussing in 2003 the news of the death of his great-grandfather – Fred Archer.

'Yes, racing's important, but I'm guilty of falling into the trap of thinking it's life and death.' Trainer **David Loder** (*Thoroughbred Owner & Breeder*, September 2004).

'When his time comes, I just hope someone stuffs him and sticks him in his conservatory with his bulls, because I think he would

Which trainer fractured his arms when falling off a supermarket trolley in Swindon in 2004?

like that very much.' **Charlie Brooks** on bullfight-loving trainer Sir Mark Prescott (*Daily Telegraph*, 29 September 2004).

'Almost 20 years ago I decided I wanted to find myself a nice plot with some agreeable people around. I had to contact the parks and recreation authority. And there was a very nice fellow, he showed me the graveyard and there was Fred Archer, Mr Dawson, Mr Waugh and lots of nice people. I found a nice corner and said "I want three plots down there" and he said, "Would that be for Sir, and Lady Prescott and your son and heir?" "Certainly not" I replied, "It's so I don't have to have any fucker next to me." **Sir Mark Prescott** in an interview by Will Buckley (*Observer*, 7 October 2001).

'"See you in 2006,"' said the man who guards the gate of the exemplary Royal Ascot Racing Club. I told him I would look forward to that, suggesting he keeps an eye on the obituary column.' **Sir Clement Freud**, a box holder, wonders whether he'll be around when Ascot reopens (*Racing Post*, 29 September 2004).

'I have to go.' Inscription on a brass plaque on the coffin of racecourse and racehorse owner **Sir Stanley Clarke**, who died in September 2004. Explained business partner Jim Leavesley, 'They were the words of a man who had so much to do, and so little time in which to do it.'

'I will carry on until I drop down dead in the yard – I don't want to die in my bed.' So said 79-year-old **Snowy Outen**, groom at Barry Hills' yard after hearing that 2004 2,000 Guineas and Champions Stakes winner Haafhd, the horse he looked after, was to be retired.

'I am afraid my luck is beginning to run out.' Owner of great filly Petite Etoile, **Aly Khan**, after his Sheshoon, hot favourite, lost the

Sylvester Kirk.

1960 Prix du Cadran in a photo finish after stumbling. Four days later Aly was killed in a motoring accident on the outskirts of Paris.

'Well beaten when falling fatally.' Connections of the alive and well Hawk's Landing were shocked to read this description of their jumping pride and joy in the new **Timeform Chasers and Hurdlers** in November 2004.

'He's been entered just in case everything else dies.' Trainer **Nigel Twiston-Davies** explained why his horse Fundamentalist was entered for Kempton's 2004 King George Chase, a race in which there was no chance of the beast running.

'All the people who gave me hope when there was precious little else to cling to.' **Bob Champion's** dedication in *Champion's Story*.

'I threw a kiss to the heavens because I knew Vinny would be looking down on us.' Cheltenham Gold winning jockey **Adrian Maguire** dedicated his 1992 victory in the race on Cool Ground to his brother, who was killed in a hit-and-run accident.

'It was a feeling like no other...it was caps in the air time. We were all screaming and hugging each other. I started running and nobody could keep up with me.' England football skipper **David Platt** on his Handsome Ridge's win in France.

'I am blowing as hard as the horse. While I used to get excited scoring a few goals for Arsenal and Ireland, this was as good as any day I've had in sport.' **Niall Quinn** celebrates the September 2004 historic third consecutive win in Doncaster's Portland Handicap by his Halmahera, of whom trainer Kevin Ryan enthused, 'I'll kick the Mrs out and put him in the bedroom' – presumably referring to horse rather than footballer!

Which footballer part-owned Champion Hurdle runner Intersky Falcon?

'We were all screaming and hugging each other. My dad who never goes like this, lost it totally. If a goal goes in he applauds. But when our horse went in we were just on this incredible high. I ended up in the middle of the track. I started running and nobody could keep up with me. The next thing I know I'm chasing the bloody horse. I was hugging stable lads and anyone I knew.' Former England skipper **David Platt** recalls his horse Handsome Ridge winning for the first time, at Maisons-Lafitte.

'People who see me now will say I was very unlucky, but I was very, very lucky to win a race at Cheltenham. Nobody can ever take away that feeling or that memory from me.' **Shane Broderick**, whose career was terminated by a fall at Fairyhouse on Easter Monday, 1997. It had left him with a severe spinal cord injury.

'We are thrilled to win this race but we feel horrible.' Owner **Mary Lou Whitney** after her Birdstone won the 2004 Belmont Stakes to foil the Triple Crown bid of public hero, and 'new Seabiscuit', Smarty Jones.

'Racing in this country is becoming an outmoded and shrivelling industry. The people in it are getting older and older. It's too slow for young people.' **John Gosden**, 13 April 1997.

'When I see Velazquez ride, I feel like I died and was reincarnated in him. It's like my mind goes right into his.' **Angel Cordero**, who suffered tragedy in his life when his wife was killed in a 2001 hit-and-run incident, on his protégé, jockey John Velasquez, January 2005.

'To get him fit you have to half-kill him with work – and a lot of other horses as well.' Trainer **H G Bedwell** on his 1919 US Triple Crown winner, Sir Barton.

Alan Shearer.

'Why it's that handy Guy named Sande bootin' a winner in!' **Damon Runyan** was inspired to versify as Gallant Fox won the 1925 Kentucky Derby under jockey Earl Sande *en route* to the 1930 Triple Crown.

'There is no more demanding a series of events in any sport than the Triple Crown, as these young horses are asked to contest three races over a five week period.' **Dan Farley** on the US Triple Crown, (*International Turf,*1998).

'He is a bit of a playboy these days. It is only when someone puts a gun to his head that he remembers he is there to do a professional job.' Best Mate's owner **Jim Lewis**, apparently revealing some odd details about the triple Gold Cup winner (*Mail on Sunday*, 21 November 2004).

'He's a real tool,' said **Jamie Osborne**, after riding a winner at Newbury on 1 November 1989 – and he was being complimentary, using a term from the early 19th century, meaning a smooth, efficient ride.

'His nickname at home is Exocet; you know he's around but you never know when he'll strike.' Trainer **Philip Mitchell** on his January 2005 Lingfield winner, Burgundy.

'Himself'. AKA Legendary jumping great, **Arkle**.

'Cash'. His real name is **Brian Keith Asmussen**.

'Weary Willie'. AKA Jockey **Bill Williamson**.

Which Ryder Cup winning golfer owns Tequila Sheila?

'Avenger of Waterloo'. First French-bred winner of the Derby – in 1865 – **Gladiateur**.

'The Run for the Roses'. AKA the **Kentucky Derby**.

'Sacred Nuts'. The 2004 winner trainer **Michael Bell** had wanted to name Goldenballs in tribute to David Beckham, only for the Jockey Club to veto the idea.

'Swerve Dancer.' – AKA Arc winner **Suave Dancer**, who had a tendency to come off a straight line.

'Such was the (Vincent) O'Brien dominance of the Irish jumping scene that behind his back he was known by members of the Irish racing press as "The Fuehrer".' ***Ruffs Guide to the Turf,*** 1978.

'The Pocket Hercules.' The 1950s jockey known as **Willie Snaith**.

'The Assassin'. Kieren Fallon's weighing-room nickname revealed by **Frankie Dettori**.

'Posh bird'. Barry Dennis-bestowed nickname for Channel 4 racing's First Lady, **Lesley Graham**.

Lee Westwood.

Jockeying for Position

Jockey was originally a term indicating a horse dealer or owner, gradually acquiring its current meaning – although the verb, to jockey, seems to retain some of the less than positive content once implied by the word. When women became professional riders, the term jockette was rather coyly introduced, but soon dropped out of favour.

I don't know many jockeys – working for a bookmaker, contact between the two professions is discouraged by the powers that be – but from my limited knowledge of them I shouldn't imagine that the word 'jocular' was coined as a result of observation of fun-filled riders of horses.

Most jockeys seem to opt for a serious demeanour and downbeat outlook on life – probably due to the stresses and strains of keeping their weight down to the archaically low levels demanded by the sport. There are exceptions, of course – several of the current crop of Irish jump jockeys seem to enjoy a laugh or two. But as far as the world at large is concerned, Frankie Dettori is the only jockey with a sense of humour.

When it comes to jockeying for position, though, jockeys have few rivals – and they are not averse to 'jocking' each other off intended mounts (usually then blaming their agents when the news leaks out). This is an art at which Lester Piggott was a past master in his prime.

Another key ability in jockeys' armoury is coming up with a perfectly plausible explanation as to why they are always entirely responsible for a masterful piece of riding when their horse wins, yet never remotely culpable when they fail to do so.

'He told me Fred had no sons, only three daughters. Dad reasoned that I'd have no unfair competition from sons so all I had to do was

Which actress rode her own horse to win a 2004 Windsor charity race?

shag the prettiest daughter and I'd be well in.' **John Francome** on his father's advice to apply for a job with Fred Winter (*Racing Ahead*, October 2004).

'To be the little fat man that I'm meant to be.' Great Aussie jockey **Roy Higgins**, announced his future ambition when he gave up riding – and fasting – in 1984.

'As far as I'm concerned, Jackdaws Castle has to move up, and if it doesn't do that, then I don't want to be there. Simple as that.' **Tony McCoy**, only recently departed from Martin Pipe to Jonjo O'Neill's stable, sets out his terms in an interview with Andrew Longmore (*Sunday Times*, 28 November 2004).

'The son of three time champion jockey Terry Biddlecombe relinquished his licence and plans to earn a living as an artist.' **Robert Biddlecombe** announced his retirement from the saddle in January 2005, aged just 22.

'The slight jockey is hunched on top, one hand on loose reins, the other unbuckling his chin strap. Not that the reins or helmet are drawn, the jockey is barely there, everything is just a suggestion, a sense. But we know all these things at a glance.' **Jane Wheatley** on Jo Taylor's racing painting of *The French Horse* (*The Times Weekend Review*, 30 October 2004).

'Was, is and always will be about boogieing, booze and black eyes.' An apt *Racing Post* description of the annual jockeys' awards bash, the 2005 Lesters.

'You don't see hip-flasks in the changing rooms like in the days of the old amateurs we keep hearing about.' Racing's top doc, **Dr Michael Turner**, dismissing fears of a booze culture among jockeys.

Claire King.

'I'm shocked and deeply disappointed. I presume we will talk, although I wish we didn't have to.' **Mark Johnston** after his jockey Joe Fanning failed a breath test for alcohol at Redcar in 2003.

'If I had a bad day I would go down to the pub. A good day, the same.' Jockey **Timmy Murphy** looks back to his bad old days. (*Daily Mail*, 9 November 2004).

'Maybe a different author will tell the tale of Jem Snowden, a famously drunken jockey who arrived at Chester to ride for the Duke of Westminster only to discover that his latest bender had caused him to miss the race meeting by a week.' **Matthew Sweet**, reviewing Mike Huggins' book, *The Victorians And Sport* (Hambledon) in *Culture* magazine, November 2004.

'My dad's older friends get a great kick out of Ruby's successes now because it keeps his name alive.' **Ted Walsh** on his jockey son Ruby, named after Ted's dad even though, 'it's an unusual name for a fella'.

'In a recent opinion poll, Lester Piggott came top as the person most people would like to see at Number 10. It's what is known as a "gallop" poll'! Comic, and, to his enormous credit, Luton Town supporter, the late **Eric Morecambe**.

'Daddy was just the same. It must be something to do with the food.' **Tracy Piggott's** comment about jockey Timmy Murphy's excellent form since being released from prison during 2003.

'For all jump jockeys, past, present and those who are no longer with us.' **Richard Dunwoody** in his *Obsessed*.

Which football team does Best Mate owner Jim Lewis support?

'To Glossary, the gamest of horses, without whose will to win my career as a jockey might have ended almost before it had begun.' **Bill Rickaby** in *First To Finish*.

'I don't particularly like riding on the dirt, but then I don't think any jockey much does. The kickback cuts your head off, you come back in and you've got barks and bumps on you.' **Kieren Fallon**, January 2005.

'Piggott may be the greatest jockey of his generation, but he is also the greatest bore…a work of monumental tedium…but then what can you expect of a man who calls his cat Tiddles.' ***Daily Telegraph* review** of Lester's 1996 autobiography.

'I thought I was as fit as anyone in the weighing room. But when they did the first tests it was embarrassing. The run on the treadmill nearly killed me, my upper-body strength was a joke and my core strength, the stomach muscles and pelvic drive which should hold everything together, was practically nil.' Jump jockey **Graham Lee** on the shock to the system when he began training with Middlesbrough FC's fitness team to boost his performance (*Sunday Telegraph*, 17 October 2004).

'You and I are aware that there is Flat racing from Wolverhampton later that day, that the season continues for 39 more days, and that the record books will award the championship to the guy who has ridden most winners between January 1 and December 31.' **Tony Morris** of the *Racing Post* jumped on his hobby horse – with some justification – to point out that although Frankie Dettori was crowned champion flat jockey 2004 on 6 November 2004, it was somewhat premature – as it is most years!

'If you deny yourself something you can end up with a craving.' **Richard Quinn** on a jockey's diet, 1996.

Aston Villa.

'I used to crave, really crave, a tomato or a grape. It became too much in the end.' Jockey turned trainer **Gay Kelleway**.

'The thing I dream about is waking up lighter than I was.' **Tony McCoy**.

'My festivities consisted of one slice of turkey and a glass of wine for lunch. Then a hot bath to lose a few pounds before rounding off the day with a light laxative for a night cap.' Jockey **Guy Lewis'** 1996 Christmas celebrations. The Boxing Day racing was cancelled.

'There's one jockey who has to go to Harley Street once or twice a year to have his stomach re-lined.' **Richard Perham** on the tribulations of wasting.

'I have seen whey-faced young men in the weighing room swill out their dry mouths with mineral water and then spit it out in desperation that they will not make their riding weight if they take a single swallow.' **Robin Oakley** in the *Spectator*.

'You take one of those pills and pee for three minutes. You can lose 5lb like that, but you daren't have anything to drink because it goes straight back on – so then you have to have another pill and you're up to two or three and before you know it its four. It's then you've got to quit, because it's either that or kill yourself.' **Frankie Dettori**, 1999.

'I can live with the fact that for the rest of my days riding, I'm never going to wake up and have a fried breakfast.' **Tony McCoy**, December 1997.

Azertyuiop's name comes from where – (a) Lord of the Rings, (b) a typewriter, (c) random use of Scrabble tiles?

'If you've had breakfast you wish you hadn't. If you haven't, you wish you had.' **Jimmy Lindley**.

'If a top jockey is riding at his absolute minimum weight, back his horse. He wouldn't have given up even his meagre breakfast if the creature had no chance.' Tip from **John McCririck** for anyone hungry for winners.

'I'd have a drink to not think about going all night without eating. Eventually I got tired and depressed.' Triple Crown-winning and champion jockey **Steve Cauthen** confessing to undergoing a 1985 alcohol dependency programme, reported in *Sports Illustrated*, July 2004.

'The food I loved – chips and anything out of the frying pan. To me it was the food of the gods but, on reflection, not of the aspiring champion jockey.' **Tony McCoy** on his pre-dedication diet.

'In later life it has been one of my favourite foods.' **Lester Piggott** on ice cream.

'Most mornings I have to lose around 3lbs by walking the dogs, running on my exercise machine in my gym and sitting in the sauna. That way I can eat a half decent meal at night, although I can't eat as much as I'd like.' **Frankie Dettori**, 2004.

'My solution was to wear a plastic running suit, which covered me from foot to neck, and turn the heater in the car on full blast. I got my weight down but my passengers didn't always enjoy their lifts.' **Lester Piggott's** secret to keeping his weight down.

(b) a typewriter – these are the top row of letters on a French typewriter.

'When he came to weigh out he was met by not only the clerk of the scales, but a traffic policeman.' **Marcus Armytage** on jockey George Moore, who had 'taken a few liberties' while driving to Fontwell once.

'I knew that the flat dream was over: the needle on the bathroom scales was stuck at eight stone ten.' The moment in 1994 when **Tony McCoy** realised his future lay over the sticks.

'Psychologically, wasting makes jockeys very angry, very tense and quite depressed. Physically it can result in exhaustion and stomach cramps because you are putting the minimum of petrol in the car.' **Michael Caulfield**, former Jockeys Association chief executive, now a sports psychologist (*Evening Standard*, 11 October 2004).

'The first thing you do every day is weigh yourself and the last thing you do is weigh yourself.' Apprentice **Jean-Pierre Guillambert** (*Evening Standard*, 11 October 2004).

'In my mind, 7st 12lb is no longer a realistic bottom weight...my feeling is that it would be better to raise the minimum weight by 4lb.' Jockey Club chief medical adviser, **Dr Michael Turner** in October 2004, adding, 'Jockeys argue that when bottom weights rise, top weights should rise too, and that makes good sense to me.'

'You could remove the brains from 90 per cent of jockeys and they would weigh the same.' Former champion jockey **John Francome** (*Sun*, 13 November 2004).

'One day I rode at 8st 6lb on the Flat and then at 11st 12lb in a chase at Warwick. I could hardly carry the saddle.' Dual code

'I'm just a broken-down old taxi driver who got lucky again.' This was a quote from whom in 2004?

jockey **Vince Slattery**, who has ridden at all 59 British race-courses (*News of the World*, 21 November 2004).

'At the end of the day, it is all I know – to ride a horse.' Former flat jockey **Keith Dalgleish**, explaining why, having lost his battle with the weight and quit riding the previous summer, he returned on 24 November 2004 as a jump jockey at 10st.

'The sandwiches were definitely on the firm side of good.' Jockey **Ian Watkinson** on the racecourse catering at defunct Teesside Park.

'The trick with pizza, as with pasta, is little but intense. Like Frankie.' Top restaurant reviewer, **A A Gill** gives 'Frankie's Italian Bar And Grill' a three-star review in the *Sunday Times* Style magazine of 26 September 2004.

I rode quarter horses until I ate myself out of a job and then I thought it would be better to train them.' **Charles William 'Bubba' Cascio**, 70-year-old Texas trainer, in October 2004.

'Eating, for me, was not very pretty. I had it down to a fine art. The whole idea is that you drank fizzy drinks when you bolted and I knew how to get it back up within minutes. The more dehydrated you were the easier it was to get it up.' **Walter Swinburn** explaining his 'bolting and wasting', which he began in 1986 (*Guardian*, 1 November 2004).

'In racing there is no point to part-time. If you ride only four days a week you still have to diet the other three.' **Marcus Armytage**, 8 November 2004.

'Ever since I was a little kid I always wanted to have my own restaurant. Now, every time I drive down this little street, I get

Ginger McCain.

goosebumps.' **Frankie Dettori**, whose 'Frankie's Italian Bar & Grill' in Yeoman's Row, London SW3 opened in autumn 2004 with Marco Pierre White as presiding chef.

'My major interest is football, I prefer it to racing.' **John Francome** (*Sunday Telegraph*, February 1998).

'I was there 10 months and I learned a little French. It's good being there for one year, but not two or three.' Panama-born, US-based jockey **Jorge Luis Velasquez** speaking in 1996 about his 1987 sojourn in France.

'Framed betting slip featuring Swain.' Restaurant critic **Matthew Norman** – 'I have harboured a grudge against Frankie ever since having the second biggest bet of my life on Swain in the 1999 Breeders Cup' – offers advice on what *not* to take with you when visiting his Italian Bar & Grill restaurant (*Sunday Telegraph*, 9 January 2005).

'Trinket Ride Oaf.' Anagram of racing personality offered to **Frankie Dettori** on *A Question of Sport* – he couldn't get it.

'Frankie rode him today.' Accepted explanation by **Reg Hollinshead** to convince stewards about the improved form of 10/1 Pontefract winner.

'The difference between having a horse relaxed and having him run away is the edge of a razorblade.' **Frankie Dettori**.

'I work hard for my money. I wouldn't put it on a racehorse.' **Frankie** in 1995.

The last ever race meeting at Manchester was when – (a) 1960, (b) 1963 or (c) 1966?

'Revenge is best served on a cold plate and mine is freezing right now.' **Frankie** after winning the Breeders Cup Turf on Daylami in 1999, having been savaged by the US media for his 1998 defeat on Swain.

'Not often enough,' **Frankie's** answer when he was asked in 1996, 'How often do you have sex?'

'Hey, the place is being pulled down. I want it for my garden.' **Frankie** kisses the wooden post marked 'First' in the winners' enclosure after riding his fourth winner of the afternoon at Ascot on 10 July 2004. Earlier he performed a flying dismount from one of his winners – and ended up on his backside, earning this reproval from Paul Haigh in the *Racing Post*: 'He ought to give this practice up now…because, well, Frankie, mate, it's just not very grown up.'

'I felt this hand reach over, and he squeezed me by the balls. He just said "That will teach you to be so cheeky" **Frankie** on Lester Piggott's mid-race revenge after Frankie had told him he was so old 'they were going to stuff him and put him in a museum' (*Frankie Dettori – The Real Story* DVD, 2004).

'He may not be everybody's glass of frascati, but like it or not, to the man on the Clapham omnibus he *is* racing.' **Peter Thomas** on Frankie, adding, 'If Frankie didn't exist, it would be necessary for the BHB to invent him.'

'Dettori is fed up with people thinking him more as a personality than a jockey.' **Brough Scott** on the driving factor behind Frankie's successful 2004 title bid.

'They're calling it good to firm. The bit I landed on was definitely firm.' **Frankie** after being unshipped from Nightfall at Royal Ascot 2004.

(b) 1963.

'Having Frankie here on a Bank Holiday puts at least 1,000 people on the gate.' Epsom Managing Director, **Stephen Wallis**, on August Bank Holiday Monday, 2004.

'The first rock 'n' roll jockey.' *Total Sport* **magazine** on Frankie.

'He's packed with vitality, skill and sex appeal.' **Esther Rantzen** on Dettori at the Variety Club Day at Sandown in August 2004.

'If Frankie is the happy, smiley, wholesome image of a jockey, Fallon is the flipside of the coin. Take him off a horse and he is a walking liability.' **Clare Balding** (*Observer*, 5 September 2004).

'Frankie has been officially declared Good For Racing, and has accordingly been granted a sort of diplomatic immunity from traditionalist censure. In the superstitious minds of the Racing Tribe, he is more than just an effective ambassador: he represents racing not just as a spokesman, but as a tribal icon. To express disapproval of racing's lucky charm would be to invite divine retribution.' Anthropologist **Kate Fox** on Frankie in her book *The Racing Tribe*.

'Seven. And I'm gonna call the last one Ascot.' **Frankie Dettori**, when asked by colleague Martin Dwyer how many children he intends to have as news of his impending fifth was revealed in August 2004.

'Ten minutes in, and our man's down to his underpants; now we're watching him urinate.' **Alex Hankin's** review of Frankie's 2004 video *Frankie Dettori – The Real Story*.

'I always wanted a beard – I've got one now.' Mud spattered on his face, **Frankie** comes in after winning at Newbury on 17 September 2004 on Sights On Gold.

The first £10,000 race run in England was (a) Eclipse Stakes, (b) Derby or (c) Ebor?

'They talk about life in the fast lane, but I'm so in the fast lane, I'm almost on the crash barrier.' **Frankie**, September 2004.

'I met him in Cuthie Suttle's betting shop in Newmarket before he had his first ride. He was chalking up the prices on the board because he had to work to pay off his gambling debts.' **Pete Burrell**, Frankie's business manager (*Daily Telegraph*, 25 September 2004).

'We know Frankie wants it and, in view of everything he has achieved and done for Ascot, we couldn't really sell it to anyone else. Frankie owns it, in effect.' **Nick Smith** of Ascot announcing in September 2004, as the course prepared to close down for rebuilding, that the first-place post from the course's winners' enclosure was to be presented to Dettori.

'I was just lucky that Ray reached me first – otherwise I would not be here.' **Frankie** in serious mood for once recalling in an interview with Donald McRae how fellow jockey Ray Cochrane saved him after their plane crash (*Guardian*, 27 September 2004).

'I decided to start riding in small meetings again, those ones on cold and horrible Monday afternoons that I'd given up years ago. And you know what? It's really hard work but I love it...I've got back everything that had gone missing from my life.' **Frankie** on his decision to chase the championship in 2004 after his wife, Catherine had told him: 'Listen, get your a**** into gear, go out there and start being a f**** jockey again.'

'Frankie Dettori is the Sergio Garcia of the weighing room.' **Charlie Brooks** (*Daily Telegraph*, 27 September 2004).

(a) Eclipse Stakes.

'God forbid he ever wins the Derby. We will never hear an end to it and his ego will be bigger than ever.' **C Miller** of Plymouth, writing to the *Racing Post* in July 2004, is clearly not a Frankie fan.

'He has also managed to fit in such extracurricular activities as modelling for Yves St Laurent, and addressing the Oxford Union, not to mention mooning out of the rear window of a coach to astonished onlookers in Japan.' **Sophie Topley** on Frankie (*Sunday Telegraph*, 24 October 2004).

'Frankie Dettori doesn't do nappies – I went right off him.' Comedian **Peter Kay**, a recent father himself, revealed his dismay to discover that while he was frequently up to his arms in bodily excretions courtesy of his newborn, Frankie had said that he declines nappy duties (*Jonathan Ross Show*, BBC TV, 4 November 2004).

'The only man in racing capable of rejecting the Michael Parkinson show in favour of Jonathan Ross.' **Colin Mackenzie** on Frankie (*Daily Mail*, 4 November 2004).

'Think of the Irishman (Kieren Fallon) as Don Revie's Leeds, perhaps, with Dettori cast as Forest under Clough.' Greg Wood, (*Guardian*, 8 November 2004).

'So addicted to the sport that he even reads John Francome's racing thrillers.' The *Observer's* **Will Buckley** marvels at jockey Carl Llewellyn.

'I hope to take part in and win the Championship at Toulouse. That's my great ambition.' Jockey **Olivier Peslier** on the other love of his life – paintballing – which in the twelve years since he took it up in 1992, 'has become a real passion'.

Which of these innovations was introduced to Britain on 8 July 1967
(a) photo-finish camera, (b) patrol camera, (c) starting stalls?

'To some people, I am over-priced and they use other people. But I ride quality horses for quality people.' **Cash Asmussen**.

'They thought I was a suicide bomber. I must admit I do look a bit like one – my nickname in the weighing room is Bin Laden.' Jockey **Shashi Righton**, who was detained by anti-terrorist officers in August 2004 while at Heathrow Airport waiting to collect his wife.

'A National Hunt Jockey can expect to fall once in every ten races, and sustain a serious injury once in every 250.' Cautionary statement by the **Injured Jockeys Fund** in January 2005.

'Whatever you do, don't start doing anything different just for the sake of it.' **Nicky Henderson** recalling words of wisdom passed on by the late Fred Winter.

'Stop where you are. Get a job outside.' Advice regularly dispensed to wannabe jump jockeys by Aussie riding legend **Les Boots**. He died in 1987 and had claimed to be the world's worst rider over obstacles. In Adelaide he boasted 41 falls in 39 starts – once falling, remounting and falling again in one race before riding in the next, falling again and being carried off the course on a stretcher – from which he fell off.

'We got as far as the third, and I broke my arm off him. We turned over the ditch and I got a kick from the following horse. It was a heck of a buzz. I was sitting there thinking, "I wouldn't have missed this for the world."' **Brendan Powell** proving you don't have to be certified to be a jump jockey, but…

'It's the left collar bone – I couldn't have broken the other one as I've already had it removed.' Jump jock **Mick Fitzgerald** after a May 1996 fall.

(a) The photo-finish camera.

'I'm brave, I'm a jump jockey. Jump jockeys don't cry.' **Sharon Murgatroyd's** reaction when a doctor told her she'd never walk again after a fall. *Jump Jockeys Don't Cry* became the title of her 1996 autobiography.

'While you have to have a certain amount of sympathy for Richard Johnson with his pelvic injury, it is just part and parcel of being a jockey.' **Willie Humphreys** should know, because he was one (*Gloucestershire Echo*, 13 November 2004).

'You can see why he will be champion jockey one day.' Trainer **Hughie Morrison** bigs up Ryan Moore after he rode his Solo Effort to victory at Newbury on 17 September 2004.

'There are fools, damn fools and those who remount in steeple-chases.' **Common horse-racing saying**.

'If saunas aren't removed, the time jockeys spend in them, and heat levels, must be very closely monitored at the least.' Turf Club senior medical officer **Walter Halley**, in October 2004, concerned at the overuse of saunas by jockeys, calling for them to be banned for use at racecourses.

'When you're in a race and especially when it gets tight, you're out there for yourself and you don't give a shit who's beside you, whether they go down or stand.' **Kieren Fallon** (*Independent*, 25 August 1997).

'The majority of flat jockeys are actually deformed – we're just small people.' Then jockey now trainer **Jamie Osborne** ponders the difference between jump and flat jocks in 1996.

When was the first running of the Prix de l'Arc de Triomphe – (a) 1920, (b) 1924, (c) 1928?

'He did turn up to ride out one morning with stubble on is chin. It was ghastly. I made my view clear on the matter. He has arrived clean shaven ever since.' **Sir Mark Prescott** on a not so close shave for his jockey Seb Sanders.

'The travelling band of certifiable madmen known as professional jockeys.' **Sue Mott** (*Daily Telegraph*, 20 November 2004).

'The Europeans ride grass better than our jockeys. Here, position is important. It's about speed. Over there, it's about finishing.' Retired US Hall of Fame jockey **Angel Cordero** on contrasting jockey styles (*Daily Mail*, 12 January 2005).

'Anyone can go out and go as hard as you can. But to be able to sit in and judge pace and judge what is around you, and get the jumps right and to be able to take a pull and fill the horse's lungs and go again. There is nothing like it.' **Timmy Murphy** on why he prefers to ride from behind rather than from the front (*Daily Mail*, 9 November 2004).

'Part of the challenge of this race is knowing where you are going. Unfortunately he wasn't up to it.' Cheltenham clerk of the course **Simon Claisse** after German jockey Peter Gehm rode dual Velka Pardubica winner Registana onto the wrong part of the course in the Sporting Index Chase on 12 November 2004, when the pair had looked close to winning. Four jockeys have previously been banned over the years for committing a similar misdemeanour.

'You can only ride what's underneath you…you can't ride what people in the stand think you have underneath you.' **Timmy Murphy** (*Sunday Times*, 21 November 2004).

'I'm a jockey because I'm too stupid to do anything else.' **Jamie Osborne** before he became a trainer.

(b) 1924.

'Jump jockeys are gentlemen but flat jockeys are a disgrace in their attitude and their jockeyship.' Trainer **Mick Easterby**.

'His booking is now generally accepted as providing his mount with a fifth leg.' **Richard Edmondson** on Tony McCoy of whom he also said, he 'would rather have a finger off than a day'.

'Put me up before you put me down.' Plea from jump jockey **Sophie Mitchell** to sceptical trainers.

'National Hunt jockeys have a hard and brutal life, but they also have free entry to the world's greatest brothel of the senses.' Sportswriter **Simon Barnes**.

'It's only because they never grew to normal height that a lot of them are jockeys, not because they're brilliant. Their egos are a lot bigger than they are.' Trainer **David Barron** (*Racing Post*, 2 July 2004).

'Jockeyship is rarely decisive, well over 90% of all winners would win with any competent rider on board.' **John Randall** (*Racing Post*, 11 July 2004).

'A flat jockey once told me that his daily life consisted of "early mornings, hours on the motorways, service station food and disappointment every thirty minutes" – a bit sad, really.' Former jockey spokesman, **Michael Caulfield**.

'Steve Smith Eccles would say "go steady, Scu" – then push past you!' **Peter Scudamore** (Radio 4, August 2004).

Which course celebrated 100 years of racing in July 1987 – (a) Windsor, (b) Wincanton or (c) Wolverhampton?

'I needed an English-speaking horse to win my first Group 1 race in France.' **Gary Stevens** is grateful to Tim Easterby's Somnus, which won him the Prix Maurice de Gheest in August 2004.

'In defeat, especially prolonged defeat, Fallon's face is a "Keep Out" sign to any with an ounce of sense.' **Alan Lee** (*The Times*, 2 August 2004).

'When you served an apprenticeship for three years you simply had to get on with the trainer. It was an honour to be an apprentice, but you had to graft. Today, you get a load of cocky young fellas who expect to get rides rather than thinking they'll be lucky to.' Trainer **Richard Fahey** (*The Times*, 4 August 2004).

'When Wally came back in after winning he'd been holding the reins so tight he could barely unclench his hands.' Still active just before his 80th birthday, former valet **Arnie Robinson** has seen at least 55 Ebors and best remembers Wally Swinburn's 1954 win on By Thunder, carrying 6st 12lb on a rain-soaked day.

'It's easier to hold a microphone than to go at 30–40mph on a racehorse.' **Jamie Spencer** responds to criticism of his riding when quizzed by Alastair Down on Channel 4 in August 2004.

'I don't think he knew what he was doing half the time, but as it was the right thing I never enquired what went on in his young head.' No, not said about Frankie Dettori, but by trainer **Jack Jarvis** in 1923 of champion jockey Charlie Elliott.

'Steve Cauthen is no 18-year-old. He's an old man. Sometimes he makes me believe in reincarnation. Maybe he had another life where he was a leading rider for fifty years.' **Laz Barrera**, trainer of the then teenaged Cauthen's Triple Crown winner Affirmed, about the Kentucky Kid.

(b) Wincanton.

'I rode Navan Boy at the October 1923 meeting and we had to wear helmets. They were neat and weighed only a few ounces, nothing like the piss pots worn now which remind me of the knights of old jousting.' Old-time jockey **H J Delmege** is scornful of the head protectors of today, recalling that crash helmets were first worn at Ely races in Cardiff.

'I never realised I'd end up being the shortest knight of the year.' **Sir Gordon Richards** on being honoured in 1953.

'Most riders beat horses as if they were guards in slave labour camps. Shoe treated them as if he were asking them to dance.' *LA Times* writer **Jim Murray** on US riding legend, Bill Shoemaker.

'The ideal jockey is short, thin, tough, quiet, hunched, reticent. The ideal trainer is tall, elegant, straight-backed, self-assured and charismatic.' **Rebecca Cassidy** in *The Sport of Kings*.

'Whether he is innocent or bent, he remains something of an anti-Establishment folk hero to the five-pint brigade.' The *Spectator's* **Robin Oakley** on Kieren Fallon, 11 September 2004.

'A very selfish life.' **Mrs Catherine Dettori's** opinion of jockeyship, expressed in the video *Frankie Dettori – The Real Story*.

'The jockey who rode him last time got off him and said "I should bring him back to seven furlongs". But I told him: "That was seven furlongs."' Reporter **Tom O'Ryan** relays a trainer's remarks, heard at Beverley on 15 September – but he spared the jockey's blushes by declining to name him.

Who sponsored the 1988 Welsh Derby? (a) British coal, (b) British Gas or (c) British steel?

'If I hadn't gone to America for those six months I would be struggling now. I don't think I would have been champion jockey without that experience. I could easily have got lost.' **Kieren Fallon** reflects on his time at Santa Anita with trainer Rodney Rash (*Thoroughbred Owner & Breeder*, September 2004).

'In 50 years I have never seen a Flat jockey as physically strong on a horse as Fallon, nor one with such an acrobatic fitness as Dettori.' **Brough Scott** (*Sunday Telegraph*, 19 September 2004).

'At least McCoy speaks to you. He tells you what he wants to do. Kieren says nothing. He just goes out there and does it.' **Frankie Dettori** on McCoy and Fallon, September 2004.

'Despite being the toughest in the weighing room, he looks distinctly vulnerable when he doesn't have the security of a horse under him.' **Charlie Brooks** on Kieren Fallon (*Daily Telegraph*, 27 September 2004).

'I have looked at many another woman, but I have never looked at another jockey.' **Sir Mark Prescott** on his stable jockey George Duffield.

'There you go, they get hold of a few bob and it all goes to their head, doesn't it?' Trainer **Terry Mills** after his apprentice Robert Miles was reported as having failed a drugs test in October 2004.

'As a jockey you never allow yourself to take a break because you're scared someone else will get your winners.' **Walter Swinburn** (*Guardian*, 1 November 2004).

(a) British coal.

'As for lengthy explanations to connections, I have edited mine down to two words – "dog" followed after a pause by "meat".' Then a jockey, now a radio presenter, **Luke Harvey**, January 1999.

'There are very few British sportsmen over the past 50 years who could claim to have been arguably the best in the world in their fields for a decade… Piggott is the only one who could argue that he was probably the best in the world for three decades.' **Will Buckley** (*Observer*, 14 December 2003).

'About two weeks ago.' After a 1967 US victory on Sir Ivor **Lester Piggott** was asked just when he thought he was going to win.

'The performance of Sir Ivor was more exhilarating than Nijinsky's, so I have to rank him my best Derby winner, with Nijinsky second.' **Piggott** in 2004's *Lester's Derbys*. In 1980 he said, 'I think Nijinsky probably on his day was the most brilliant horse I've ever ridden.' In his 1995 autobiography, 'Of all my nine Derbys, Sir Ivor's was the most exciting.'

'The austere regime further isolated him from his fellow men, promoted irritability and fostered the gunfighter's delusion of being above the law.' **Peter O'Sullevan** reflects on how a wasting lifestyle affected Piggott.

'I would not say it is the greatest day of my life.' **Lester** was a little underwhelmed in 1954 at becoming the youngest-ever Derby-winning jockey as Never Say Die won at 33/1. He later said, 'I went home and cut the lawn. I haven't cut the lawn since.'

'He's got an arse like a cream bun.' A **character** in the 1977 Howard Brenton stage play, *Epsom Downs*, describes Lester.

When Michael Dickinson saddled the first five home in the 1983 Cheltenham Gold Cup, how many runners were there – (a) 8, (b) 11 or (c) 14?

'The telephone rang and it was Lester Piggott. He said "Don't blame yourself. It was not your fault." Those words meant everything to me.' **Jamie Spencer** recalled how the maestro boosted his confidence after being slated for losing the 2002 Guineas on much vaunted Hawk Wing during an interview with the *Sun's* Claude Duval who, in another article, had unflatteringly dubbed young Jamie as 'Frank' Spencer.

'At Newbury races he slipped into my hand a neatly folded square of white paper which, in those days, was a £5 note. When I politely rejected the gift on the grounds that, as a journalist I was fully recompensed by being first with the news he clearly regarded my reaction as indicative of possibly dangerous imbalance.' **Peter O'Sullevan** recalls Lester's attempt at rewarding him for fixing him up with a winning ride back in his early days (*Horse Racing Heroes*, 2004).

'God gave him a great gift and he exploited it to the full.' Legendary trainer **Vincent Brien** on the man with whom he shared many of his greatest triumphs – Lester Piggott.

'He once crossed me; rode right across my nose. "What do you think you're playing at?" I asked him in the paddock afterwards. "I'm sorry, sir" he said, "I'm a little deaf and I didn't hear your hooves."' Russian jockey **Nikolai Nasibov** with a typical Lester yarn.

'Piggott received apologetic phone calls from both the Duke of Devonshire, Her Majesty's representative at the course, and Johnny Wetherby, a trustee. He declined their belated pleas to attend.' **Alan Lee** in *The Times* on Ascot's oversight in forgetting to invite the greatest jockey of all to their 'Finale' dinner prior to the closure of the course in September 2004 for rebuilding.

(b) 11.

Stewards' Inquiries

S tewards must get more inquiries about whether Stewards Enquiries are actually Steward's, or Stewards', Enquiries, or Inquiries, than anything else with which they have to concern themselves. Very few of us know which is right and what the difference is. You wouldn't offer too long odds about every steward knowing, either, would you?

Permit me to explain. A few moments of your attention now will shed light on this perpetual uncertainty and avoid having to return to the subject. To inquire means, 'to make a search or investigation' – and that would seem to fit the bill, wouldn't it? To enquire, my dictionary assures me, means 'to seek (information) by questioning'. So, both seem to be appropriate, which is a pain, really.

Upon referring to someone whose opinions and knowledge I trust – Gerald Hammond, Reader in English at the University of Manchester – I discover that, according to his *Book of Words*, it is in fact "e' before 'i', except...' And as for the Steward part, well unless it is just one Steward doing the, er, enquiring, it has to be Stewards'.

In case you were also wondering, a Steward is, 'a person appointed to supervise the arrangements or maintain order at a race meeting' and a 'Stewards' Enquiry' indicates that the running of a race is to be reviewed so the result is not yet official.

Stewards were first officially appointed in 1770, and as I was writing this in early 2005 there was much excitement about the prospect of Inquiries being held in public – well, parts of them, anyway. Yet, way back in 1919 a Stewards' Inquiry did take place in public, when top jockey Steve Donoghue was beaten on red-hot favourite Diadem in the King George Stakes at Goodwood. The jockey himself felt this was done as a sop to aggrieved punters and declared, 'I should not think that the experiment was considered to have been so successful as to warrant its being established as a precedent.' He got off, though.

When did Henry Cecil first take out a trainer's licence – (a) 1968, (b) 1969 or (c) 1970)

'Can you believe the stewards tried to make us ride in the race after it had happened. F***ing bastards.' **Ruby Walsh** remembers the Kilbeggan fall, which ultimately killed 25-year-old jump jockey Kieran Kelly (*Observer Sport Monthly*, January 2005).

'The Stewards, that selfless body of men generations of whom, over the last 200 years have given of their time and wisdom to build up and maintain the traditions of the Royal Calcutta Turf Club.' **W G C Frith's** dedication in the eponymous history of that august establishmen from 1976 – I have as yet, oddly enough, failed to trace a book dedicated to *our* Stewards!

'Unprofessional conduct.' The reason given by **stewards** for fining teenage female jockey Liz Morris $300 in August 2004 after she had thrashed the buttocks of senior rider Carlos Marquez Jr with her whip at Arlington Park, Chicago when he cut her up.

'When you are dealing with two-year-olds, ratings cannot tell you how good horses are, they can only tell you how bad they are not.' Official juvenile assessor **Matthew Tester** in 1997.

'I'm talking about a global form book. As I see it, this will solve many of the problems facing the racing industry. It will enable punters to understand the "mystery horses" who contest the biggest races and it will give them the same global perspective which fans of other sports now have.' **Nick Mordin's** solution to the difficulty of keeping tabs on foreign form (*Weekender*, 18 August 2004).

'Melbourne stands alone as the greatest horse-racing city in the world. The entire population seems to exist on racing.' **J Snowy** in his 1896 tome *The Stanley of the Turf*.

(b) 1969.

'This course is part Hampton Court maze and part Fontwell on drugs.' **Alastair Down** on the Czech marathon race, the Pardubicka.

'I've had four winners from just six rides in Norway this summer and as they don't have many jump races, that was enough for me to be champion.' **Sean Curran** claims the Norwegian title, October 2004.

'Nothing good ever came out of France except for good-looking women.' **Ginger McCain** didn't specify just what else he could wish for from the country when making this comment in November 2004.

'A perverted form of amusement which did no good to man nor beast.' **John Lawrence** (now Oaksey) on one-and-a-half mile three-year-old hurdle races, abolished in 1953 by the National Hunt Committee.

'How could the horse tell the difference between an owner and a punter?' Question for which **Newmarket racecourse office** reportedly had no answer when they tried to justify the denial of access for the general public to the course's pre-parade ring as a 'health and safety issue' because someone might be kicked.

'They are saying that Saxby won. What they should say is that he ought to have won.' Judge, **Mr C E Robinson**, after awarding a close finish to the 1913 2,000 Guineas against the apparent first past the post, Craganour. The horse was ridden by W Saxby who was, after that comment, jocked off Craganour, which came in first in the Derby but was disqualified.

'Stewards' Inquiries are a chilling evocation of the public school prefects' den.' *Guardian* writer **Melanie McFadyean**.

What do the initials R C stand for in the middle of trainer David Elsworth's name – (a) Robert Charles, (b) Richard Christopher or (c) Raymond Cecil?

'My 1997 *Rules of Racing* weighs a skinny 6 ounces. However, the 2004 version comes in at a heavyweight 11 ounces.' *Racing Post* letter writer **Richard Brooks** bemoans the 'over-regulation' of racing in August 2004.

'Rules of Racing are largely, and increasingly, standard throughout the world. Their enforcement varies considerably, in regard to such things as medication and rough riding. Standardization ought to be as complete, as universally accepted, as in tennis. We shall not see this until we watch Flying Childers, Lexington and Sea Bird II contest the Prix du Styx on the turf of the Elysian Fields.' Racing writer **Roger Longrigg** in 1972.

'Who's to say the call of three men, good and true, on appeal is better than that of three men, good and true, on the day?' **Malcolm Wallace**, Jockey Club director of regulation, ponders the appeals procedure (*The Times*, 28 July 2004).

'There's still too much rudeness in racing. If I go in front of the stewards and they talk down to me, I tell them to talk to me like a human being and we might get somewhere.' Trainer **Jamie Poulton**, October 2004.

'Punters are now convinced that, short of the jockey actually pulling a revolver and shooting one of his rivals dead, it's virtually impossible these days for any horse who passes the post first to get disqualified in any race.' **Paul Haigh** on the 'absurdity' of the rules relating to disqualification (*Racing Post,* 10 July 2004).

'He, Steve Smith Eccles and myself had agreed to share our prize money if any of us won. When Francome admitted that in a news-paper article, we all got done by the stewards.' **Peter Scudamore** on how Donegal Prince's win under John Francome in the 1982 Schweppes Gold Trophy got three top riders in trouble.

'I have received a letter of apology from Sir Claude de Crespingy which I have accepted but it does not alter my opinion that he is quite unfit to be a Steward at a meeting and I hope I can have an assurance that after your next meeting he will not figure in the list of Stewards. I am asking other Clerks of the Course where he is a Steward to take the same line.' This letter, written by **Frederick H Cathcart Esq**, the man credited with popularising Cheltenham and launching the Gold Cup and Champion Hurdle, was dated 6 October 1921 and addressed to an anonymous Clerk of the Course about one of his Stewards who had not stewarded to Cathcart's satisfaction. Sir Claude was an amateur rider of distinction.

'I asked why he had been so far back on Susu and he used a swear word in reply.' Jockey **Gary Hind** was fined £500 for using a profanity in the unsaddling enclosure after finishing second on Susu in Dubai and being reported for swearing by his trainer, Satish Seemar, 31 December 1998.

'Put a cabbage in front of that man and he'd interview it.' US journalist watching **Derek Thompson** at work in 1997.

'The July meeting is one of those lazy, hazy occasions where the first race should never be before 2.15pm. The only reason for it being so early is that *Countdown*, the Channel 4 quiz show, apparently is not a moveable feast.' **Alan Lee** of *The Times* on why TV insisted on starting the 2004 Newmarket meeting at 1.20 p.m.

'For her next trick she will climb the north face of the Eiger in high heels and full make-up. Then change into Lycra when she reaches the summit and slalom effortlessly down the other side.' Notoriously hard to please Paul Haigh is impressed by **Clare Balding** in July 2004.

What colour was Arkle – (a) bay, (b) brown or (c) chestnut?

'Michael Stoute is hard work. It is difficult to try and get him to say anything of import.' **Clare Balding**.

'Just listen to any random fifteen minutes of coverage, on either racing channel, and see how many crackings, juices or zests you hear.' *Racing Post* letters' page correspondent **Martin Godfrey** is not happy at the overuse of current 'buzz words' on the box in August 2004.

'No one is a bigger horseracing enthusiast than me, but the manner in which my sport is presented on television sends me to sleep. It's so boring.' **Richard Birch** (*Racing Post*, 11 September 2004).

'We joke that Clare spent most of her life being known as "Ian Balding's daughter". She couldn't wait for me to be known instead as "Clare Balding's father". Now that's happened.' Clare's dad, **Ian** (*Sunday Times Magazine*, 19 September 2004).

'Willie (Carson) had his usual problems with the English language.' **Paul Haigh**, 4 October 2004.

'Jockey, author, broadcaster, *Sun* newspaper columnist, womaniser – the man must be scared to unzip his flies in case the next thing he touches also turns to gold.' **John Anthony** on John Francome (*Racing Ahead*, October 2004).

'I've got into the probably unwise habit of watching almost all sports, including horseracing, with the volume off. I'm not quite sure how it started. I think it was Derek Thompson.' **David Ashforth** (*Racing Post*, 9 October 2004).

(a) Bay.

'Anything I tip, I back... I'll have four figures on a horse when everything is right.' *Morning Line's* **Jim McGrath**, March 2001.

'At one point, this most organic of roving reporters (Derek Thompson) was seen asking a horse, Mr Ed, if it thought it was going to win and then holding the microphone to its lips in anticipation of a reply. The horse was silent, by the way – and well done to all punters who were sensible enough to take that as a "no".' **Giles Smith** (*The Times*, 18 October 2004).

'I'm pretty seething, actually. At a time when Channel 4 is considering its long term future in racing, the sport, or a few individuals within, is ill-advised to hinder innovation to make the sport more attractive.' Channel 4 Head of Sport **David Kerr** was not best pleased when plans to use new speed sensing technology to show viewers precise details of a horse's position and speed throughout a race were scuppered when the connections of two runners in races being shown on 23 October refused to have speed-sensing chips inserted into saddle cloths. Said irate Kerr, 'We make a loss on racing and one of the reasons we keep involved is we can innovate. If we can't, it's another reason for us to think about walking away.'

'Shock horror. Big Mac's passport was six months out of date.' **Claude Duval** reveals how John McCririck's disastrous attempt to fly out to Las Vegas in October 2004 was scuppered at Heathrow (*Sun*, 23 October 2004).

'What if a horse kicks out with both barrels and either injures the interviewer, the sound technician, the jockey, the lad or a member of the public? What if the valuable thoroughbred lashes out and hurts itself? Someone, somewhere, is going to get sued.' **Simon Milham** calls for the banning of 'inane TV jockey interviews' (*Pacemaker*, November 2004).

How many horses did See You Then beat when winning three Champion Hurdles – (a) 46, (b) 52 or (c) 58?

'The idea that racing is so big that people should pay lots for it, or at least for anything besides the Grand National, the Classics, Cheltenham, Ascot, York and maybe Goodwood, no longer holds.' **Brough Scott** warns people not to take free TV coverage of the sport for granted (*Guardian*, 9 November 2004).

'Coops grabbed his racecard and tore it up!' **Peter Scudamore** revealed a *contretemps* between *Attheraces* host Robert Cooper and a 9-year-old boy who'd secured his autograph on a racecard before telling Coops 'I hate ATR' (*Daily Mail*, 17 November 2004).

'I gave it up because I was being recognised by the public more for my appearances on it than for being a jockey.' **Frankie Dettori** on why he quit hit TV show *A Question Of Sport*, November 2004.

'What total bollocks… Dry up, girl! Horses are for racing, and no one enjoys the spectacle of your dewy-eyed hand-wringing.' *Racing & Football Outlook's* 'Off The Bit' column takes issue with **Clare Balding's** contention that Best Mate had endured a 'hard race' in winning his four runner comeback race at Exeter in November 2004.

'We were so elated that we sat and stared at the teletext racing results all evening.' **Mark Johnston** recalls how he and wife Deirdre celebrated their first-ever winner, Hinari Video at Carlisle in 1987 (*Racing Ahead*, July 2004).

'We'll get the place fumigated before the next meeting.' **Course foreman** at Gowran Park reassures itchy journalists after the press room suffered a flea infestation in May 2004.

'It is deception, even if Mitchell insists that he did it for the sake of the foal.' *Racing Post's* **David Ashforth**, unimpressed with Philip

Mitchell of Juddmonte Farms, who registered Endless Summer as being born on 2 January 1998 instead of the true date of 26 December 1997. Of course, all horses have a birthday on 1 January.

'Full marks for offering a few Cheltenham ante-post lists. Fewer gold stars, though, for putting in Gold Ring as Triumph (Hurdle) favourite. He won't be winning as he is already four!' **Nicholas Godfrey** pointing out Totesport's faux pas, 26 September 2004.

'As our racehorses are as upper class as the Jockey Club, perhaps they enjoy a good thrashing now and then.' **Peter Moverley** of Bristol in a letter to the *Observer*.

'Some people seem more worried about horses being hit than they are about granny-mugging or child abuse. There is more cruelty going on around them in this country than there is on the race-course.' **George Duffield** after three jocks were suspended for whip offences following the 1996 2,000 Guineas.

'The horse is a creature of flight, not fright. Whoever heard of Mother Nature using the whip on the fleetest mustang as it leads the pack.' **Roy David** of the *Manchester Evening News*.

'Maybe jockeys should carry Ken Dodd-style tickling sticks instead of whips and wear skirts instead of breeches – then, at least, they would look like the fairies the stewards want them to be.' **Jack Berry**, after Dettori and Eddery were suspended for whip offences having finished first and second in the 1996 St Leger.

'I went to switch my whip and it flew off. I had to do something so I took off my goggles and hit him with them.' US jockey **Alex Sollis** on how he won a hundred grand race at Hollywood Park on Swiss Yodeller in July 1996.

Lester Piggott's first St Leger winner was (a) Pindari, (b) St Paddy or (c) Aurelius?

'I think more horses are whipped out of the money than into it.' All-time great jock **Willie Shoemaker**.

'If there were no whips at all I would not mind.' **Ian Balding**.

'I was excessive, but you don't think of that during the Gold Cup and I wouldn't have won otherwise.' **Adrian Maguire** explains his whip Catch 22 in the 1992 Gold Cup on Cool Ground.

'In the course of my career as a commentator, one practice which developed, in both flat and jumping, which I found disturbing was the habitual misuse of the whip. I considered it unnecessary, unproductive and offensive.' **Peter O'Sullevan**.

'We also have to remember that horses are bred and trained to run as fast as they can – and if it takes a few taps with the whip to make them do what they were bred for, so be it.' **Lester Piggott**, 1995.

'When they (jockeys) enter the paddock, they stride out confidently, heads high, often swinging their whips about or flicking them against their boots. Frankie Dettori is the most flamboyant baton-twirler, but I noticed that many jockeys seemed to indulge in some form of whip display as they entered the parade ring.' Really, what could anthropologist **Kate Fox's** observation signify!

'Well, I don't know. I just gave him one crack of the whip and he did jump tremendous.' **Thomas Aldcroft**, jockey of shock 1856 20/1 Derby winner, Ellington – in those days a 'crack' would have meant just that!

'The only reason she banks with Lloyds is because of the black horse on their logo.' **Sue Mott** on Jenny Pitman.

(b) St Paddy.

'When I was riding I did have one indulgence. I spent £25,000 on a season racing cars in Formula First. I was 34 and it was great.' **Richard Dunwoody** confesses to splashing out (*Sunday Times*, 22 August 2004).

'To saving Mill Reef's life: £25,000.' Bill from vet **Jim Roberts** to trainer Ian Balding after he operated on the stricken Derby winner's shattered leg in 1972. It seems cheap now but at the time Balding felt it was 'an extortionate liberty'.

'One of Red Rum's racing plates, worn for his third Grand National triumph in 1977, set off a lively battle of nods, finally won by a young man in a suit, whose clinching nod was for £3600.' **David Ashforth** reporting on a November 2004 auction.

'You go between two horses for money, not for fun.' US jockey **Eddie Arcaro**.

'It infringes owners' intellectual property rights and they should recognise that and pay for it.' Owner **Jenny Foster**, leading criticism of Turftrax speed-sensing systems being affixed to runners, producing a response in the *Racing Post* letters' page from Ken Jude of Herts, 'Planet earth to Jenny. If you don't want the public to know about the results of your trainer's work, leave your horses at home to race against each other.' November 2004.

'The racecard described us as a "relatively new stable". I started training thirty years ago.' **Merrick Francis** on 17 January 2005 after his Fard du Moulin Mas won at Doncaster.

'Up here when you have a winner they say "Well done" and mean it. Down south they say it, but whisper "You jammy so and so".' Trainer **Alan Bailey** – from 'oop north'.

At which course did jockey George Duffield ride his first winner – (a) Warwick, (b) Wolverhampton or (c) Yarmouth?

'I love racing in the north. When I meet the M5 I'd much rather turn left than right.' Llancarfan-based trainer **Evan Williams**.

'It is nonsense to say that bookmakers hate 16 runner handicaps and that we are all clapping our hands at the thought that they will go. Remember that a lot of the business on these races is win only.' William Hill executive **Ian Spearing** counters claims that bookies were behind BHB plans to introduce a maximum field size of fourteen – twelve during June, July and August – for all bar certain 'heritage' handicaps from 2006.

'It is time for mathematicians, marketing men and punters to think about a new range of place terms.' **David Ashforth** in response to the above plan.

'The Jockey Club, which runs racing, has no jockeys among its members.' *A Book of Words*, **Gerald Hammond**, 1992.

'They are just inter-changeably posh.' TV critic **Nancy Banks Smith** on stewards.

'The viewer is left with the impression that to qualify as a steward you need to be one of life's fat cats, with the time and the money to buy the necessary trilby or panama to suit the occasion.' **Colin McKenzie** in 1997 Channel 4 documentary *The Englishman And His Horse*.

'Those running racing often seem, like the current government, impervious to criticism. If we say it is true, it must be – so the argument goes.' **Sue Montgomery**, (*Independent*, 5 June 2004).

(c) Yarmouth.

'At times he can't understand why people can't understand.' New BHB Chairman **Martin Broughton's** assessment of his predecessor, Peter Savill.

'Oh, he'd be perfect. He's deaf, he's blind and he knows sod-all about racing.' Triple Grand National winning trainer, **Neville Crump**, asked about the chances of a racing figure becoming a steward.

'Dictator of the English turf.' **Admiral Henry James Rous** (1795-1877), who drew up the weight-for-age scale and became handicapper of the Jockey Club for 22 years.

Linda Sheedy rode Foxbury in 1984 and became the first woman to take part in which race?

Thoroughbred Types

I 've never come a cross a thoroughbred that can type, but I can tell you something about them, 'The thoroughbred is a British creation, and is part of our national heritage, which is worth preserving...the foreigner looks to the thoroughbred as a typically British creation... It is the duty of the Turf authorities to try to preserve the supremacy of the British thoroughbred as far as possible...and if they fail in this duty racing is liable to be debased to the level of roulette, and does not deserve to survive.'

That's not really me talking there – in fact it is from 1965's 'Report of the Duke of Norfolk's Committee on the Pattern of Racing'. A little patriotic, perhaps, maybe even jingoistic, but a stirring evocation of the importance to the nation of the thoroughbred. Not such a tribute to the virtues of roulette, though, and one wonders whether it might not have been penned after an unsuccessful stint at the tables in a casino somewhere – Monte Carlo, possibly, which I visited in the year 2002. Whilst staying in the Monte Carlo Grand I visited that hotel's casino and soon realised that they must have taken on board the Duke's Committee's Report because they had installed a gambling game based on horse-racing. I rapidly became very proficient at it, and, indeed, financially successful, a trait that soon led to my good lady escorting me from the premises before I could squander my hard-earned winnings rather than spend them in what she saw as a fit and proper manner – on her.

Thoroughbred types on a racecourse do not all wear saddles and stirrups, many of them are from well-bred human families, albeit often spoiled slightly by excessive in-breeding. I don't need to tell you which ones they are, I'm sure you can work it out for yourself.

The word thoroughbred is believed to have been used for the first time in 1713 by the Earl of Bristol – but how would

Cheltenham Gold Cup.

anyone else have known what he was on about if he was the first one to use the word?

I don't know why, but I do tend to worry about little things like that...

'It's said his best friend was a parrot who would squawk psalms and popular songs.' **Sharon Wright** on the first thoroughbred superstar, 18th-century champion, Eclipse (*Daily Express*, 11 October 2004).

'There is nothing in racing to compare to that glorious late turn of foot, that magical moment when a horse takes wing and metamorphoses before your eyes into Pegasus. That shocking instant of disbelief has in it the quintessence of sport.' The incomparable **Simon Barnes** on Dancing Brave's 1986 Arc victory (*The Times*, 6 November 2004).

'There is nothing unreasonable or unfair about barring from the richest and highest prestige races the horse that has been not-so-subtly relieved of some of the physical and mental burdens that are part and parcel of the proper test of the equine athlete.' **Tony Morris** on why geldings should be banned from Classic races, July 2004.

'Owners marketed three alcoholic drinks, Funny Cide Light Beer, Funny Cide Chardonnay and Cabernet Franc Reserve, making him perhaps the first horse to have an alcoholic beverage named after him since Red Rum.' **Richard Edmondson** on the US gelding that won the 2003 Kentucky Derby and Preakness Stakes (*Independent*, 29 October 2004).

'I learnt from the pigeons that you should look at the animal, not the pedigree.' Racing pigeon trader turned racehorse purchaser **Fergus Wilson**, whose ambition is to win the National – is he strictly for the birds? (*The Times*, 6 January 2005).

What trade did Jonjo O'Neill's father pursue – (a) butcher, (b) cobbler or (c) farmer?

'All that the breeder can do is to try to arrange matters so that there is a reasonable chance of the right genetic shakeup emerging, and hope for the best.' One of the best breeders, **John Hislop**, effectively admitting it is all a bit of a lottery.

'How could anybody have envisaged a scenario in which your father is also your brother, while your mother and grandmother are one and the same?' **Graham Green** tries to work out who is related to who and how after mare Flopsy Mopsy and sire Does It Matter produced a colt called Moses. Does It Matter's dam was Flopsy Mopsy. Don't ask! (*Racing Post*, 14 July 2004).

'The owner and breeder premiums are so good, I believe that France is the last bastion of the owner/breeder.' The Aga Khan's daughter, **Princess Zahra**, who is actively involved in the management of his horses (*Pacemaker*, August 2004).

'My dad told me a long time ago, "if you find something that you love, you'll never have to work another day in your life. And I love what I do."' Former jockey **Steve Cauthen** believes he has now found his true calling, as a breeder, July 2004.

'Every so-called expert told me it was breeding suicide.' **Lord Derby**, who made his own decision to send his mare Selection Board to Cape Cross – producing dual 2004 Oak and Breeders' winner, Ouija Board. He added, 'No matter how much money you throw at it, racing is not an exact science.'

'Throughout the long history of the British Thoroughbred, no single breeder has exercised more influence on the breed than the late Earl.' **Obituary** in the *Bloodstock Breeders' Review* to the 17th Earl of Derby (1865–1948), who won a record number of Classics as both owner and breeder.

(b) Cobbler.

'I have mett with so many disappointments, besides those commonly attending all studs…from the ignorance, carelessness and drunkenness of grooms, etc, that I am finally determined to carry it on no farther.' Breeder the **Earl of Bristol** decides he has had enough – in 1737.

'The bloodstock market is founded on a central uncertainty. Nobody knows what a good racehorse is, or rather what exactly it is which enables one racehorse to run faster than another. Equally, nobody knows how to set about producing a superior racehorse, or how to select one from a mass of relatively similar yearlings.' **Jocelyn de Moubray** in *The Thoroughbred Business*.

'I bred and retained a filly by Nicholas Bill. Knickerless was apparently not considered decent, yet I got away with Nicholess.' Breeder **Bob Urquhart**, 23 September 1998.

'The trouble is, it's a bit like losing your virginity. After you've done it once, you want to continue doing it until you cannot do it any more.' **Tony Morris** on attending a bloodstock sale (*Racing Post*, 8 October 2004).

'I realized a long time ago that animals love you regardless of what you are, who you are, what you're worth and what you're not worth. They are true friends.' The former heavyweight and middleweight world champ and for many years regarded as the best pound for pound boxer in the world, **Roy Jones**. He breeds horses in Pensacola, Florida (*Sports Illustrated*, 1 November 2004.)

'What's the difference between the world's most famous Jagger and the racehorse of the same name? Well, one is a feisty if greying performer who has failed the odd dope test but still puts his heart and soul into every performance. And the other. Well, the

In how many consecutive Grand Nationals did Peter Scudamore's father Michael ride – (a) 16 (b) 17 or (c) 18?

other is the lead singer with the Rolling Stones.' **Graham Cunningham** on the equine Jagger, fancied for the 2004 Ebor.

'The prime position in the room, bang above the middle of the fireplace, goes not to any golfing memento, but to Desert Orchid. And it's not a picture but a beautifully crafted bronze model which I purchased from a catalogue for £600.' Racing fan and punter, golf star **Laura Davies** in her 1996 autobiography *Naturally...*

'It would be idle to pretend that those five races (the Classics) now matter more than any others where breeders are concerned, and we can no longer trace the development of the Thoroughbred through the events that formerly were recognised as landmarks in its progress.' **Tony Morris** (*Pacemaker*, September 2004).

'Stamina, once a prized quality on the turf, has become almost a cuss word. Winning what remains a great race is now a passport to the damned country of National Hunt stallions. As a breeding house for Flat breeding horses, the St Leger is dead.' Contemporary racing writer **Richard Edmondson** of the Independent.

'For my sire and dam.' **Kevin Conley**'s dedication in his breeding book, *$tud*.

'Saturday the sixteenth of September next, will be sold, or set up for sale at Skibberdeen. A strong, staunch, steady, sound, stout, safe, sinewy, serviceable, strapping, supple, swift, smart, sightly, sprightly, spirited, sturdy, shining, sure-footed, sleek, smooth, spunky, well-skinned, sized and shaped, sorrel steed of superlative symmetry, styled Spanker. His sire was the sly Sobersides on a sister of Spindleshanks, by Sampson, a sporting son of Sparkler who won the sweepstakes and subscription plate last session at Sligo. His selling price, sixty seven pounds, sixteen shillings and sixpence, sterling.' A **handbill** distributed in Manchester in 1829.

(a) 16.

'The thoroughbred is a delicate animal, women's tender feelings may help a horse.' Top Japanese jockey **Yutaka Take** backs women entering the sport in his homeland in 1996.

'Over jumps, big-priced winners tend to be flukes. They come looking for you, carrying a big stick. You are seldom pleased to see them. On the Flat, you can get out there and find them.' **Chris McGrath** of *The Times*.

'A thoroughbred steak is like butter, it is the healthiest form of red meat, very low in fat, cholesterol-free and iron-rich.' Food writer **Michael Raffael**.

'I wouldn't have my house if it wasn't for Cois Na Tine. The house is a shrine to him. There are no football pictures up, just racing pictures.' Republic of Ireland international striker **Niall Quinn** named his house after his Group 3 winner.

'Once upon a time there was a horse named Kelso – but only once.' US writer **Joe Hirsch** on America's Horse of the Year 1960–64.

'There is no horse like this horse.' **Sheikh Mohammed** on the ill-fated Dubai Millennium who died aged just five years old after suffering from grass sickness. Frankie Dettori called the horse, who won 9 out of his 10 races, 'One of the best horses I've ridden.'

'Not many horses are truly great, but this one is.' **Mick Kinane** on 2001 dual Derby winner, Galileo.

'The toughest little dude I've ever seen.' Jockey **Bill Shoemaker** on US horse of the year 1981 and 1984, gelding John Henry.

Who was the first jump jockey to ride 100 winners in consecutive seasons?

'Like a surfer hitting a good wave.' **Frankie Dettori** on sprinter Lochsong.

'Taking disaster by the throat and turning it into victory, they have surely earned a place of honour that will be secure as long as men talk, or read, or think of horses.' **Lord Oaksey** on the 1962 Grand Steeple-Chase de Paris of Mandarin and Fred Winter after the horse's bit broke and the jockey had to ride with no means of steering for 17 fences.

'Pebbles acts as a tonic to any race in which she competes.' ***Racehorses of 1985*** on 1,000 Guineas and Breeders Cup Turf winner.

'I have seen a handful who matched his quality and durability, but don't expect to lay my eyes on more than a couple in his league this side of the Reaper carrying out his raid.' **Alastair Down** on Florida Pearl.

'The nearest thing to a bullet in animal shape that I ever met.' The Tetrarch's jockey **Steve Donoghue** who rode the rocket-like two-year-old in his 1913 season.

'He looked like Muhammad Ali walking around the parade ring. He is the best horse in the world and always has been.' **Luca Cumani** on 2003 Hong Kong Cup winner Falbrav.

'One well-known, hard-bitten trainer watched the Jockey Club Cup in the betting shop at Newmarket racecourse and – with tears in his eyes – he said that losing punters were cheering.' Owner **Jeff Smith** on another Persian Punch triumph.

Terry Biddlecombe.

'When he first came to Mr Dreaper's his action was so bad you could drive a wheelbarrow through his hind legs!' Jump legend Arkle's jockey **Pat Taaffe**, who also paid tribute to him as 'A Rolls-Royce of a horse. A horse in a million.' Trainer **Dreaper** added, 'Champions are made in Heaven,' while owner **Anne, Duchess of Westminster**, pledged, 'I will never let my Arkle run in the National, because I adore him, because he is one of the family, and because he is much too precious to me.'

'Arkle was a freak, an unrepeatably lucky shake of the genetic cocktail, the nearest thing the sport has ever seen to the perfect machine.' **John Randall** and **Tony Morris** in their *A Century of Champions*.

'If there has ever been a more superlative example of stern, unre-lenting courage in a thoroughbred horse, no one has yet made it public.' **Patrick Robinson** on Triple Crown winner Affirmed in *Decade of Champions*.

'The man is a colossus, we have never seen his like before.' **John McCririck** on Tony McCoy.

'There are two types of stallions – Northern Dancer and the rest.' **Robert Sangster**.

'A god on four legs.' Racing journalist **Sidney Galtrey** on five times Cheltenham Gold Cup winner, Golden Miller.

'I unhesitatingly describe him as a genius. There has been no train-er like him, and there never will be another.' Great jockey **Sir Gordon Richards** on Fred Darling (1884–1953), winner of 19 Classics, of whom he also said, 'I don't think Mr Darling ever understood friendship at all.'

What is Terry Biddlecombe's middle name, which begins with W?

'The most devastating solo tour de force ever seen at that level of competition.' Verdict on Sea-Bird's 1965 Arc victory, which encouraged **John Randall** and **Tony Morris** to declare him 'Horse of the Century' in their *A Century of Champions.*

'Trying to fault Secretariat's conformation was like dreaming of dry rain.' US writer **Charlie Hatton** on America's Horse of the Century.

'Lanzarote is a Henry Cooper of a horse – a powerful tiger on the course, yet gentle and quiet off it.' **Brough Scott** on the 1970s Champion Hurdler.

'He's the all-time bravest horse I have ever trained and consistency is his hallmark.' **Dermot Weld** on Vinnie Rose after that horse won the Irish St Leger for the fourth successive year in 2004.

'Great racehorses make races great, not the other way round.' Discuss! **Julian Muscat** (*The Times,* 21 September 2004).

'It's like when you look at a woman and you never quite know why, but sometimes you turn your head. When I saw this one, I really turned my head.' Trainer **Michael Hourigan** on making the acquaintance of his jumper, Beef Or Salmon, October 2004.

'For me, he is a great horse, although I cannot rate him as a great horse yet in terms of what he has achieved.' BHB handicapper in charge of jumpers, **Phil Smith**, on triple Gold Cup winner Best Mate, 21 October 2004.

'If another person tells me what a great horse Best Mate is and that he rivals Arkle as the greatest of all time, I'll push their face under John McCririck's sweaty armpit.' **Paul Jacobs** (*Inside Edge,* December 2004).

Walter.

'A steeplechaser as an icon, the only animal a sizeable proportion of the population could recognise.' **Brough Scott** on Best Mate (*Sunday Telegraph*, 21 November 2004).

'My idea of the greatest trainer who ever lived.' **Hugh McIlvanney** on Vincent O'Brien.

'He was the fastest chaser and fastest jumper I have ever seen.' **John Francome** on Tingle Creek, 1 December 2004.

'She was a grey and she loved to have a grey in front of her in the string and more particularly a grey behind her when she went out to exercise. In my experience this was unique.' Legendary trainer **Noel Murless** on 1959 Oaks winner, Petite Etoile.

'To be on him was like riding a creature that combined the power of an elephant with the speed of a greyhound.' Great jockey **Steve Donoghue** who partnered great grey The Tetrarch, nicknamed The Spotted Wonder. The horse was rated the best two year old of the 20th century, and won all seven of his 1913 races.

'It appears, however, we are not yet out of the backwoods and on to the plains of modern thinking. The evening before the greys, Newmarket stages a race of similar conditions for all other shades of horse, as instructed by the BHB. Restrictive sales races for hundreds of thousands of pounds are tolerated but a £15,000 runaround for greys brings in the lack of thought police.' **Richard Edmondson** is not impressed that a race only for grey horses cannot take place without an equivalent for all other colours (*Independent*, 4 August 2004).

'Desert Orchid is a ham. He may not be able to read all those gushing superlatives in the cuttings book, but he knows that when

Which service did Dick Francis join during World War II?

he walks towards a crowd, wild-eyed people jump in front of him with clicking cameras.' **Brough Scott** on perhaps the most famous grey of them all.

'If you got drunk in a pub with him, you'd want him on your side in the gutterside brawl afterwards.' Owner **Graham Roach** on his Viking Flagship.

'Bad horses are no good to any fella. But, trouble is you get attached to the bastards.' **David Nicholls**.

'He was a sod, a real lager lout.' Trainer **Robin Dickin** on his three year-old Prairie Minstrel.

'He had the head of an Arkle, despite the body of a Mr Bean.' Trainer **Richard Phillips** on Time Won't Wait.

'He just adores affection and lots of cuddles. If he were a man I would have married him by now.' **Linda Perratt** on her two year-old Jacmar.

'A great picture stays great forever. A horse is only great for two or three years. And, unlike art, horses bring you disappointment.' Art dealer and racehorse owner **Daniel Wildenstein**.

'The thoroughbred racehorse is one of the most romantic things on earth. A beautiful and ruinous lover, he inspires dreams and offers eternal hope.' Writer **Laura Thompson** (*Daily Telegraph*, 6 November 2004).

'The sight of a great racehorse at full gallop has a power to thrill so profound that it is ultimately mysterious, inexplicable except

RAF.

perhaps in terms of some long-buried folk memory.' **Hugh McIlvanney** (*Sunday Times*, 7 November 2004).

'He's the best horse I've ever trained. He may be the best horse anyone has ever trained.' US trainer **William I Mott** on 1995 Horse of the Year, Cigar.

'The colt was supposed to be a wobbler.' **Michael Goodbody** whose Shamardal was Cartier Two Year Old Colt 2004.

Every single grey thoroughbred traces back to the Alcock Arabian, imported to Britain during the early 18th century.' **Sue Montgomery**, (*Independent*, 12 August 2004).

'Arkle got his name from a mountain facing the Duchess of Westminster's home by Loch Stack in Sutherland.' Racing writer **John Scally**.

'Charles II even took his nickname, "Old Rowley" from his favourite horse.' **Rebecca Cassidy**, *The Sport of Kings*.

'Many of today's thoroughbreds can be traced back 40 generations, which means that with time on your hands, the relevant references and a very large piece of paper, you can construct a tree consisting of 2,199,022,250,550 names.' **Tony Morris's** startling 1998 observation.

'Country music at 50% was the most popular genre, followed by rock, oldies, alternative, classical and jazz.' A summer 2004 **survey** in the US by Equine.com revealed that 70 per cent of respondents used music 'to soothe their runners' in their barns or training yards.

Who rode Peter O'Sullevan's Attivo to win the Triumph Hurdle?

'The Jockey Club is like the monarchy, paranoid about the press, secretive about its inner workings and run by people who inherit the power and seek to protect it.' **Riete Oord**, director of *The Englishman And His Horse*. Surely not!

'Has there ever been a racing authority that was not incompetent, lacking in imagination and dynamism, or out of touch with the industry's needs?' **Chris Hawkins** of the *Guardian* in December 1996.

'The Jockey Club is very autocratic – it was about five years before anyone said good morning to me.' Starter **Alec Marsh**, 1978.

'To those who abhor self-perpetuating, self-elected autocracy in any form the Jockey Club is anathema.' Racing author **Jack Waterman**.

'He apparently has never heard of premium telephone lines and he certainly doesn't know anything about betting.' Former trainer **Charlie Brooks** on Jockey Club Chief Executive Christopher Foster (*Daily Telegraph*, 5 July 2004).

'The commission finds some of the current nomenclature such as "lad" and "lass" outdated and inappropriate.' Conclusion of BHB-appointed **commission** looking into conditions for stable staff – almost as inappropriate, perhaps, as an incident of which they were told when a member of staff reported to their employer, 'I have hurt my shoulder', to be told bluntly, 'Well, you'd better fuck off home then.'

'During a race I attempt to look as male as I can.' Cunning tactic by jockey **Sophie Mitchell**.

Robert Hughes.

'I would advocate banishing women from all betting offices and indeed from racecourses, unless they were an owner, trainer or breeder. I have yet to meet a woman who can hold a rational conversation about horse racing.' **Martyn McVeigh** of Fleetwood, Lancashire, in a 1997 letter to the *Racing Post,* would play with Clare Balding, Alice Plunkett, Lydia Hislop, Lesley Graham, *et al,* I'm sure.

'Gentleness, firm contours and a sense of humour.' **Richard Pitman's** ideas of a woman's most attractive characteristics. The jockey turned commentator was once married to Jenny Pitman.

'Go down to the paddock and back anything that appeals to you, anything that gives you a wink – unless it is Jamie Osborne, in which case it means that he can see all the way down your cleavage.' **Richard Pitman** giving tipping advice to a group of female novice punters at the 1996 Cheltenham Festival.

'If she had a pair of bollocks she'd be getting 10 rides a day.' Trainer **David Nicholls** on then apprentice Iona Wands in 1997.

'As strong and invigorating as a double brandy.' Andrew King on apprentice **Hayley Turner's** riding abilities. She says, 'The only difference between me and the boys is, I've got a different changing room' (*Racing Post,* 11 August 2004).

'I'll have to go to America and ride there, because it's ten times harder for a girl to get on in Ireland. Most people just wouldn't give a girl the chances that a lad would get.' **Cathy Gannon**, as she battled in September 2004 to become Ireland's first female champion apprentice.

'Ugly cries of "fix" and "not 'er again" split the air, and suddenly Thompson, hemmed in on all sides by walls of disgruntled flesh,

Which non-British jockey was runner-up in the Cheltenham Gold Cups of 1991 and 1992?

found himself in some danger of suffering the same fate as first-day winner Caesar Beware, who is no longer in possession of a working set of nuts.' **Alastair Down** on the rumpus when Thommo judged the Best Dressed Lady at the 2004 St Leger meeting's Ladies Day at Doncaster – only to select the 2003 winner, Rebecca Walker, again.

'Women jockeys are OK on the flat. But I don't think they are physically strong enough to hold their own against the men over the jumps.' **Henrietta Knight** (*High Stakes*, Winter 2003–4).

'Not unpleasing to the eye, not only was she decked out in a rather fetching pink outfit, but her joint is also pink and to top it off her umbrella is of the same colour and decked out in pink roses. The endless line of lads waiting to bet with her obviously approved.' Bookie **Simon Nott** on a female member of his breed at Stratford racecourse in September 2004.

'One thing I've been working on is a theory that people don't really understand racehorse pedigrees in this country, outside the breeding industry. It's an underused factor in betting. I think there's some mileage to be got out of assessing the going preferences of a horse's ancestors and whether they acted round certain tracks.' Top private tipster, **Henry Rix**, in 2002.

'The pedigree of a racehorse is of more value in judging of its probable success than its appearance.' **Charles Darwin**.

'This ever more selectively bred animal (the thoroughbred), which is drenched in sophisticated medication to a degree inconceivable back in the 1970s may also be becoming weaker in terms of its immune system and susceptibility to infection.' An uplifting thought from **Alastair Down** in July 2004.

Adam Kondrat.

'The President came out with tears in his eyes.' *Seabiscuit* author **Laura Hillenbrand** after a White House screening of the film.

'Past history tells us that the bloodstock market is often two years behind the general economic trend, so, with the British economy in robust health, it should equate to a strong bloodstock market for the next year or four at least.' **Darry Sherer**, Editor, *Pacemaker*, October 2004.

'Keep yourself in the best company and your horses in the worst.' Attributed to 19th-century turf administrator, **Admiral Henry Rous**.

'Well done, Arthur, but the joint is rather too big for the dish now, you know!' Unflattering observation regarding his weight by a **female racegoer** after top jump jockey Arthur Yates had won his 460th race, on Settling Day at Kempton in December 1884. Upon hearing the cry he quit. He had once won a race at Croydon, after falling but catching the horse by the tail, and remounting. Reported the *Sporting Life*: 'In racing reports it is oftentimes said that a jockey has cleverly won by a head; But Yates has performed, when all other arts fail, a more wonderful feat – for he won by a tail!'

'The toffs laugh at the proles; the proles sneer at the toffs. What fun! Two decades ago the only Labour voters here would have come to identify those who should be first against the wall.' **Tania Branigan**, the *Guardian*, on Royal Ascot 2004.

'Royal Ascot used to be a day devoted to the beauty of Britain's fairer sex. Today, it's about as stylish and classy as a hen night during Happy Hour.' The headline over **Lisa Armstrong's** *Times* article on 17 June 2004.

In which year did betting shops open legally in Britain?

'What I'd really like is a Royal Ascot winner. Not sure if they'd let me in the royal enclosure in a shellsuit, though.' Footballer turned trainer **Mick Quinn**.

'When I wake up every morning now my first thought is whether Mr Wylie is well. I told him it's a sign of age. The first thing I used to think about was sex.' **Sir Mark Prescott** is concerned for the well-being of a wealthy owner (*The Times*, 19 January 2005).

'The few women who broke into horse-racing were exceptional and from middle or upper-class backgrounds. Lower-class women only held supporting, subservient roles such as stable girls, cloakroom attendants, payers-out at the Tote windows, barmaids, trainers' wives, daughters and sisters.' The conclusion of **J Hargreaves** in the 1982 book *Sport, Culture and Ideology*.

'An arrant rogue, a thief, a horse so temperamentally unsatisfactory as to be practically worthless for racing purposes.' **Definition** of the Timeform 'double squiggle' rating, introduced in 1951 and 'awarded' to the very worst examples of the ungenuine equine thoroughbred.

'The police could not prevent women from rushing the cordon and picking hairs out of his tail for mementoes.' Trainer **Basil Briscoe** on the fever surrounding his five-time Cheltenham Gold Cup winner, Golden Miller.

'Cotty's Rock and The Reverend came over from Ireland in a small lorry which they had to share with 500 dead pheasants. The stink was unbelievable. I went mad.' **Howard Johnson** on how two of his new purchases had arrived with him, 10 November 2004.

'Mr McGoldrick is the man who performed a heart bypass operation on me about eight years ago.' Owner **Richard Longley**

1961.

explains why his chaser Mr McGoldrick was so-named in January 2005.

'When I go down to the post on those two-year-olds and I feel their little hearts beating between my legs, I think, why not let them have an easy race, win if they can, but don't frighten them first time out.' Quite a modern outlook by jockey **George Fordham** (1837–87) who had 16 Classic victories to his credit.

'Two year old racehorses are like teenagers. All the good breeding in the world won't guarantee they won't run off with a rock band, join a circus or drop out and spend the rest of their lives breaking your heart.' US writer **Jim Murray**.

'The number of horses now brought out to run on the course as two year olds, by which their powers are not only strained to the utmost, and to an extent beyond what their natural powers warrant from insufficient development, but they undergo in training an exertion preparatory to the race itself which not only tends to weaken, in most cases, the natural physical powers of the animal, but in many must destroy it altogether.' The **anonymous author** of 1863's *Horse Racing* was not big on two-year-old races.

'As Charlie Whittingham, the great American trainer once told me, 'No one with a young horse ever committed suicide.' **Simon Barnes** (*The Times*, 25 August 2004).

'I prefer to train two-year-olds so I can watch them develop. It's a better feeling when they win. It takes a lot of time and patience but I feel good about it.' US trainer **Dominick A Schettino** from New York, who began training two-year-olds in 1992.

Name Jersey's racecourse.

'He was a very tough man and I don't think he had much affection for his animals – he was very hard on them.' **Noel Murless** didn't think his predecessor at Beckhampton stables, Fred Darling, who won 19 Classics, was over-enamoured of his charges.

'The Wild Horse Racing team consists of a shanker, a mugger, a rider and of course a wild horse. The object of the race is to saddle, mount and ride the horse to a designated finish within the time limit – usually two minutes, depending on the distance of the track.' **Rules** of 'Wild Horse Racing', which takes place, you guessed it, in the States.

Les Landes.

The Final Furlong

I have always wondered who comes up with the names of the 'virtual' jockeys who ride the 'virtual' horses who contest the races that have proved so popular in betting shops over the past couple of years. For example, I recently spotted someone called 'Dave Furlong' down to ride in one of them – and I happen to know that he is a 54-year-old former schoolfriend of mine now living in Ivybridge, Devon, who is anything other than virtual, but who has never sat on the back of anything in his life – well, anything equine, that is. So, he may be the final Furlong to which this chapter heading refers. Although there are other candidates...

Back in 1935, Old Harrovian Frank Furlong rode Reynoldstown to win the Grand National. The horse was trained by Major Noel Furlong and owned by Major Noel Furlong, leading papers to headline 'Grand National Won By Three Furlongs' – so was Noel or Frank the final Furlong here?

You might well wonder just why furlongs remain so important within racing when you never see them used on maps or motorway mileage signs. Well, don't ask me, I'm nothing to do with the Jockey Club or the BHB. But what I can tell you is that, according to Gerald Hammond, author of *A Book of Words: Horse Racing*, 'The word (furlong) is derived from "furrow" plus "long", ie the length of a furrow.'

Is that final enough for you?

'Anyone immune to the delicious lunacy of racing is suffering a deprivation for which mere solvency cannot compensate.' A man who is far from immune, writer **Hugh McIlvanney**.

Where is Duindigt racecourse?

'All religions need a sacred text and Timeform is racing's bible.' Former Archbishop of Canterbury, **Lord Runcie**, on the world's self-appointed leading horse-racing publisher.

'Watching Secretariat win the Belmont by 31 lengths.' Multi Grand Slam event golfer **Gary Player's** answer when asked for his greatest sporting memory by Thommo (Derek Thompson).

'The racecourse commentator kept saying, "he's always ridden from behind" – which is news to me.' Trainer **Roger Charlton** after his Dorothy's Friend stormed through to win at Ascot on 7 August 2004.

'However much I try I cannot countenance paying £150,000 for an unraced something.' **Toby Balding**, on the eve of his late 2004 retirement.

'GRATEFULLY – To the thousand of horses and people who've given me such fun in racing; CHARITABLY – To the sour handful who tried to spoil it.' Dedication from **Ivor Herbert's** *Arkle.*

'My learning stopped when I had read *Treasure Island* and my education only started when I began to read Timeform.' The late **Jeffrey Bernard**, who penned the *Spectator's* 'Low Life' column.

'I'm going to be remembered for two things; being hit by Jenny Pitman in the weighing room at Ayr, and arrested on fraud charges.' An optimistic, perhaps, **Jamie Osborne** in 1998.

'A good tutor of jockeys, a good schooler of horses, and a hard bastard.' **David Nicholson's** self-composed epitaph.

Holland.

'Champion racechorse and champion sire, whose achievements in life stirred our hearts, and whose influence as a sire will continue to be a fitting tribute upon the breed.' Walmac International **tribute** to dual Arc de Triomphe winner Alleged when he died in June 2000, aged 26.

'Tis the Pace that Kills.' **Epitaph** on gravestone of long-time champion flat jockey George 'The Demon' Fordham, 1837–87.

'He had the three most important bones anyone can have – a wishbone, a funny bone and a backbone.' Father **Paddy McMahon** paying tribute to trainer Jimmy Fitzgerald at his October 2004 funeral.

'A cocky little bastard.' Trainer **Noel Meade's** thoughts on the young lad who had turned up at his stables and who grew up to make a name for himself – jockey Barry Geraghty.

'The morning of her life was rich in color and conquest and the evening shadowed in tragedy and defeat. Out of the west she came, unheralded and unsung, her flashing chestnut coat a banner of beauty and speed flung from ocean to ocean, her winged hooves feathering the racetracks of a nation.' Anonymous **tribute** to top late 19th-century US sprinter Geraldine, winner of 68 of 184 starts and a top-class performer in her prime, but over-raced until the age of 11 at low-quality tracks.

'Corrigan would ride them out, by danger undismayed; He never flinched at fence or wall, he never was afraid.' Tribute to Aussie champion jump jockey **Tom Corrigan** (1854–94) who died in a race fall, by poet A B 'Banjo' Paterson.

The Emperor Napoleon attended the 1857 opening of which racecourse?

'Florida stone crabs, Conch chowder, spaghetti Bolognese (no cheese), Cesar salad with plenty of anchovies, Dover Sole with sauté potatoes (well done), creamy rice pudding, Baileys coffee, dark chocolate mints, a Nebuchadnezzar of Dom Perignon champagne, a gallon of diet coke, vintage port and a couple of my best cigars.' **John McCririck**, when asked, 'What would you order for your last supper?' (*Sunday Express*, 5 April 1998).

'Odds-compilation is an art, not a science and don't let anyone convince you otherwise. All those maths lessons, spent learning about percentages, ratios and the like may come in handy but, when it comes to issuing prices about horses, the best odds compilers in the business use a healthy slice of instinct and gut feel.' **Simon Clare**, spokesman for Coral.

'For their employers they must be biggest price about the losers and shortest price the winners.' That's how pressurised is the lot of an odds-compiler as William Hill PR man and former jockey **David Hood** points out.

'At least two ghosts are supposed to haunt there – one of the headless Sir Harry (Vane, beheaded in 1662), the other of Lady Fanny Fane, the finest minuet dancer in England and also by some accounts, a nymphomaniac.' Writer **Ivor Herbert** on Queen Mother's trainer, Peter Cazalet's, Fairlawne, Kent stables, 1967.

'He spelled out where he shot himself, the house where he lived – which has been knocked down – and told them to back Unblest before he made his debut. Unfortunately, his starting price was only 5/4.' **James Fanshawe** recalls how his stable lads used a ouija board to make contact with the ghost of Fred Archer, who is believed to haunt Pegasus Stables, the Newmarket yard he built in 1884 and which Fanshawe took over (*The Times*, 26 June 1998).

Longchamp.

'There was no way anyone could have fiddled it. It gave me cold shivers and made me sweat.' Stable lad **Alex Cairns**, who took part in the above séance in which Fred also 'asked us to visit his grave'.

'A friend of mine saw her. She was knitting in a chair and there was a smokey blue aura round her. He was really shaken.' Carpenter **Bob Glass** on the ghost known as the Blue Lady believed to haunt Frankie and Catherine Dettori's Stetchworth, near Newmarket, mansion (*Sun*, 2 July 1998).

'I'm not prepared to bet against it.' **Sir Mark Prescott** when asked in 2001 whether he believes in a life after death.

'Kick him in the belly three out, and don't stop kicking until you kick me in the winner's enclosure.' Instructions to his jockey from trainer **Charlie Moore**.

'I was pouring money down a black hole, so I knocked it on the head before it knocked me on the head.' Newmarket trainer **Gordon Johnson Houghton** giving up in August 1998.

'Retire? Where am I going to go at 4.30 in the morning after all these years?' The 66-year-old US trainer **Sonny Hines** after his Skip Away won the 1997 Breeders Cup race.

'I can't understand why he's giving up when he's so young – he must have made more money than I did!' **Lester Piggott** on 51-year-old retiree, Pat Eddery.

'Not riding again is not out of the question.' Top US jock **Julie Krone**, the only woman to win a Triple Crown race, possibly quitting – possibly not – in July 2004 with 3,704 winners to her credit.

Quorum-Mared (MagicRed) is which horse's breeding?

'He's been stalking round the grounds with a rifle in his hands taking potshots at millions of rabbits digging up the grass. His new mission is to eliminate them. And now, he's started on the pigeons.' Peter Savill's wife **Ruth** reports on his activities following his retirement from the job of BHB Chairman (10 July 2004).

'Nothing will ever come near or be the same as race riding, but there's a great deal to life beyond race riding.' Retired champion jump jockey **Peter Scudamore**, August 2004.

'When I retire I'll always look back and feel privileged to have ridden against Scu, Dunwoody, McCoy, and to be mentioned in the same breath as them. If only, as Lorcan Wyer said, you could bottle that feeling of riding and unscrew it to get a little bit of the fizz whenever you wanted it.' **Mick Fitzgerald**, August 2004.

'I kept falling on it and sometimes I couldn't lift my right arm. They had to put quite a lot of metal in my shoulder to keep it together.' French jump jockey **Thierry Doumen**, partner of Baracouda and First Gold, announces his retirement, aged 25, on 11 August 2004, because of a shoulder injury.

'It would hardly be stretching things to say that many punters will be approaching the new jumps season with a lighter heart now that this fella will not be part of it.' The *Racing & Football Outlook* 'Off The Bit' **column** welcomes the news of Thierry Doumen's retirement from the saddle.

'I want a Kentucky Derby and ten English Derbys – then I'll get in my rocking chair.' So said 70-year-old trainer **Clive Brittain** in August 2004.

Red Rum.

'I did feel at one time that there was a vendetta against me among the stewards in the north.' **Mary Reveley**, thinking back as she retired in August 2004.

'I'm 65 going on 100 and it's time for my son Robert to take over.' Trainer **Terry Mills** in 2004.

'It is a known fact that trainers, stud owners and breeders do not retire – they just become increasingly more bad tempered and eccentric.' Author of *Equine Tax Planning*, **Julie Butler**.

'Retired jump jockeys to whom I spoke cited injury as the reason behind the end of their career and always attributed to others a loss of "bottle".' Anthropologist **Rebecca Cassidy** in her 2002 study of racing, *The Sport of Kings*.

'God told me it's an appropriate time to leave.' Aussie champion jockey **Darren Beadman**, announcing his decision to quit to become a minister of religion in August 1997.

'As a son you don't want to live in your father's shadow forever. I'm glad that I've had a chance to make a name for myself before he's retired.' **Ed Dunlop** on dad, John (*Guardian*, 2 October 2004).

'I've either skinted or killed my client list.' **Toby Balding** on the eve of retirement in November 2004. He added, 'I have spent my whole adult life playing with someone else's toys at their expense' (*Independent*, 5 November 2004).

'I ache for the life I was forced to leave behind.' Retired champion jockey, **Richard Dunwoody**. 'My lifestyle is good but it's as if I've been emasculated.'

Grey Mirage-Flower Child (Brother) is which horse's breeding?

'I was riding out one day and just got stuck on a horse and couldn't get off.' Scottish jockey **Iona Wands** who, after 52 winners, had to quit through back trouble in her late twenties and became a betting shop cashier in 2004.

'If he'd finished second we'd have stopped. I'd be farming by now, probably somewhere back towards Wales.' **Nigel Twiston-Davies** reveals how close he came to retirement at the 2002 Grand National won by Bindaree (*Independent*, 30 November 2004).

'I looked up and the winning post appeared to be about four miles away. I realised then it was time to hang up my riding boots.' **Lord Oakesey**'s last ride was on fourth-placed Kabayil at Ascot on 25 September 1992, a race won by Brough Scott on Kitaab, his final winner.

'I wanted to go out on a winner rather than on a stretcher.' **Ron Barry** quits after his 1984 Ayr winner on Final Argument.

'Listen, I'm going to tell you something now. You're at the top of the tree, you're leading the jockey's table, why don't you get out now? The Queen Mother doesn't want you to ride her novice chasers any more.' **Lord Abergavenny** to Royal jockey, Dick Francis in January 1957 when, aged 36, he was out injured with a damaged spleen. He quit.

'I had to fight with them and ended up getting a licence which was restricted to one ride a day. It was costing me money to ride – it was a joke!' **Jonothan Lower** on being diagnosed as an insulin-dependent diabetic in 1998 and being treated unsympathetically by the Jockey Club and left with no option but to quit the saddle. (*Racing Ahead*, December 2004).

Desert Orchid.

'To go on training until I die. I can't think of a better life.' **Bill Marshall**, 86, had no plans for retirement when he was asked in January 2005 about his future.

'Delight makes all of the one mind.' **Yeats**, in his poem 'At Galway Races', naming racecourses as the place where this happens.

'A bad day at the races is still better than a great day at the office.' Bookie **Gary Wiltshire** whose own 'bad' day came when he lost the best part of a million at Ascot on 'Frankie day'.

'The hell with this, fellas, I'm leaving.' Jockey **Eddie Arcaro** deciding to go for broke after half a mile of the 1941 Belmont Stakes on Whirlaway, who duly won by five and a half lengths to complete the Triple Crown.

'I'll be applying for two riding fees for that race.' Aussie jock **Andrew Payne** who, in January 1997, started a race aboard one mount only to be catapulted onto another in mid-race.

'The whip is out on Smarty Jones! It's been 26 years! One furlong away!' Racecourse commentator **Tom Durkin** as Smarty Jones came to win the 2004 Belmont Stakes to complete the US Triple Crown for the first time in over quarter of a century, only for outsider Birdstone to foil the late run by a length.

'Why do we do it? We do it because it's like falling in love. And as long as the joy exceeds, even marginally, the inevitable and unavoidable pain... I'll never stop. Never.' **Jamie Reid**, racing writer on his passion for the sport.

Archive-Bright Cherry (Knight of the Garter) is which horse's breeding?

Racing Calendar

Every racehorse becomes a year older on 1 January, but obviously this isn't his or her actual birthday, just the official one – only one horse ever won the Derby on his real birthday. That was Sailor on 18 May 1820. Many trainers and jockeys win big races on their birthdays, but no one knows why that might be – or at least they aren't admitting to it if they do.

Dates are important to racing and betting in many different ways. For example, 29 February may only come round every four years, but on that date in 1984, John Francome rode his 1,000th winner over the sticks in Britain; 1 May 1961 was the date when betting shops became legal and on 25 December 1753 The Godolphin, one of the three stallions from which all of today's thoroughbreds are descended, died.

Not a day goes by without some bon mot said about horse-racing, so it is appropriate to include a selection of interesting, amusing, significant, crazy and serious sayings for specific days of the year in a collection of quotes – otherwise you might never have known that it was on 5 May 1994 that Brough Scott declared, 'Newmarket is full of statues of naked horses but there's not one of Mistress Gwyn and her famous charms.' It would, 'opined the respected observer of the racing scene, 'jolly things up'. Or that on 30 April of the same year, then trainer Charlie Brooks gave a unique insight into his way of narrowing down a field of possible winners: 'I never back a horse being led round the paddock by a blonde stable girl.'

My favourite racing and betting date is 20 August 1980 when my eldest son, Steeven, was born. A friend referred to him as 'Sharpo' whereupon I observed that a horse of that name was running in a race sponsored by the company I worked for – so I backed it. It won at 3/1.

Arkle.

1 January 'The flat season began at Southwell on January 1 and it will not end until Wolverhampton closes proceedings on December 31.' *Racing Post* columnist **Tony Morris** could not get his head around the fact that the 2004 flat season featured 'several hundred' races run on the flat that did not count towards the flat jockey championship – 'The BHB [British Racing Board] should never have sanctioned this lie, and they had better outlaw it now, before a bogus champion is hailed.'

2 Jan 'Mostly unprintable.' How Irish trainer and prolific amateur rider **John Fowler**, born on this date in 1946, described his favourite recreations in the *Directory of the Turf*.

3 Jan 'And which sport are you involved in?' Jockey **Gee Armytage**, appearing on this date in 1988 on TV quiz programme *Sporting Triangles* vaguely recognised her fellow contestant – Manchester United and England skipper, Bryan Robson.

4 Jan 'They told me it was not a fast food store.' A suitably chastened **Frankie Dettori** after being cautioned while riding at Sha Tin in Hong Kong on this date in 1992, for – chewing gum.

5 Jan 'It will take a very, very good man to catch me. Plenty have tried, but I'm only in love with my horses at present.' Jockey turned trainer **Gay Kelleway**, who also said, 'Although I achieved several firsts, I never felt as if I was accepted as a jockey in the eyes of the public.' She saddled her first winner, Aberfoyle, at Lingfield on this date in 1993.

6 Jan 'If you lose a race it's a matter of passing the buck: the owner blames the trainer, the trainer blames the jockey, the jockey blames the poor old horse.' Sadly, Classic winning jockey **Tony Murray** had no one left to blame on this date in 1992 when he was found dead at his Wiltshire home aged just 41.

Never Bend-Milan Mill (Princequillo) is which horse's breeding?

7 Jan 'His large mutton-chop whiskers were the most striking features of an appearance over which he took little trouble; his clothes were generally old and shabby and he never wore a collar and tie if he could help it.' Even so, jockey **John Osborne**, born on this date in 1833, won all five Classics at least once each.

8 Jan 'In 1773 I could ride horses in a better manner than any person ever known… In 1775 I could train horses better than any person I ever yet saw.' So claimed the modest five-times Classic winning **Sam Chifney Sr**, who died on this day in 1807.

9 Jan 'He became, as some stallions do, quite savage in later years and towards the end of his life only George (Roth, his groom) could handle him.' **Ian Balding** on Mill Reef who, on this date in 1973, left his stables to stand at the National Stud.

10 Jan 'I know it sounds very grand but I think we might be the horseman's horseman.' Yes, trainer **Christian Wall**, born on this date in 1959, was sounding somewhat grand and, perhaps, pompous when using the Royal 'we' to describe his stable's training philosophy.

11 Jan 'It is not enough to say racing is a sport. We must all show sportsmanship,' declared Classic-winning owner **Sir David Robinson**, who died on this date in 1987, aged 82.

12 Jan 'If a racehorse could talk, one of the first things he'd tell his jockey would be "If you don't know where the bloody winning post is, I'm sure I don't."' Jockey **Harry Wragg**, who knew well enough where the post was to pass it in front in thirteen Classics, retired from training on this date in 1983.

Mill Reef.

13 Jan 'The racing fraternity consists very largely of a bunch of crooks out to relieve you of your money.' Few would disagree with this observation by **Mr Justice Melford Stevenson**, who was presiding at a court case on this date in 1967.

14 Jan 'Munro, if you don't win this race I'll kill you.' The somewhat unorthodox but unarguably clear instructions given to jockey Alan Munro – born on this date in 1967 – by owner **Sir Clement Freud**, as he saddled up on Nagnagnag at Lingfield in 1994. The threat failed, as Munro finished second, but survived.

15 Jan 'We think that as the trophy was won in the West Country it is probably at Windsor Castle.' **Alastair Aird**, the Queen Mother's representative admitted to *Sporting Life* that the Queen Mother had no idea where the trophy for the Lilo Lumb Handicap Chase, to be run for at Wincanton on this date in 1998, could be. She had won it in 1996 with Norman Conqueror and kept it for an extra year when the 1997 running was abandoned. It had to be run without the trophy present.

16 Jan 'Because it is Fibresand, people think it is a fluke. I don't.' Trainer **David Barron** in 1989 acclaiming Alex Greaves for becoming the leading jockey on Southwell's all-weather track.

18 Jan 'I just think it's a load of bollocks.' Richard Dunwoody's response (he was born on this date in 1964), when his riding abilities came in for criticism in 1994.

19 Jan 'It ain't right. I know I ain't did it.' The plaintive, and ignored, claim from jockey **Sylvester Carmouche**, who was banned for three months after being found guilty of hiding his mount, Landing Officer, in thick fog at Delta Downs, Louisiana, for a whole circuit of a mile race, before rejoining the race and winning by an impressive 24 lengths on this date in 1990.

Which is the bigger price – 6/5 or 11/8?

20 Jan 'Everyone thought I was a four-stone better jockey two minutes after the race than I was two minutes before it.' Former jump jockey **Graham Bradley** – who was fined £500 after dropping his hands at Ludlow on this date in 1988 – on the reaction to his brilliant ride on Morley Street to win the 1993 Martell Hurdle.

21 Jan 'Eating and cigars.' So declared jockey **Walter Wharton**, born on this day in 1959, when asked for his favourite recreations. Not, one hopes, at the same time.

22 Jan 'Once, Richard received a trophy for Michael at Longchamp while his brother was taking a shower.' Writer **Jonathan Powell** recalls a typical incident involving twin jockeys Michael and Richard Hills, born – both of them, oddly enough – on this date in 1963.

23 Jan 'Their back ends are similar,' answered owner **Tony Hill**, when asked why he named Ann Hill, who won on this date in 1993 at Lingfield, after his wife.

24 Jan 'The longer a young rider goes on without a winner, the better. Too much success early on and they begin to think their job's easy.' So the name of jump jockey **Hywel Davies'** first winner, Mr Know It All, on which he won at Fontwell on this date in 1977, was strangely appropriate . . .

25 Jan 'Many horses are fast but they don't all win races.' Deceptively simple homily from former jockey **Anthony Webber**, who rode his 200th winner, Applalto, at Leicester on this date in 1982.

26 Jan 'Sue Lawley explained that no other living creature is allowed... I opted for snorkelling equipment instead.' Refused his

choice of favourite horse, Sabin du Loir, as his luxury item when he appeared on *Desert Island Discs* in 1994, Champion jump jockey **Peter Scudamore** – who fell but remounted and went on to win in a race on this date in 1993 – opted instead for a more practical item.

27 Jan 'He only eats straight bananas.' So revealed **Chester Barnes**, born on this date in 1947, about his boss Martin Pipe's fussy dietary fads.

28 Jan 'When he was found by his owner, Jacques Van't Hart he was lying on a thin carpet of wet snow, a barely moving little black shape contrasting with the white background.' **Henrietta Knight** recalls this date in 1995 when future triple Gold Cup winner, Best Mate, was born in County Meath.

31 Jan 'We at Headline are so convinced that you will love John Francome's *Dead Weight* that we are offering to refund your money if you disagree with our guarantee.' ***Greatest Jockey's*** **publishers** came up with this no-lose offer for purchasers of his 2001 novel. It's too late to send back your second-hand/charity shop/boot sale copy and hope for a refund, though – the offer closed on 31 January 2002!

1 February 'I think we only had one eye between the two of us coming to the first two fences. Mine were tight shut.' Born on this date in 1914, **Ken Oliver**, perhaps Scotland's most successful trainer, recalls his debut victory, aged 21, on a one-eyed horse called Delman.

2 Feb 'I can't make a living out of the game any more,' declared 138 winning mounts jump jockey **Dale McKeown** upon retiring on this day in 1993, aged 28.

Funnily enough, who owned Grand National winner, Miinnehoma?

3 Feb 'It may have been the only time during his long career that Shoemaker was cheered for finishing out of the money on a favorite.' Writer **William Murray** was one of 65,000 present at Santa Anita on this date in 1990 for 'The Legend's Last Ride', the final race in which legendary jockey Bill Shoemaker, then 58, contested, finishing fourth on Patchy Groundfog.

5 Feb 'Slow.' For the first time in nine years, the **official going** at Lingfield was announced on this date in 1998 as something other than the usual 'Standard'.

6 Feb 'Do something about them or I will do it myself. It's happening all the time and I shouldn't have to put up with it.' Matters came to a head on this date in 1992 when Aussie jockey **Jim Cassidy** finally snapped and issued threats aimed at punters who he claimed had been giving him a hard time about losing on a string of short-priced favourites at Warwick Farm, Sydney.

11 Feb 'Doh!' The not recorded, but almost certainly relatively accurate quote from punter **Edward Hodson** from Wolverhampton who, on this date in 1984 landed a 5p yankee bet of a lifetime boasting world record odds of 3,956,748-1 – only to discover that his bookie had a £3,000 payout limit.

15 Feb 'In case of air raid the public is requested to act promptly on the instructions of the police. The presence of enemy aircraft in the vicinity will be notified to the public by short blasts on police whistles.' **Racecard notice** for Plumpton's meeting on this date in 1941.

20 Feb 'The success came as little surprise to Walwyn, who had backed the horse before Christmas.' In its 1991 obituary on this date of great jumps trainer Fulke Walwyn, 80, the ***Daily Telegraph*** demonstrated his shrewd awareness of the ability of his runners, including 50/1 1965 Champion Hurdle winner, Kirriemuir.

Freddie Starr.

25 Feb 'He is pretty irresponsible sometimes and too loud for the BBC.' **Clare Balding** on McCrirrick (*The Times*).

27 Feb 'Meet back at the weighing room after we've caught him.' This was the pessimistic advice given to connections of Last Suspect, before the off of the Grand National, which the 66/1 shot won. The advice was given by triple National-winning trainer **Tim Forster**, who was born this day in 1934.

28 Feb 'The Duke of Devon lost £1900 at a horse race at Newmarket,' recorded diarist **John Evelyn**. That amount would be a fair setback today – but how much must it have been worth on this day in 1699, which is when this happened?

1 March 'It is a very hard way to make easy money.' Pro punter **Dave Nevison**, once 'something in the city,' in the *Independent* on this date in 2000.

2 Mar 'Beating John Francome in a photo finish the day before my 21st birthday.' This was jump jockey **Lorna Vincent's** career high-light. She was born on this day in 1959.

3 Mar 'Contracting pneumonia on eve of intended association with equally unskilled partner in wartime novice chase at Plumpton,' was rated his, 'most fortuitous racing experience' by legendary commentator **Peter O'Sullevan**, whose birth date was today in 1918.

4 Mar 'His coup de grace came when he featured 7 of the 8 run-ners. Needless to say, the unmentioned nag, Rosgill, won at 9/1.' A **disgruntled reader** wrote to the *Daily Telegraph* in 1993 to com-plain about the tipping of top racing writer, Tony Stafford, who was born on this date in 1946.

Jumping first took place at Ascot in 1945, 1955 or 1965?

5 Mar 'Shall I, shan't I. Should this be my last ride as a jockey as he is my first winner as a trainer?' **Jimmy Frost**, four days a trainer, did quit riding on this date in 2002 after partnering Bohill Lad to win a hurdles race at Exeter.

7 Mar 'We rode to Farne race where I run against Sir Edmund Ashton, Mrs Morte, Mr Mackworth and Capt Warburton' noted the **anonymous diarist** of the *Chester Recorder* in 1691. The race was won by Mrs M and her mount.

10 Mar 'Now is the time to bet like men!' *Guardian* racing writer **Richard Baerlein** after Shergar won the 1981 Guardian Classic Trial. From 12/1 the horse's price shrunk to 10/11 pre-Derby as readers followed the advice, which Baerlein took himself – even naming his house Shergar. He died on this day in 1995, aged 84.

13 Mar 'He'll be useful if they give him a bit of time.' Jockey **Joe O'Gorman**, having won at Ayr on this date in 1989 on Panegyrist, who was getting his head in front after 38 unsuccessful attempts – at the age of 14.

16 Mar 'Some man. Some horse. Some day.' **Hugh McIlvanney** on this date in 1986, brilliantly and succinctly summing up the performances of Jonjo O'Neill on the great mare Dawn Run in the Cheltenham Gold Cup a couple of days earlier.

17 Mar 'This is my biggest ever bet. I am quietly confident of winning. If not I expect a rough ride when I face the wife because I never mentioned how much I was placing on Best Mate.' North Wales garage boss, **Mark Brilley**, admitting on this date in 2004 that his other half didn't know about the £20,000 bet he placed on Best Mate for the Cheltenham Gold Cup at 6/4. Luckily for Mark's marriage, the horse duly obliged next day.

1965.

18 Mar 'One of the greatest training feats I have seen in my life.' The much-respected **Fulke Walwyn** said this about Jane Pilkington's achievement in sending out 13-year-old Willie Wumpkins to win Cheltenham's Coral Golden Hurdle for the third consecutive year on this date in 1981.

19 Mar 'A Horse Race at Newmarket; at which the King (James I) tarrying too long in his Return from Newmarket, was forced to put in at an Inn at Wichfordbridge by reason of his being indisposed.' Recorded by **William Camden** in his *Annales*, about this date in 1619.

21 Mar 'They used to tie her to this wooden wheel and then some idiot with a blindfold on would throw knives at her.' **Frankie Dettori** explains his mother's circus job (*Sunday Times*, 21 March 2004.)

23 Mar 'In point of interest and attraction this race is second to none in the kingdom; it is a joyous and animating scene, and worthy of being paid a visit, not only by lovers of sport, but by those of the beau monde who delight in seeing and being seen, for the attendance is always numerous and fashionable.' A glowing testimonial in *Colburn's Kalendar of Amusements* for the 1840 Leamington Grand Steeple Chase, being run on this date.

24 Mar 'Brilliant Scobie Breasley! That was the spontaneous reaction after the veteran Australian had won the Lincoln Handicap.' *Sporting Life* reporter **Len Thomas** wrote this on this date in 1966. On 25 March 1965 he had written: 'Brilliant Scobie Breasley! That was the spontaneous reaction after the veteran Australian had won the Lincoln Handicap.' Thomas had wondered whether anyone would notice he had repeated himself! They did.

27 Mar 'Ironic that a race named "Initial Steeplechase" should have been the last.' Racing historian **Chris Pitt** on the last afternoon's racing ever at Bedford on this day in 1901.

Where was The Thinker's trainer Arthur Stephenson when the horse won the 1987 Cheltenham Gold Cup?

29 Mar 'I deeply regret the incident, and the adverse publicity it might have brought to the ceremony and to my profession. I was upset at Roger Marley's arrest and this unfortunately led to my own.' **Richard Dunwoody**, after he and Mr Marley had been arrested for disorderly behaviour hours after attending the Jockeys Association Awards in London on this date in 1993.

3 April 'They failed to accept my explanation and fined me the minimum.' Amateur rider **Simon Claisse**, who pulled up his mount Forest Musk in a race at Ashford Valley point-to-point on this date in 1999. He was found guilty of riding a non-trier – ironic as Jockey Club official Claisse's duties included advising stewards on how to watch out for non-triers.

4 Apr 'Here hapned a dispute upon the greatest point of Criticall learning that was ever known at Newmarket. A match between a horse of Sir Rob. Car's, and a gelding of Sir Rob. Geeres, for a mile and a halfe only, had engaged all the Court in many thousand pounds, much depending in so short a course to have them start fairly. Mr Griffin was appointed to start them. When he saw them equall he sayd Goe and presently he cried out Stay. One went off, and run through the Course and claims the money, the other never stird at all. Most possibly you may say that this was not a fayre starting, but the critics say after the word Goe was out of the mouth his commission was determined and it was illegal for him to say Stay.' Sadly **Lord Conway** does not record the verdict in this controversial 1682 race.

5 Apr 'The racing public had a picture in their minds of Walls in one of his typical Aldwych farce roles and found it impossible to take such an accomplished comedian quite seriously.' *History of The Derby Stakes* explains why comic cum trainer Tom Walls staggered the racing and entertainment worlds in 1932 when he saddled the 100/6 Derby winner – called April The Fifth, and foaled on that very date in 1929.

Hexham racecourse.

6 Apr 'This day there was a race at Sapley neere Huntingdon, invented by the gentlemen of that country (*sic*): at this Mr Oliver Cromwell's horse won the syluer (*sic*) bell and Mr Cromwell had the glory of the day.' A page from the 1602 diary of one **John Manningham**.

7 April 'Bookmakers are like leeches.' Trainer **Luca Mateo Cumani**, who was born on this day in 1949.

8 Apr 'He can safely be ignored, even in a race noted for shocks.' *Daily Express* pundit **Charles Benson** on Foinavon in his preview of the 1967 National. Foinavon won at 100/1.

13 Apr 'The bookmaking fraternity were represented by large numbers of their members; the Ethiopian serenader, the juggler and the professor of the three card trick were also present.' **Report** of the first Llanymynech (near Oswestry) steeplechase meeting in 1886.

15 Apr 'Mrs Jenny Pitman is one of the more unpleasant people I have met in racing and reminds me of a manatee who employs a blind milliner.' **Jeffrey Bernard**, perhaps not a fan, made this remark in the *Spectator* on this date in 1997.

16 Apr 'He got a pretty severe kicking, but he couldn't wait to get back into the weighing room to hear the end of the joke.' **Steve Smith Eccles** recalled the 1986 hurdles race at Cheltenham on this date when he and Jonjo O'Neill were cruising along comfortably enough for the former to begin telling an anecdote, only for Jonjo to take a tumble mid-yarn.

17 Apr 'We think this guy is the biggest single winner in the history of betting shops.' **Simon Clare** of Corals on an anonymous,

Racing at which Home Counties course began in 1890 with a jumps meeting?

51-year-old hotel worker from Poole in Dorset who, betting on the Tote Scoop 6, picked six winners on this date in 2004 and walked away with £878,939 for his £2 stake.

18 Apr 'John Higgins fractured a bone in his left leg in a fall from Mrs Higgins on Monday,' reported the **Sporting Life** on this date in 1977, presumably referring to a racecourse rather than bedroom accident for the jockey.

19 Apr 'It's not good day, it's good bye.' The reported farewell message by jockey **Mick Williams** as he set off to Kelso to partner Master William in the Roxburghe Chase on this date in 1909. Williams had had a premonition that Kelso was unlucky for him – he and the horse were both killed during the race.

21 Apr 'That was a brilliant piece of training. I don't know why I've got empty boxes back home at Newmarket.' Jump jockey turned flat trainer **Paul Kelleway**, who died aged 58 on this date in 1999, to the press in the winners' enclosure after one of his representatives came back triumphantly.

22 Apr 'That's it lads, I'm finished.' **Walter Swinburn** announcing his retirement from the saddle on 22 April 2000.

23 Apr 'He fought 38 bouts as a middleweight club fighter, winning 23 of them, 15 by knockout.' His entry in the New York Racing Association media guide suggests you'd do well not to argue with trainer **Peter Vestal**, who was born on this date in 1951.

24 Apr 'My overwhelming feeling on passing the post was one of relief.' **Pat Eddery**, for whom Alvaro's win at Epsom on this date in 1969 was his first ever, at the tender age of 17.

Lingfield.

25 Apr 'Their move was scandalous and an insult to the public' stormed the *Sporting Life* this day in 1989 when Another Clem won the 5.45 at Punchestown but no one could back him – after bookmakers' clerks, tote staff and the official timekeeper all went on strike, objecting to the eight racecard ending so late.

28 Apr 'When you go out to ride him you don't feel you're going out to ride a horse; it feels like you're going to meet one of your old mates for a pint.' Which is how so many racegoers felt about the gallant stayer, Persian Punch, whose rider **Martin Dwyer** had paid tribute to him in this way and who, on this day in 2004, died at the end of his race at Ascot. I was there and the eerie silence that surrounded the course as Persian Punch breathed his last was very moving.

29 Apr 'I was too small to become a window cleaner and too big to be a garden gnome.' **Adrian Maguire's** explanation for why he became a jockey – he was born on this date in 1971.

2 May 'Ten stall urinals, six wc's and three hand basins all for seven nicker, but then, to the connoisseur, racing at Wye was always a bargain.' The ***Sporting Life*** commenting on the sale of ablutions from Wye racecourse, which staged its final meeting on this date in 1974.

3 May 'Eclipse first, the rest nowhere.' One of racing's most famous quotes was instigated on this date in 1769 when the legendary Eclipse made his racecourse debut at Epsom with his professional gambler owner, **Dennis O'Kelly**, using the phrase to strike a bet. Eclipse had to win so easily that the vanquished runners would be too far behind even to be officially placed. The bet was duly landed.

Which was England's first enclosed racecourse?

4 May 'By his skill, consistency and longevity in the saddle, and his strength of character out of it, he brought more credit to his profession than any other jockey has ever done.' Turf historians **John Randall** and **Tony Morris** in the *A Century of Champions*, in which Sir Gordon Richards, born on this day in 1904, was declared Jockey of the Century, beating Lester Piggott into second.

7 May 'When Lord Glasgow died in 1869 he made tacit acknowledgement of the wrong he had done Aldcroft by leaving him £500.' *Biographical Encyclopaedia of British Flat Racing* **comment** about jockey Thomas Aldcroft, who rode General Peel to win the 1864 2,000 Guineas for owner Lord Glasgow – who later accused him erroneously of dodgy dealings. Aldcroft died on this date in 1883.

8 May 'The stewards did not exchange hats, nor did the bookmakers pay out any bonuses.' So noted a **contemporary report** of this date's 1,000 Guineas day at Newmarket in 1945, which coincided with VE Day.

10 May 'I still think I lost – but I'm gonna take the money anyway.' The reaction of US trainer **Gary Jones** on this date in 1992 after the horse he had brought over to England, Kostroma, was awarded the race in a photo finish.

12 May 'I'm afraid my luck is beginning to run out.' **Prince Aly Khan** when his Sheshoon stumbled and lost a race at Longchamp when he had looked like a sure winner. Just four days later, on this date in 1960, the great owner was killed in a Paris car crash.

16 May 'Hang me, you see I won, that's enough for you!' Jockey **William Clift**, who won the 1793 Derby on Wray on this day in 1793 was an irascible type who once dismissed a query from the Duke of Dorset, for whom he had just ridden a winner, with the phrase mentioned here.

Sandown.

17 May 'I never dreamed the old boy would go so quickly.' **Charles Howard**, owner, on hearing the news that America's favourite horse, Seabiscuit, had died on the morning of this date in 1947, little dreaming that the story of the brave horse would win the William Hill Sports Book of the Year in 2001 and become the subject of an Oscar-nominated movie.

19 May 'I don't care how he dresses. He's a good enough jockey for me.' **Sir John Hawley** - whose Beadsman was ridden to victory on this date in the 1858 Derby by John Wells, a flamboyant chap known to ride out 'in an Alpine hat with several feathers, a suit of clothes made from a Gordon plaid and a pair of red morocco slippers.

18 May 'Whatever beats me will win.' **John Francome** in 1985 before a race at Warwick in which he rode Shangoseer and Lester Piggott rode Liquidator. Francome was spot on as Piggott won the two-horse flat race.

21 May 'Depend on it, that Eleanor is a hell of a mare' gasped **Mr Cox**, trainer of the horse of that name, as he lay dying, shortly before the horse became the first of her sex to win the Derby on this day in 1801. The first death-bed tip, perhaps?

22 May 'We can but deeply deplore the blackguardism which, once a year, has been allowed to establish its saturnalia in the quiet village of Harpenden.' The ravings of **The Hertfordshire Advertiser** of this date in 1857 suggest that the race meeting at Harpenden was a lively affair.

25 May 'Training with the St Helens rugby team,' answered jockey **Julie Bowker**, when asked for her favourite recreation. She rode her first winner, Misha, at Doncaster on this day in 1985.

All were born on 7 April but which trainer is the oldest? Luca Cumani, Colin Tinkler or Mark Tompkins?

26 May 'A poor wretch was detected picking a gentleman's pocket at Epsom Races, and was so severely ducked, that he could not have escaped with his life, but for the interposition of his R H the Duke of Cumberland, who displayed upon this occasion a humanity that must endear him to all considerate Englishmen.' From the **Morning Chronicle** of this date in 1773.

28 May 'Because Sir Bevys was the hero of one of my early poems,' beamed poet laureate **Alfred Tennyson** explaining why he staked £5 on the horse of that name –who was the 20/1 winner of The Derby, the 100th running, on this date in 1879.

29 May 'All persons are desired to keep their dogs at home; and if any be found upon the Race-ground, it is hoped the Populace will destroy them.' Doggone harsh warning in the **racecard** for this day's 1777 Silver Cup meeting at Sheffield & Rotherham.

30 May 'In case of no claimants, then the money, for that year only, to be paid by the trustees to the winner of the next Town Plate.' Part of the extraordinary Will of **John Perran** of Newmarket, dated 30 May 1772, which left £21 to be given each year either to a parishioner of the local All Saints church who should be wed on the Thursday in Easter Week – or donated to the purse for the big race! 'The money had not been claimed above 20 times in the last thirty years,' it was reported in 1837.

1 June 'I now regret that decision,' reflected **John Francome**, ten years after he had, on this date in 1982, ridden his 120th winner of the season, to level with the injured Peter Scudamore. Francome then quit for the season to share the title.

2 June 'He's the best I've ever sat on.' **Pat Eddery** had had a few to choose from, although not all were Derby winners, like Golden Fleece was on this day in 1982. The horse was trained by Vincent O'Brien and owned by Robert Sangster.

Luca Cumani.

5 June 'Not having won the Derby is beginning to get to me.' **Frankie Dettori** on 5 June 2004, shortly before he failed again to ride the winner.

8 June 'Little fish are sweet.' The career-long motto of the dual-purpose trainer **William Arthur Stephenson**, whose The Thinker won the 1987 Cheltenham Gold Cup, and who on this date in 1946 sent out his first winner as a trainer when he also rode T.O.D. to win at Hexham.

9 June 'With his face lined like a map of hard roads travelled, his capacity for pulverising put-downs and the inspired audacity of his jockeyship, he became one of the most magical presences in sport over the last fifty years.' On this date in 1991, **Hugh McIlvanney** summed up the essence of Lester Piggott.

12 June 'A purse of 30 guineas was run for weight 12st, 3 guineas entrance, and won by Lord Molyneaux's Bay Gelding, Tickle Me Quickly.' This happened, according to **John Cheny's** *An Historical List of Horse Matches Run*, at Oswestry in Shropshire on this day in 1729.

18 June 'I heard Walter scream at me on the home turn and I couldn't see what had happened. I thought perhaps I had pulled out in front of him.' In fact, Swinburn was warning **Frankie Dettori** that his horse, Arcadian Heights, was trying to take a chunk out of the Italian's rear end during the 1992 Ascot Gold Cup.

20 June 'Now coming to his best.' The optimistic claim included on this date in 1967 in the **prospectus** for the sale of a half share in the shock 100/1 winner of the Grand National, Foinavon – possibly the least illustrious winner ever of the race.

Major Dick Hern was born in Devon, Dorset or Somerset?

21 June 'Who was the last jockey to ride in two Derbys without getting round in either?' **Ray Cochrane**, after his mount Green Foot was left in a closed stall as the rest of the field set off in the 1992 Austrian Derby – just days after Cochrane's mount Young Señor was withdrawn from the Epsom equivalent for refusing to enter the stalls.

23 June 'There was a very extraordinary horse race between a six year old horse and one aged twenty one. They ran 14 miles round the said course and performed it in 39 minutes for 100 guineas – which were won by the former by only a horse's length. There were great wagers laid and the greatest concourse of people ever seen there.' This event was held on this date in 1744 at Lincoln, reported the **Westminster Journal**.

25 June 'Don't be ****ing silly. I've got to go out there and earn my £14 riding fee in the next race.' **Lester Piggott's** reported remark to the course doctor at Leopardstown on this date in 1977 where he had already won the Irish Derby on The Minstrel before falling from Glencoe Lights when his stirrup broke, after which he was advised to give up his remaining rides.

1 July 'A day at the races cost the Queen £11,843 last year – the amount charged by Railtrack to take the Royal train 21 miles from Victoria to Tattenham Corner for the Derby. The cost of £564 per mile compares unfavourably to the normal day return fare of £10.' **Alan Hamilton** (*The Times*, 1 July 1998)

9 July 'I've never known anything like it,' said jockey **Mark Birch** after his mount in a Ripon race on this date in 1990, Bescaby Boy, clashed heads with Ernie Johnson's charge, It's Me, drawing blood on the race to the line. Following the inevitable steward's inquiry, Birch's horse was given the race.

Somerset.

10 July 'I suddenly thought, it's all daftness. It was getting out of hand.' Jockey **Phil Tuck** in 1988, denouncing all the superstitions that had previously blighted his life, such as wearing the same holey socks, the same tattered T-shirt, using the same pin, saluting magpies – even naming his house The Magpies. He was born on this date in 1956.

11 July 'The prevalence of superstition in the racing world is irritating, not endearing. Superstition is another word for stupidity.' **John Randall** dismisses the treasured idiosyncracies of so many in racing in the *Racing Post* in 2004.

12 July 'The hardest thing was the changing room – it was mixed, with no curtains, so everybody could see in. There was one toilet cubicle and a couple of showers, but they were mixed as well. It was an uncomfortable experience.' Nonetheless amateur rider **Charlotte Towsley** made history on Sunday, 4 July 2004 when she won at Warsaw to become the first British woman to ride a winner in Poland.

17 July 'I obviously feel let down to some extent,' observed **Michael Hills** philosophically, on this date in 1990, having just been sacked as stable jockey by his father, trainer Barry Hills.

20 July 'I don't want it to stop now, it would be like retiring from breathing.' So 70-year-old trainer **Clive Brittain** scuppered retirement rumours on this date in 2004.

21 July 'This morning I galloped 12 horses. When I got done I went home and cleaned tomatoes and juiced a dozen quarts. And tonight I'll go dancing.' **R A 'Cowboy' Jones** elaborates on the 2004 day on which the 61-year-old rode Jarrett to win the first race at Ellis Park, Kentucky – meaning that he had ridden a race at the track in each of the last six decades.

Trainer Ian Balding was born in New Jersey, New York or New Zealand?

22 July 'The horse started at 16/1 only because she's married to me.' Radio 5 Live pundit and former jockey **Luke Harvey** after his trainer wife Georgina won at Bath with Tight Circle in 2004.

24 July 'I have lived here for 18 years and the British people have taken me to their hearts as if I was one of them.' One of, what precisely? No, we know what **Frankie Dettori** meant as he celebrated his 2,000th winner at Ascot in July 2004.

25 July 'Sorry, I ballsed up'. **Darryll Holland** apologises to trainer Michael Bell after failing to get a run on Glorious Goodwood 2004 odds-on favourite Sacred Nuts – who would have been called Goldenballs had the authorities not vetoed the name.

27 July 'I think Barney Curley would have been a better name for him!' declared **Luca Cumani**, after his Mephisto [by Machiavellian out of Cunning] won at Goodwood's 2004 'Glorious' meeting.

28 July 'I have done a lot of horses before, but not many racehorses,' said artist **Andrew Baynes** in 2004, hard at work at a site near Goodwood's Richmond Enclosure, sculpting Persian Punch, kneeling, full size, in, er, ten tons of sand.

29 July 'He had it in his head that the start was at 5.30pm,' reported **Michael Clower** in the *Racing Post* of starter Peter McGouran at the 2004 Galway Festival, which was unfortunate for those wanting a bet in the Guinness Handicap, which went off at 5.31 p.m instead of its advertised 5.35 p.m.

31 July 'The crying shame is that he's imprisoned in a body two sizes too big for flat racing.' **Tom O'Ryan** on the talented but over 6ft tall Keith Dalgleish – who failed to turn up for four booked rides at Hamilton sparking reports that weight problems had forced his retirement, aged just 21, in 2004.

New Jersey.

1 August 'The first people were here at 7.15 a.m.' reported clerk of the course **Ed Stretton** of the 2004 Chester Sunday meeting, which attracted a record crowd of 46,137 and began at 2.20 p.m.

3 Aug 'Fast youths, fancy men, gamblers, blacklegs and women of easy virtue.' The reasons listed by **The Airdrie & Coatbridge Advertiser** on this date in 1861, for banning the annual race fixture at Airdrie.

4 Aug Twice Nightly finished ninth at Newcastle on this date in 2004. Owner and TV's *Countdown* presenter, **Richard Whiteley**, explained that Terry Wogan had named the horse on the basis of Whiteley's daily double stint on the C4 show and Yorkshire TV's Calendar, but Richard added: 'That's the official explanation – if others want to read in other reasons for it, they can!'

7 Aug 'Surprisingly, considering Dettori's record at the course, there was not a single bet of three figures or more seen for the winner.' Frankie gained his first Shergar Cup winner during the 2004 running of the event at Ascot when 10/1 shot Justaquestion came from last to first – but, said ring reporter **Kel Mansfield**, his fans seemed reluctant to back him with big bucks.

8 Aug 'He has stabled a handful of his lovers in lavish houses around the world and visited them in turn, for days or weeks at a time, in the same way that a champion stallion is taken to cover beautifully bred mares.' Some might say, 'nice work if you can get it,' in response to this 2004 *Sunday Telegraph* **revelation** about wealthy owner and trainer Ivan Allan.

9 Aug 'I have a three year old gelding by Mtoto… He has big honest eyes, a lovely countenance and a very friendly demeanour. I had to hold him for an hour the other day while another horse was being treated. He was so patient I'm going to call him Alec.'

What is the first name of US trainer D Wayne Lukas – Darrell, Darren or Darius?

Charlie Brooks pays a quirky tribute to trainer of Mtoto, Alec Stewart, who had just died tragically of cancer aged 49 in 2004.

10 Aug 'Dr Arbuthnot, the Queen's favourite physician, went out with me to see a place they have made for a famous horse race tomorrow, where the Queen will come.' So wrote **Jonathan Swift** in his 1711 diary. The 'place' was Ascot, the Queen, Anne.

11 Aug 'We'd love to hear from any single men who want an evening to remember on Saturday.' **Gabrielle de Brie** of Rapid Romance, organisers of the first ever speed-dating session to be held at a racecourse, Goodwood, in 2004.

12 Aug 'I've got the worst bunch of two year olds I've ever had. I was hoping something was wrong with them but we had them tested and the only thing wrong with them is that they are slow.' **Mick Channon**, mistaking his swans for geese on this date.

13 Aug 'The meeting was originally scheduled for May 3, but that was lost through waterlogging. So it was rearranged to this meeting which was again waterlogged.' Newcastle commercial manager **Kay Forster** about the second waterlogging abandonment of their 2004 charity meeting in aid of, er, Water Aid, which is dedicated to the provision of safe domestic water to the world's poorest countries!

16 Aug 'We want to make sure that nothing untoward happened.' The **Jockey Club**, after a massive 2004 gamble saw Exponential, offered at 280/1 on the exchanges, 100/1 in the early bird market, but starting at 8/1, win on his second appearance – having finished last first time out. Bookies reported three-figure bets at three-figure odds for the Stuart Williams-trained, David Allan-ridden two-year-old that cost bookies hundreds of thousands – at least.

Darrell.

17 Aug 'Few sons exceed the achievements of famous fathers in the same field, but Frankie has managed that rare trick and, by the beam on Gianfranco's face he is one proud dad.' **Alastair Down** marvels at another Frankie Dettori feat as, in front of his ex-champion jockey father, he won York's 2004 Juddmonte International on 3/1 shot Sulamani.

18 Aug 'The first time in 25 years.' **Robert Sangster**, quantifying how many times Lester Piggott had previously done what he did before riding Rodrigo De Triano to win York's Juddmonte International on this date in 1992 – which was to ask for advice on how to ride the horse.

19 Aug 'It's like making love, luv!' An excited **David Nicholls** after his nine-year-old Bahamian Pirate became the oldest horse to win a Group One in Britain with the 2004 Nunthorpe Stakes at York.

20 Aug 'A good jockey by profession rather than a brilliant horseman by intuition.' **Anonymous** contemporary assessment of Elnathan Flatman, the first-ever champion jockey, in 1846, and on six other occasions, who died on this date in 1860.

21 Aug 'It's Variety Club day at Sandown when people who once graced many a black and white TV set are wheeled out in front of a baffled public… All for a great cause, of course, but I'd bet 1–10 any racegoer under the age of 50 has no chance of recognising any of the celebrities.' **Richard Birch** of the *Racing Post* was underwhelmed by the charitable delights of the 2004 meeting.

22 Aug 'I danced with the devil and got burned – twice.' Jockey **Dean Gallagher**, twice suspended for drug use, after surprisingly being given the chance to resuscitate his career in 2004 after François Doumen invited him to succeed his son, Thierry, as stable jockey.

Lester Piggot rode Sandal to win at Newmarket on 28 April 1972. It was which trainer's first winner?

23 Aug 'He's disappointed us more times than the late Rock Hudson disappointed women.' What *could* trainer **Ian Semple** have meant after his Templet won a Hamilton maiden in 2004?

24 Aug 'The ground has been laid out in accordance with the latest ideas, with the result that the course is one of the finest and most completely adapted for racing purposes in all England.' If Hull's racecourse was so good on this date in 1888, according to the local *Express*, it seems odd that it did not survive beyond 1909.

26 Aug 'Rather than go on holiday to Spain or France, we went to Thirsk or Ripon.' Eight-year-old Jamie Thomas from Cardiff was at Musselburgh on this date in 2004 – visiting the last of Britain's 59 racecourses that he and his father Tony had been to during a 'pilgrimage', which began when Jamie was three months old and taken to Hereford. 'I don't drive so we've done them all by bus and train,' added Tony.

27 Aug 'Sacred to the memory of Leopardstown – finally and brutally strangled at birth by gross incompetence, bungling and mismanagement – August 27 1888.' Spoof obituary published by an **Irish sporting paper** after the new course's first meeting was bedevilled by problems that threatened to make it also the last.

28 Aug 'This is the last evening meeting of the year at Redcar. But we're going out with a bang because this is Ladies Night.' **Peter Naughton** welcoming TV viewers to the final 2004 twilight action.

29 Aug 'I'm calling the ground as it is, and bugger convention.' Gowran clerk of the course **Paddy Graffin** is defiant after the Turf Club picked him up over describing the going as 'good to soft' rather than the traditional, Irish, 'yielding', for what the *Racing Post* described as, 'what could well be the first time on an Irish racecourse'.

Michael Stoute.

30 Aug 'This is the first time two Irish horses have run against each other in England with no English horse in the race in National Hunt history.' County Tyrone trainer **J J Lambe** after his Caislean Ui Cuain beat stable mate Zurs in a novice chase at Cartmel on this day in 2004.

31 Aug 'It feels like a bag of marbles.' The words uttered by vet **Barry Williams** as he examined the suspected broken leg of Derby and Arc winner Mill Reef on this date in 1972.

1 September 'They picked me up before five in the morning and let me out at seven in the evening. I spent most of those hours in a cell and it was pretty unpleasant. They made sure I felt like a criminal.' Champion jockey **Kieren Fallon** told *The Times* how it felt to be one of three jockeys, one trainer and a dozen others arrested as part of a race-fixing investigation on this day in 2004.

4 Sept 'Oh, yes – he has no balls, so he definitely will.' Trainer **Tim Easterby** confirming that his Somnus, winner of the Sprint Cup at Haydock in 2003 and runner-up on this date in 2004 would be back for another tilt in 2005.

5 Sept 'That's total bollocks.' On this date in 2004 trainer **David Nicholson** did not agree with Cheltenham MD Edward Gillespie, who justified a change of name for the Festival's Stayers Hurdle because, 'we always thought the word stayers implied plodders'.

6 Sept 'A plate as has been usual will be run for on Langton Wolds, near Malton, and another on the Thursday, according to articles.' The *London Gazette* **advertisement** for a 1692 meeting taking place on this date.

What is Jenny Pitman's middle name?

7 Sept 'Since Richards had none, and he was riding for J C Waugh, a W was inserted.' **Gordon Richards**, born on this date in 1930, was gifted his middle initial, having none of his own, in order to differentiate him from namesake and prolific flat champion, Gordon Richards. GWR died in October 1998 and this story was reported in his *Daily Telegraph* obituary.

8 Sept 'That place wanted bombing. It still amazes me how horses used to race round there, ridiculous really. There's no way I'd be calling for it to reopen, it wants to stay closed. It was dangerous, it wasn't good for horse or rider, they were always falling over.' Unlike John McCririck, **Willie Carson** was no fan of 'The Frying Pan' track at Alexandra Park, which was closed on this date in 1970. Big Mac, by contrast, yearns, 'My greatest ambition in life is for somebody to come along with £20m to revive Alex.'

9 Sept 'In general, racing is clean. I said that when I started 12 months ago. I stand by that...but there are a core of people who are trying to cheat. I'm putting structures in place to catch those people; either catch them or persuade them not to do what they are doing. I'm talking about people both inside and outside racing.' Jockey Club head of security **Paul Scotney** on BBC Five Live's *Sport on Five* on this date in 2004.

10 Sept 'Unable to sanction National Hunt racing,' declared a **government announcement** on this date in 1942, suspending the sport until January 1945.

11 Sept 'You need to be a horseman as well as a jockey over here,' reflected 23-year-old Australian jockey **Kerrin McEvoy**, who arrived in England as second jockey to the Godolphin stable at the beginning of the season in 2004. On this date he won his first Classic, the St Leger, on 3/1 joint favourite, Rule Of Law. His response: 'This is heaven! Winning a Classic in a foreign country has to be the tops.' Whether he knew why they followed

Susan.

a long-standing tradition of shoving a baggy cap on his head immediately afterwards is another matter!

13 Sept 'In the post parade he suddenly stopped, turned towards the Tote board and just stared. It was as though he was reading the odds on him and couldn't believe it. Then he turned squarely around, faced the stands and stared at the people. He really brought down the house.' Jockey **Jerry Lambert** remembering one of the last races run by Native Diver, the first Californian equine prize money millionaire who won 37 of 81 starts and died on this date in 1967.

14 Sept 'I thought it was a terrible track. The pull up wasn't much good, there was no rail to ease the horse after the finish. If you were on a real puller you went down the hill and finished up by Lewes prison. And, thinking back, I know one or two jockeys who should have been in it.' **Willie Snaith** rode at Lewes when it staged its final meeting on this date in 1964.

16 Sept 'What! Ride such a cripple as that?' This was the reported comment of jockey **John Jackson**, who also burst into tears upon learning that he had been handed the ride on 200/1 no-hoper Theodore in the 1822 St Leger – which they then won on this date, landing for one optimistic punter a bet of '£1000 to a walking stick'.

17 Sept 'The result was expressed to Manchester by J Richardson, Junior in the short space of 2 hours and 20 minutes!' boasted the *Yorkshire Gazette* after the named messenger had travelled the 58 miles, including two of them on foot, to relay the result of this day's 1836 St Leger.

18 Sept 'We are happy to say this gay scene was attended with only two accidents. Lord Macartney's groom in running had his

When training Jack Berry always wore what colour shirt – blue, white or red?

left leg broke from his horse falling. And Mr Maxwell, his lord-ship's secretary, had a narrow escape of his life, having tumbled into a pond, coming from the Ball.' The *London Morning Chronicle* **report** of an early race meeting in Cape Town on this date in 1797.

19 Sept 'Most men lack courage when they have to tell their wives something, so I said, 'I've bought you a racehorse, darling. That went down like a lead balloon.' **Sir Stanley Clarke**, who died on this date in 2004 aged 71, explained how he broke the news that he was going into racing. He became a trainer from 1961–6 but became better known when he eventually took over the running of nine racecourses, which he floated on the Stock Exchange in October 2003 as Northern Racing.

21 Sept 'The world record for the most number of people in a Mini is 21, so it's a shade disappointing that, at Chester, only 16 jock-eys could be squeezed into one.' **Marcus Armytage**, reporting on a failed record attempt on behalf of charity on this date in 2004, adding, 'For Franny Norton, it was quite an ordeal – he's claustro-phobic – so he had the boot to himself.'

22 Sept 'Sorry, love, but there's a big meeting at Goodwin (*sic*) today. We ordered 63 copies but they didn't send any.' Response by **WH Smith shop assistant** when I tried, but failed, to buy a *Racing Post* at Victoria Station on this date in 2004.

23 Sept 'There is a move to stamp out the tradition that stretches back 50 years. In the belief that parents are the beneficiaries, it is being cited as cruelty to children and police are being encouraged to take action.' **Rodney Masters** on this date in 2004, on the prac-tice of youngsters standing in the River Feale near Listowel race-course, begging for racegoers to 'throw me down sumtin, mister'.

Red.

24 Sept 'It must have wedged in her foot,' explained jockey **Michael Wigham** after his mount Pas De Reef was brought down during a race at Hamilton on this date in 1990 – by a golf ball straying onto the track from the adjacent golf course.

25 Sept 'If he was human he'd be having serious medication for schizophrenia.' **Alastair Down** on Rakti, winner on this date in 2004 of Ascot's Queen Elizabeth II Stakes. He was known to his trainer Michael Jarvis as a 'horse of moods'.

26 Sept 'Since I was 21 I have been drunk almost every night; I never sold a race, and I never kissed a lass against her will.' The reported last words on this day in 1848 of 50-year-old jockey **Bill Scott**, rider of 19 Classic winners. Of the three claims the middle one was the most controversial!

28 Sept 'I'm just warming up – is there any more racing? **Frankie Dettori** after riding all seven winners at Ascot on this date in 1996 and almost putting the bookmaking industry out of business single-handedly as they had to shell out £40 million to winning punters.

30 Sept 'Buy a new Rolls Royce – mine is getting on a bit.' What **George Rhodes** of Aldershot told me in 1984 he would be doing with the £86,056.42 he had just won after landing world-record odds of 1,670,759/1 for his 5p ITV bet.

2 October 'She's the best horse I've ever trained – there's no shadow of a doubt.' Praise indeed on this day in 2004 by **Mark Johnston** for his talented first-ever 1,000 Guinea double winner Attraction, which had just won the Sun Chariot Stakes at 11/4.

3 Oct 'James Willoughby poured cold water on it, but I should know my horses better than he does. He is the best I have trained.'

Why was the 1955 Royal Ascot postponed for a month?

Jubilant trainer **Jonathan Pease** celebrates with a swipe at the *Racing Post* writer, after his Bago won the Arc de Triomphe on this date in 2004.

5 Oct 'Arazi is not just the best horse I have ever owned – he's the best horse anyone has ever owned.' So claimed **Allen Paulson** after the colt had won for the sixth successive time in the 1991 Grand Criterium at Longchamp. He would be proved not far wrong.

6 Oct 'He was like a father to me... Without him I probably wouldn't still be in the game – he was always there when I went off the rails.' **Kieren Fallon** paid tribute to Gold Cup-winning trainer Jimmy Fitzgerald who died on this date in 2004, aged 69. Fellow handler Kim Bailey said of him, 'When the money was down, Fitzgerald's horses didn't get beaten.'

11 Oct 'The transformation whereby Nearly-man became Been-everywhere-man took place on Monday.' **Sir Clement Freud**, celebrating the fact that on this date in 2004 he visited Irish racecourse, Roscommon, thus having visited every racecourse in Britain and Ireland.

12 Oct 'He surrendered dignity and respect by confronting photographers who were merely doing their job.' *The Times* racing writer **Alan Lee** on Kieren Fallon who, on this day in 2004, was unable to resume riding at Leicester less than 24 hours after a fall the day before that had left him battered and bruised. Nevertheless he decided to take out the frustrations of that and other situations which had dogged him all season on the assembled snappers. On the same day, with Dettori 14 winners ahead of Fallon and just 24 racing days of the season left, Ladbrokes decided to pay out on the Italian – 'It's all over as far as we're concerned, and punters can form an orderly queue,' said their spokesman Michael Dillon.

A railway strike.

13 Oct 'The French have always done the Breeders' Cup well... Their horses don't bust their guts in midsummer the way ours still do.' **Paul Haigh** on this date in 2004.

14 Oct 'I know some of the jockeys can't wait to get skating.' On this date in 2004 Lingfield racecourse's Marketing and PR Manager **Kate Hills** announced that the track would boast a 'customised, undercover ice rink' for six weeks between late November 2004 and early January 2005.

15 Oct 'Are you worried about Lester's return?' **Walter Swinburn** was asked on this day in 1990, which saw the return to the saddle of L Piggott five years after his retirement. Swinburn had just ridden five winners that afternoon at Leicester. He wasn't worried.

16 Oct 'I've got beaten on some great horses in the Champion – Daylami, Halling, Noverre, Best of the Bests – I don't even want to remember them.' **Frankie Dettori** before racing at Newmarket's Champions' Day on this date in 2004. Before racing began he had failed ever to win the Dewhurst, the Cesarewitch and the Champion Stakes. By the end of the afternoon he still hadn't won any one of those three races.

17 Oct 'Put it this way, I think I've got more championships left in me than Frankie. Frankie knows he's got a gift this year.' Extraordinarily ungracious admission of defeat by **Kieren Fallon**, quoted in the *Sunday Times* on this day in October 2004, admitting that Frankie Dettori would be taking his flat jockey championship from him. He also told the paper's Andrew Longmore, 'A lot of people didn't want me to be champion. I was getting silly little suspensions and Frankie was getting away with a lot.'

18 Oct 'I think granddad planned this. I think my granddad is riding Red Rum again up there. It's no accident that they died on the

In how many races did Desert Orchid run before winning – 0, 4 or 6?

same day.' On this date in 1995 Red Rum, legendary triple Grand National winner, died. On the same day in 2004 his devoted lad, Jackie Grainger, died, aged 84. His granddaughter, **Joanne Thisleton** was in no doubt that this was more than coincidence.

21 Oct 'If Chifney were suffered to ride the Prince's horses, no gentleman would start against him,' the Prince of Wales was told after a **stewards' inquiry** was held when, on this date in 1791, the Prince's Escape, partnered by Chifney, won at decent odds at Newmarket, having been beaten the day before when favourite. The Prince elected to stand by his rider and refused ever to race at Newmarket again.

23 Oct 'Because of a spillage of aviation fuel on the course.' Unusual **official explanation** for the abandonment of racing at Newbury in 1992 after a light aircraft crashed – without casualties – onto the flat course.

24 Oct 'It is surprising to think what a height this spirit of horse-racing is now arrived at in this kingdom, where there is scarce a village so mean that has not a bit of plate raised once a year for the purpose.' *The Post* reported on the spread of racing on this day in 1776.

25 Oct 'I gotta horse.' The trademark shout of flamboyant, Abyssinian, racecourse tipster **Prince Monolulu**, the John McCririck of his day, remembered on what would have been his 111th birthday in 1992 at a pub bearing his name in Maple Street, London.

26 Oct 'For a cost of £2.70 for a ten day listing, it is a bit cheaper than Tattersalls.' On this day in 2004, Newmarket-based blood-stock agent **Rick Dale** explained why he had put Rae Guest-trained three-year-old winning filly Magic Verse up for sale at

£10,000 on the Internet auction site eBay. The horse wasn't sold, though – eBay removed it after declaring that the site prohibits the sale of live animals.

28 Oct 'The sort of horse who would much rather sit at home watching daytime television than compete in a three and a half mile handicap chase around Stratford,' is how reporter **Lee Mottershead** described Prokofiev after he had won on this day in 2004 to complete the tenth century of Tony McCoy's career.

30 Oct 'I love America,' shouted an emotional **Frankie Dettori** as 28/1 outsider Wilko won the Breeders Cup Juvenile on this date in 2004 at Lone Star in Texas. Kieren Fallon, who partnered Ouija Board to a 10/11 win in the Breeders Cup Filly & Mare Turf, was less frenetic – 'She done it nice.'

1 November 'As a jockey you never allow yourself to take a break because you're scared someone else will get your winners' **Walter Swinburn** (*Guardian*, 1 November 2004).

2 Nov 'Makybe Diva is the legend, I'm just the lucky bastard who is sitting on her back.' Jockey **Glen Boss** on partnering Makybe Diva when she became the first mare ever to win back-to-back Melbourne Cups on this date in 2004.

3 Nov 'That's gambling for you,' was his reported comment on this date in 2004 when it was revealed that 75-year-old **Jack Lee** from Newcastle was the man whose potential winning bet of £957,714 for £2 had turned into a return of £90 for a place accumulator after stewards at Newmarket relegated first past the post Babodana to second place in the Ben Marshall Stakes four days earlier.

In 1838 Amato won the only race he ever contested – was it The Derby, The Grand National, or The St Leger?

4 Nov 'I'm surprised they have gone so huge,' commented British Jockey Club Director of Regulation, **Malcolm Wallace**, in the *Racing Post* of this date in 2004, after Frankie Dettori was suspended for one month, the heaviest ban of his career, for careless riding on Mamool in the Melbourne Cup.

5 Nov 'There is no malice at all. I hope she finds the whole thing funny.' This was probably wishful thinking on behalf of racing fan **John Milton** who, on this date in 1997 at Newton Abbot, sponsored a race in honour of his former wife – 'The J C Milton She's Finally Gone Handicap Hurdle'.

6 Nov 'Confessions of a Master Fixer' was the **front-page headline** of the American magazine *Sports Illustrated* on this date in 1978. Jockey Jose Amy confessed that he 'restrained' seven horses for $1,500 a time. He was banned, but in October 2004 was allowed back to ride and screamed 'I'm back' after finishing eighth of nine on Julia's Signal at Belmont Park.

7 Nov 'If I unexpectedly came into £5m I would buy a thoroughbred racehorse for £1m and aim for a Derby win.' Former Cockney Rebel star, **Steve Harley**, quoted in the *Sunday Times* on this date in 2004, adding, 'Owning racehorses is an expensive hobby that you should only do if you are prepared to lose money.'

8 Nov 'The rumour was discredited, but when enquiry had proved it to be true...the news spread like wildfire and furnished an absorbing topic for discussion and comment on all sides.' The *Newmarket Journal's* **report** of the death on this date in 1886 of the legendary champion flat jockey Fred Archer.

9 Nov 'In the middle of 2000 I decided to leave the industry and do something I really wanted to do. I spent a lot of my time learning karate.' Derby-winning jockey **Alan Munro**, now a black belt, the

The Derby.

Racing Post reported on this date in 2004, was planning a come-back to riding in Britain after a four-year sabbatical, after which, 'I also recognised that learning martial arts is never a business.'

10 Nov 'Hermit's Derby broke my heart. But I didn't show it, did I?' Shortly before he died on this date in 1868, aged just 26, owner and gambler the **Marquis of Hastings** made this remark about his £102,000 losses sustained by betting against Hermit winning the 1867 Derby.

11 Nov 'The most beautiful sight in the world,' the late **Quintin Gilbey** wrote, 'is Gordon Richards two lengths in front and his whip still swinging, when you have bet twice as much as you can afford.' This quotation appeared in the *Daily Telegraph* obituary, published on this date in 1986, a day after the great man died, aged 82.

12 Nov 'Farewell, best jockey ever seen on course; Thy backers weep to think by Fate's decree; The rider pale upon his great white horse; Hath beaten thee.' Tribute by poet **Edgar Lee** to legendary champion jockey Fred Archer, whose funeral took place on this day in 1886 following his tragic suicide.

13 Nov 'I'll answer that when you tell me why they call you "big fella".' **Emma Gorman** put a blush on Derek Thompson's face with her riposte on this date in 2004 when he asked her on *The Morning Line* TV show why John McCririck called her "Goo-goo". Neither question nor answer received a definitive response.

15 Nov 'When we started off in 1991 I never dreamed that we would be in this situation with winners of the Gold Cup and the Champion Chase – it's beyond our wildest dreams.' Trainer **Paul Nicholls**, celebrating the win of Noble Action at Folkestone on this date in 2004 – his 1,000th domestic success.

Having just ridden The Reject, which champion jump jockey announced his retirement?

16 Nov 'Peter just got it spot-on, when he said that you spend a while at the crease and then you get your first run!' After Grand Show won at Lingfield to give **Walter Swinburn** his first winner as a trainer on this date in 2004 he took a call of congratulations from father-in-law Peter Harris, from whom he took over.

17 Nov 'We are thought to have a decisive influence, but in reality there are far more important factors in a horse's performance than the weight it carries. The key things are its health, the ground and the trip.' Former maths teacher and non-league footballer, **Phil Smith**, the BHB's senior jumps handicapper, was quoted by the *Racing Post* on this date in 2004, casting doubt on so many serious punters' tenet that weight is everything.

19 Nov 'Most of all it was a day of very public derision for the po-faced view that racing can only be about field sizes and betting turnover.' **Alan Lee** in *The Times* on the reappearance, on this date in 2004, of triple Cheltenham Gold Cup winner Best Mate at Exeter in a four-horse race that attracted a crowd of over 6,000 to a fixture usually attracting a third of that total.

22 Nov 'This is not a one-off. It took far too much work.' **Jim Lawless** accepted a £1 bet in November 2003, to win which he had to learn to ride and partner a horse in a race under official rules. With the help of former jockey Gee Armytage he partnered Airgusta at Southwell over 1 mile on this date in 2004, finishing seventh of fourteen, to win the bet.

23 Nov 'The weighing room is something of a cultural desert. This is not a criticism, because the ability to recite poetry is bugger all use to you as you sail down to Becher's.' Former jockey **Marcus Armytage** (*Daily Telegraph*, 23 November 2004).

John Francome.

24 Nov 'Later in the evening he clambered on to a table and amid much ribaldry gave an impressive delivery of a poem on the mildly vulgar theme of breaking wind.' Writer **Jonathan Powell** recalls what jockey turned novelist Dick Francis was up to at a function at the Queen's Hotel in Cheltenham on this date in 1954.

25 Nov 'He may not be the best amateur around but I can assure you he is better at riding than I am at bomb disposal.' Trainer **Len Lungo** paid tribute to Guy Willoughby, who had ridden his first winner under Rules, Inn From The Cold, at Carlisle on this date in 2004 before going back to his day job as an explosives expert.

27 Nov 'Having the speed of a 100 year old,' was the dubious accolade paid to the horse Centurian in the annual *Mackenzie & Selby Hunter Chasers and Point to Pointers*, officially published on this date in 2004. Of a horse called Knickers, the annual commented, 'Never looked like coming down.'

28 Nov 'In the darkest days when I was very low I vowed I'd do something to help.' **Jonjo O'Neill** – a former patient himself – in 1989, handing over a cheque for £225,000 for Cancer Research to Prof Derek Crowther of Christies Hospital in Manchester.

29 Nov 'It's great fun coming into a bookie's, there's nothing quite like it in the world.' To which I say 'Hear! Hear!' echoing the words of **Anita Graham**, voted *Racing Post* Betting Shop Manager of the Year on this date in 2004, the first representing the Tote, for whom she works in Eastleigh near Southampton.

30 Nov 'Is this on-screen persona of a reactionary, elitist, sexist oaf really the image racing wants to be portraying of itself in the 21st century?' Letter writer **Ian Davies** of Basingstoke is no fan of John McCririck, according to his missive in the **Racing Post** of this date in 2004.

De Rigueur and No Bombs were both disqualified after eating what?

1 December 'And; why does Graham Goode always sound as though he thinks every race he commentates on could be of interest only to intellectual pygmies?' Er, I'll have to get back to **Paul Haigh** – for it was he who said this on 1 December 2004 – after pondering on whether he is referring to pygmies of great intellect or intellectuals of small stature.

3 Dec 'The last heat was not over at six o'clock when lights were erected at each corner of the course, to direct the riders.' A very early example of floodlit racing at a meeting at Baltinglass, Ireland on this date in 1791, reported by the ***Irish Racing Calendar***.

4 Dec 'Sleeping,' answered jockey **Hywel Davies**, born on this date in 1956, when asked his favourite recreation.

5 Dec 'The first brick of the Grand Stand at Ascot was laid on the 5th of December, 1838.' This **contemporary report** is believed to be the first time that the term Grand Stand was recorded in a British publication.

7 Dec 'I desire no other monument. This is the greatest thing I have ever done and I am satisfied.' **Elias Jackson 'Lucky' Baldwin**, one of the great pioneers of American racing, made this comment on this date in 1907 as the course he had just created, Santa Anita, opened for the first time.

11 Dec 'As a general rule we cannot have people going into the winners' enclosure and biting the jockeys' arses.' Few would disagree with that observation from clerk of the course **Major Tim Riley**, born on this date in 1928. He was officiating at Cartmel when waitress Chrissie Kent, a great fan of Phil Tuck, took a nip at the jockey's rear end.

Mars Bars.

14 Dec 'There hasn't been a day since that I have not missed riding,' said **Richard Dunwoody**, champion jumps jockey with 1,699 winners from 9,399 rides. He announced his retirement on this date in 1999.

15 Dec 'I get to 70 and suddenly start learning things. Watch out for me in 10 years – I could be dangerous.' **Clive Brittain**, born on this date in 1933, on reaching his three score and ten.

17 Dec 'They all come to me on bicycles and leave in Bentleys.' Wealthy owner **Major Lionel Holliday** on his trainers. He had three Classic winners during 1951–65. He died on this date in 1965, in his 85th year.

22 Dec 'I feel that I've had my best days as a jockey and the right thing to do is to be honest with myself and the people I ride for.' Signing-off comments of Derby-winning (on Benny The Dip) jockey **Willie Ryan**, born on this day in 1964, who announced his retirement in October 2004.

25 Dec 'Christmas Day has never even been considered before,' said the British Horse-racing Board's **Alan Delmonte** on hearing the news in October 2004 that the government's new Gambling Bill made provision for racing to take place on that day of the year for the first time.

26 Dec 'I guess it was a case of the right horse but wrong jockey.' Apprentice **Andrew Payne** who was riding at Caulfield, Australia on this date in 1996, partnering Hon Kwok Star. Jason Patton, riding Cogitate, was thrown from his horse, which cannoned into Hon Kwok Star, throwing Payne into the air – only to land in Cogitate's saddle. Payne rode on to finish the race on Cogitate. 'We will have to sort out whether young Andrew can claim two losing fees for one race,' said head steward Des Gleeson.

Arkle was born in which year – 1957, 58 or 59?

27 Dec 'He hated wearing jackets, finding them too tight under the armpits, and would refuse dinner invitations unless allowed to wear a sweater. He was also reluctant to go out if *Emmerdale Farm* was on the television.' Little-known facts in the *Daily Telegraph* obituary of triple Grand National winning trainer **Neville Crump**, who was born on this date in 1910 and died, aged 86, in January 1997.

30 Dec 'When he took his hands out of his pockets I just swung at him with my left hand,' explained US jockey **Alex Sollis** after a spectator accused him of riding a bad race on this date in 1992. This comment incited Sollis to break the racegoer's nose with a devastating punch.

31 Dec 'Good thing neither was ridden by Mr W Lambton, who scored a double at Keele Park's February 1898 meeting.' Racing historian **Chris Pitt**, noting that on this date in 1896 the two horses fighting out the finish of the Keele Park Chase were both named Lambton.

1957.

BIBLIOGRAPHY

Abelson, Edward & Tyrrel, John, *Horse Racing Records*, Breedon Books, 1993.

Ahern, Steve, *Riches From Horses*, Stanley Paul, 1964.

Ashforth, David, *Crown Jewels of Thoroughbred Racing*, Blood Horse Inc, 1997.

Ashforth, David, *Ringers & Rascals*, Highdown, 2003.

Baerlein, Richard, *Joe Mercer*, Queen Anne Press, 1987.

Batt, Peter, *Mick Channon*, Highdown, 2004.

Beasley, Bobby, *Second Start*, WH Allen, 1976.

Bird, Alex, *The Life and Secrets of a Professional Punter*, Queen Anne Press, 1985.

Brannan, Philip (managing ed.), *Vodafone Derby Day 2004*, Sportsguide Press, 2004.

Brogan, Barry, *The Barry Brogan Story*, Arthur Barker, 1981.

Brown, John, *Lucky John, From Teaboy to Chairman of Multi-billion Pound Firm*, Highdown, 2004.

Cartmell, Stephen, *From Aintree to York*, Aesculus Press, 2002.

Cassidy, Rebecca, *The Sport of Kings*, Cambridge University Press, 2002.

Champion, Bob & Powell, Jonathan, *Champion's Story*, Gollancz, 1981.

Chinn, Carl, *Better Betting with a Decent Feller*, Aurum Press, 2004.

Church, Michael, *Ripping Gambling Yarns*, Raceform, 2001.

Clower, Michael, *Mick Kinane: Big Race King*, Mainstream, 1996.

Cox, Harding, *Chasing and Racing*, William Clowes, 1925.

Conley, Kevin, *$tud*, Bloomsbury, 2002.

Davies, Laura, with Mair, Lewine, *Naturally...*, Bloomsbury, 1996.

de Moubray, Jocelyn, *The Thoroughbred Business*, Hamish Hamilton, 1987.

Drager, Marvin, *The Most Glorious Crown*, Winchester Press, 1975.

Dunwoody, Richard, *Obsessed*, Headline, 2000.

Eddery, Pat, *To be a Champion*, Hodder & Stoughton, 1992.

Fitzgerald, Arthur, *Royal Thoroughbreds*, Sidgwick & Jackson, 1990.

Fitzgerald, Mick, *A Jump-Jockey's Life*, Mainstream, 1999.

Fleming, Mary, *A History of the Thoroughbred in California*, CTBA, 1983.

Only one horse ever won four UK Classics in one year – who was it?

Fox, Kate, *The Racing Tribe*, Metro, 1999.

Francome, John, *Born Lucky*, Pelham, 1985.

Frith, W, *The Royal Calcutta Turf Club*, The Royal Calcutta Turf Club, 1976.

Frost, Jimmy with Johnson, Lucy, *Touched by Frost*, Highdown, 2003.

Gallier, Susan, *One of the Lads*, Stanley Paul, 1988.

Gascoigne, Paul with Davies, Hunter, *Gazza: My Story*, Headline, 2004.

Green, Reg, *A Race Apart*, Hodder & Stoughton, 1988.

Hammond, Gerald, *A Book of Words: Horse Racing*, Carcanet, 1992.

Hannan, Martin, *Rock of Gibraltar*, Cutting Edge, 2004.

Hargreaves, Jennifer, *Sport, Culture and Ideology*, Routledge, 1982.

Harman, Bob, *The Ultimate Dream*, Mainstream, 2000.

Haskin, Steve, *Horse Racing's Holy Grail*, Eclipse Press, 2002.

Herbert, Ivor, *Arkle*, Sphere Books, 1967.

Herbert, Ivor, *The Queen Mother's Horses*, Pelham Books, 1967.

Hey, Stan, *An Arm & Four Legs*, Yellow Jersey Press, 2000.

Hillenbrand, Laura, *Seabiscuit*, Fourth Estate, 2001.

Holland, Anne, *Steeplechasing*, Little, Brown, 2001.

Hollingsworth, Kent, *The Archjockey of Canterbury*, The Blood Horse, 1986.

Knight, Henrietta, *Best Mate: Triple Gold*, Highdown, 2004.

Laird, Dorothy, *Royal Ascot*, Hodder & Stoughton, 1976.

Lawrence, John, Mortimer, Roger, Seth-Smith, Michael & Willett, Peter, *The History of Steeplechasing*, Michael Joseph, 1966.

Lee, Alan, *Fred*, Pelham 1991.

Livingston, Barbara D, *Old Friends*, Eclipse Press, 2002.

Longrigg, Roger, The History of Horse Racing, Macmillan, 1972.

Lord, Graham, *Dick Francis: A Racing Life*, Little, Brown, 1999.

Lyle, R, *Royal Newmarket*, Putnam, 1945.

Macdonald, Malcolm with Malam, Colin, *Super Mac*, Highdown, 2003.

Magee, Sean (ed.), *Coming to the Last*, Partridge Press, 1997.

Magee, Sean, *Complete A–Z of Horse Racing*, Channel 4 Books, 2001.

Magee, Sean, *Ascot: The History*, Methuen, 2002.

March, Russell, *The Jockeys of Vanity Fair*, March Publications, 1985.

Marsh, Marcus, *Racing with the Gods*, Pelham, 1968.

McCoy, Tony, *McCoy the Autobiography*, Michael Joseph, 2002.

McCoy, Tony & Duval, Claude, *The Real McCoy*, Hodder & Stoughton, 1998.

McCririck, John, *World of Betting*, Stanley Paul, 1991.

McEvoy, John, *Great Horse Racing Mysteries*, Eclipse Press, 2001.

McIlvanney, Hugh, *McIlvanney on Horseracing*, Mainstream, 1995.

Mortimer, Roger, The History of the Derby Stakes, Michael Joseph, 1973.

Mortimer, Roger, Onslow, Richard & Willett, Peter, *Biographical*

Sceptre.

Encyclopaedia of British Flat Racing, Macdonald & Jane's, 1978.

Mottershead, Lee, *Persian Punch*, Highdown, 2004.

Murgatroyd, Sharon, *Jump Jockeys Don't Cry*, Romney Publications, 1996

Murray, Amanda, *Race to the Finish*, Robson Books, 2003.

Murray, William, *The Wrong Horse*, Little, Brown, 1992.

Nash, Stewart, *Plumpton*, Plumpton Racecourse Ltd, 2000.

Nasibov, Nikolai, *Life in the Saddle*, Progress Publishers, 1977.

Oaksey, John, *The Story of Mill Reef*, Michael Joseph, 1974.

Oaksey, John, *Mince Pies For Starters*, Headline, 2003.

O'Sullevan, Peter, *Calling the Horses*, Stanley Paul, 1989.

O'Sullevan, Peter, *Horse Racing Heroes*, Highdown, 2004.

Owen, Michael with Hayward, Paul, *Michael Owen: Off The Record*, Collins Willow, 2004.

Pierce, Peter & Kirkwood, Rhett, *From Go to Whoa*, Crossbow, 1994.

Piggott, Lester, *Lester*, Partridge Press, 1995.

Piggott, Lester & Magee, Sean, *Lester's Derbys*, Methuen, 2004.

Pitman, Richard, *Good Horses Make Good Jockeys*, Pelham, 1976.

Pitt, Chris, *A Long Time Gone*, Portway Press, 1996.

Potts, Alan, *Against the Crowd*, Aesculus Press, 1995.

Quinn, Mick, *Who Ate All The Pies?*, Virgin, 2003.

Rajpipla, Prince Rajsingh, *Counter Attack*, Raceform, 2002.

Randall, John & Morris, Tony, *A Century of Champions*, Portway Press, 1999.

Reeves, Richard Stone, *Crown Jewels of Thoroughbred Racing*, The Blood Horse, 1997.

Reid, Jamie, *Emperors of the Turf*, Macmillan, 1989.

Reid, Jamie, *A Licence to Print Money*, Macmillan, 1992.

Reid, Jamie, *Days Like These*, Mainstream, 2003.

Richards, Jim, *Jonjo*, Stanley Paul, 1985.

Rickaby, Bill, *First to Finish*, Souvenir Press, 1969.

Roddy, Daniel, *The Irish Derby 1962–1995*, Gill & MacMillan, 1995.

Scally, John, *Them and Us: The Irish at Cheltenham*, Mainstream, 1999.

Scott, Brough, *On and Off the Rails*, Gollancz, 1984.

Scudamore, Peter & Lee, Alan, *Scudamore on Steeplechasing*, Partridge Press, 1988.

Sharpe, Graham, *Turf Accounts*, Guinness, 1990.

Sharpe, Graham, *Odds, Sods and Racing Certs*, Robson Books, 1996.

Sim, Andrew, *English Racing Stables*, Dial Press, 1993.

Smalley, David, *Ultimate Horse Racing Fact & Quiz Book*, Stopwatch, 1999.

Smiley, Jane, *A Year at the Races*, Faber & Faber, 2004.

Smith, Eph, *Riding to Win*, Stanley Paul, 1968.

Thousandfold was the thousandth winner for which champion jockey?

Smith, Martin (ed.), *The Daily Telegraph Book of Sports Obituaries*, Macmillan, 2000.
Snowy, J, *The Stanley of the Turf*, Chapman & Hall, 1896.
Stafford, Tony, *Little Black Racing Book*, Collins Willow, 1994.
Stevens, Gary, *The Perfect Ride*, Highdown, 2004.
Thompson, Laura, *Newmarket*, Virgin, 2000.
Townson, Nigel, *The British at Play*, Cavallioti, 1997.
Tyrrel, John, *Running Racing*, Quiller Press, 1997.
Unattributed, *Horse Racing*, Saunders, Ottley, And Co, 1863.
Walton, Elizabeth, A Slice of Glory, Stanley Paul, 1992.
Ward, Andrew, *Horse Racing's Strangest Races*, Robson Books, 2000.
Waterman, Jack, *The Punter's Friend*, Lennard Queen Anne Press, 1999.
Willett, Peter, *The Classic Racehorse*, Stanley Paul, 1989.
Williams, Prof. Leighton Vaughan, *Betting to Win*, High Stakes, 2004.
Wilson, Julian, *Lester Piggott*, Macdonald Queen Anne Press, 1992.
Wilson, Julian, *Some You Win*, Collins Willow, 1998.

Steve Cauthen.

Index